BETTER THAN

A practical guide to renovating

by Albert Jackson and David Day

Edited by Ron Bloomfield

STERLING PUBLISHING CO., INC.   NEW YORK

The authors would like to thank the following individuals
and companies for their assistance:

David Ward
Fred Large
Greta Briggs
Jim Moore
John Coles
Les Reed
Mike Gaillard
R E Rustin
Rustins Ltd
D L Forster
Furniglass Ltd
The Art Veneer Company

The chair shown on the front cover was supplied by
Phelps Ltd, 133 St Margarets Road, Twickenham, Middlesex
and photographed by Mark Fiennes

The tools shown on the back cover, pages 113, 115, 117, 118 and
119 to 129 were supplied by Buck and Ryan Ltd, 101 Tottenham
Court Road, London W1 and photographed by Mark Fiennes

The diagrams throughout the book were drawn by David Day,
Albert Jackson and Robin Harris

This book accompanies the BBC Television series
Better than new, first broadcast in Spring 1982

Library of Congress Cataloging in Publication Data

Jackson, Albert, 1943–
　　Better than new.

　　Includes index.
　　1. Furniture—Repairing.　2. Furniture finishing.
3. Upholstery.　I. Day, David, 1944–　　.　II. Title.
TT199.J33　1983　　684.1′044　　83-370
ISBN 0-8069-7730-2 (pbk.)

Copyright © 1982 by Albert Jackson and David Day
Published in 1983 by Sterling Publishing Co., Inc.
Two Park Avenue, New York, N.Y. 10016
First published in Great Britain in 1982 by the
British Broadcasting Corporation, 35 Marylebone High St., London W1M 4AA
Distributed in Australia by Oak Tree Press Co., Ltd.
P.O. Box K514 Haymarket, Sydney 2000, N.S.W.
Distributed in Canada by Oak Tree Press Ltd.
% Canadian Manda Group, P.O. Box 920, Station U
Toronto, Ontario, Canada M8Z 5P9
Manufactured in the United States of America

Contents

CHAPTER ONE

Introduction

The magic of old furniture

Most of us have friends who, either from a lucky inheritance or by dint of constant rummaging in junk shops and auctions, have some desirable old furniture in their home. Perhaps they have taken the trouble to clean it up and to repair any gross damage. Standing there with its elegant lines and beautiful grain figure, old furniture adds a dignity and sense of history to a living space and, ironically enough, it usually costs far less than its modern counterpart in the high street furniture store.

Of course, the appeal of old furniture goes a lot further than purely financial considerations. A lot of it is made from materials which are either unobtainable today or which are so expensive that they can only be used in the most costly handmade pieces. Old furniture may also incorporate techniques such as marquetry, which are so time consuming that nowadays they are largely out of the question.

It is often said that old furniture is better made than anything produced today. The very best antique furniture is undoubtedly superbly made and finished, but the bulk of old furniture was the result of the 'mass production' of its day. The parts that show were nicely finished and, within the limitations of contemporary glues, the furniture was strongly constructed. Nonetheless, as anyone who has had occasion to dismantle an old table or chest of drawers will tell you, much of the wood on the inside came straight from the saw. Some of the old construction techniques leave much to be desired, ignoring as they do the inevitable shrinkage of timber and the problems which arise from it. If you inspect the dovetail joints on the side of an old drawer you will almost certainly find the gauge marks across the timber. In better quality work these would have been planed off, but when making furniture of this kind there was simply no time. The craftsmen were paid by results, not by the hour, so short cuts had to be found if they were to make a living.

Far from detracting from the appeal of old furniture, these failings only serve to humanise their makers. Furthermore, the split panels, lifted veneers and other defects which are a result of these short cuts allow us to pick up a bargain, as long as we are prepared to put in some work to renovate it. And renovate we mean, not restore. The painstaking restoration of valuable old pieces to as near as possible their original condition is, and always will be, the province of the professional. What we are interested in is the renovation of good quality mass produced furniture from, say, Victorian times onwards.

The mystique of renovation

Furniture renovation is a traditional craft and, like any activity which is based on information handed down from craftsman to apprentice, it gathers round it a mass of detail which seems almost impenetrable to the amateur. A professional will use the methods and materials with which he is familiar because he has a limited amount of time to spend on any project and there is little point in experimentation. However, if traditional methods are never subjected to critical examination, they are in danger of becoming dogma and anyone who wants to try out more modern methods and materials may well feel he is not a 'proper' restorer.

We have tried to penetrate the mystique which surrounds the subject by talking to manufacturers and restorers, attempting to distinguish prejudiced advice from that based on sound principles. In many cases there is no substitute for the tried and tested traditional methods but on the other hand, where we feel it appropriate, we have suggested alternative materials which may be easier to obtain from local suppliers and which will produce reasonable results with the minimum of experience.

Recognising our limitations

Most restorers, amateur and professional alike, have a genuine love of old furniture and therefore wish to preserve the character of the piece they are working on. However, many professionals are fearful that an inexperienced amateur will inadvertently ruin a desirable piece which should have been left to an expert to renovate. To be realistic, however, whilst the idea of finding an unrecognisable gem in a junk shop is an exciting dream, the odds are against it. Most dealers handle a great deal of furniture and know a valuable item when they see one. If you are paying a few pounds for a piece you can reasonably assume that it falls into our 'mass produced' category, or that it is so damaged that it is not worth the dealer's time to restore it.

If you have inherited a piece of furniture it is much more difficult to judge its value. If you take it to a reputable dealer or auctioneer he will usually value it for you free of charge. If it is a bulky item he may visit your home to give you a valuation, but there will probably be a small charge for the service. Many dealers will give you advice if you show them a photograph of the furniture, but most will insist that their valuation is a guide only, as photography can be misleading. Incidentally, most valuers prefer a black and white photograph, as the hues in coloured photographs can vary so widely.

It is always worth taking the trouble to have furniture valued before taking a step such as stripping, which is irreversible. The colour of old furniture which we all admire is a product of ageing and if you strip the finish unnecessarily you may devalue it for ever. Although you can replace it with a similar finish it will never be the same again. If the piece is valuable, it really should be restored by a professional. You can always discuss the possibility of doing some of the work yourself to reduce the cost.

Genuine or reproduction?

Dating old furniture can be very difficult. That is a subject for another book and there are far more eminent historians to write it. However, when looking at old furniture, one often wants to know whether a particular item is a genuine old piece or a modern reproduction. A dealer will know the difference, and hopefully he will point it out to you, but there are a few things you can look for yourself.

Some reproductions just do not look old enough. Genuine old furniture does not have sharp crisp edges

to corners or mouldings, especially in those areas which are constantly handled. The colour of reproduction pieces is often too even and bright. Remember the patina of an old finish, and even the wood itself, mellows with age. Polish is likely to be worn away, for example on the arms of carver chairs, and is often faded more on one side of a cabinet which has faced the light. Scratches and dents should be in areas where they would occur naturally, such as around handles and locks and on the legs of chairs and tables.

If the damage is too evenly distributed, suspect a little deliberate 'distressing'. Distressing is the art of putting all the dents, scratches and stains characteristic of an old piece of furniture on to a new reproduction. If skilfully done it is not easy to distinguish, but look at the backs of cabinets and the bottoms of drawers. The back of a genuine old piece will be made up from several pieces of solid timber whereas most reproductions will have a one piece plywood panel. Similarly, if the bottom of a drawer is plywood instead of solid timber the piece could be a reproduction, or else a modern repair has been made on an old drawer. Look for other clues to confirm your suspicions. The dovetail joints on a handmade drawer will have large tails and small pins. A machine made drawer will usually have pins and tails of equal size. Remember also the gauge mark left by the craftsmen under pressure, another clue to a handmade drawer.

Where to obtain old furniture

Antique shops are the most obvious sources for old furniture, but you will need to choose carefully if you are to pick up a bargain. The shop price usually bears a heavy 'markup' to cover the dealer's profit and a proportion of his overheads. It is possible to buy broken furniture

from even top class dealers before they have had time to renovate it. They are always happy for a quick sale, especially when it saves them extra work. If you can get on friendly terms with your local dealers they might start to hold pieces for you once they are aware of your interest. Small secondhand furniture shops are a better bet as even the humblest dealer can obtain really nice items from house clearances and you are likely to pay less. Most dealers we have spoken to agree that the marked price includes some leeway for haggling, so always make them an offer and see how you get on. Bartering is rather embarrassing at first, but it frequently produces results.

However careful you are, there is always the remote possibility that you will pay too much for a piece of furniture or that it will be wrongly described to you. One protection against this is to buy only from dealers who are members of an established traders' association. For the sort of furniture most of us are seeking, the dealer will most likely belong to the London and Provincial Antique Dealers Association and you will probably see its sign in his shop window. LAPADA has the advantage that it will arbitrate between buyer and dealer in cases of a disputed sale. Dealers selling more expensive furniture often belong to the British Antique Dealers Association.

Bidding at an auction is an enjoyable way of buying furniture. Don't be put off by the old joke about buying a complete dining set by scratching your ear. There is plenty of time before the auction to view the lots and in most showrooms a list is displayed which shows the expected price of any item. The staff of the saleroom are usually willing to discuss individual pieces and will even bid for you up to an agreed limit if you cannot be present for the auction. A catalogue will be available briefly describing each lot so that you can note the items you are interested in and mark it with the price you are prepared to pay. Stick to your estimate and you will not get carried away with auction fever. As a private buyer you are in an advantageous position at an auction. A dealer will need to add a profit margin to his estimate whereas you can outbid him and still pay less than you would in his shop. Auctions are held at more or less regular intervals. Look in your local paper for addresses and dates.

Local papers themselves are an excellent source for secondhand furniture. You will always see a few items for sale in the 'small ads' which you can expect to buy quite cheaply.

Jumble sales are sometimes worth visiting but unfortunately most organisers invite dealers to inspect any furniture they are offered before the sale.

You will of course be aware of any inherited items you have at home but other members of your family may have unwanted furniture stowed away in attics or garages. It is surprising how many people will discard old furniture as fashion dictates something new.

For the same reasons you will find furniture on rubbish dumps, in 'skips' where a house is being renovated, and even at the side of the road. You can't get furniture any cheaper than that but do ask permission before taking it away.

Assessing the work

In this book, we have tried to include examples of all the common faults you are likely to find in old furniture and how to go about rectifying them. Most of the materials we recommend are available from local DIY shops, but there are some

products which are sold only in specialist shops or by mail order. A list of suppliers is included at the back of the book. It is, of course, in no way comprehensive and you will soon get to know of the specialist suppliers in your locality. The section on upholstery is limited to dining chairs because these illustrate all the basic upholstery skills. Beyond this level you should refer to specialist upholstery books.

We have divided the chapter on structural repairs into what we call 'furniture families' – chairs, tables and cabinets. Each family is subdivided into individual groups where we describe the kind of damage that you are likely to find and the reason for it. This should help you assess the amount of work that is necessary to renovate a piece. Inspect any furniture carefully before you buy it. It is all too easy to get carried away by an interesting find only to discover that it is riddled with woodworm, or is so dilapidated that it is too difficult to repair. Point out any defects you find to a dealer. He may not be aware of all of them and he may be prepared to reduce the price.

Obviously you should repair any broken components and damage to the solid wood surfaces or veneers before you refinish the furniture, but we have laid out the book in the reverse order to encourage you to think in terms of doing as little work as is necessary. This should not be taken for a slipshod attitude but as a means of preserving as much of the original fabric of the piece as is possible. In other words, adopt the simplest approach first and only take more drastic action as the job dictates.

But can I do the work?

In our view, anyone with a reasonable level of competence in woodworking should be able to tackle

any repair we have suggested in this book. In addition, it would be a help to have some sort of workspace with a reasonable range of tools.

If you do not feel confident of your woodworking skills, we have included a section on some basic techniques at the back of this book, but by far the best idea is to attend an evening class in woodworking, where you can gain the necessary practice. Nonetheless, even a beginner can clean and wax a piece of furniture without damaging it and derive a great deal of satisfaction from so doing. Then you can move on to slightly more complex tasks and learn as you go. Similarly, you are unlikely to have a fully equipped workshop from the start. Many renovating jobs can be done in the living room or kitchen, but remember that jobs like stripping and sanding down produce a lot of mess. In sunny weather, it is pleasant to work out in the open air. Remember too that renovation can be a lengthy business, so don't be in a hurry for results.

Wherever you work and at whatever level, remember SAFETY. Woodworking tools must be kept sharp and they cut fingers as readily as timber. Stripping solutions can burn the skin. Some volatile solvents are dangerous when inhaled. Wear protective gloves and a mask where appropriate. Never allow naked flames into the workspace and turn off all electrical devices after using.

Having said all that, the main message is 'have a go and enjoy it'. Start with a cheap and simple piece of furniture, analyse its faults and follow the book instructions carefully. Once you have witnessed the transformation of a tired and run down piece of furniture into something bright and beautiful with a new future ahead of it, you are unlikely to need any further encouragement.

CHAPTER TWO

Finishes and polishes

Producing an attractive finish on an old piece of furniture is perhaps the most satisfying aspect of renovation. It is the moment you have been waiting for throughout a lengthy job, when the richness and colour of the wood is brought out.

Finishing is a long-established craft which has acquired a mystique of its own. Although the basic techniques are more or less agreed on, each craftsman develops his own methods over the years, often based on materials which are no longer widely available. Many restorers make up their own finishes from the basic raw materials and advise amateurs to do the same, but unless you are intending to do a great deal of renovation this is an awful lot of work for a comparatively modest financial saving. We have taken the view that where possible it is best to use materials that are available from your local DIY centre, whether specially formulated commercial products or more traditional materials.

As explained in the opening chapter, the general aim of renovation is to do as little as possible to an old piece of furniture. Just as you don't dismantle a chair unless you really have to, so you don't strip off the finish unless it is absolutely necessary. Sometimes all that is required is to wash the furniture to remove accumulated grime, or to 'revive' it, that is to cut back the top surface of the finish. At the next level you may have to remove stains and blemishes from the finish and then repolish it, but of course there are many occasions when you will be forced to take the bull by the horns, strip down the furniture to the bare wood and completely refinish it. This process often involves re-staining the wood as well as polishing it.

It is important to remember that many of the chemicals used in furniture finishing are dangerous. Always wear rubber gloves and work in a well-ventilated room. **Many of the solutions are inflammable: never allow naked flames in your workshop and do not smoke.** Store all stains and polishes outside the house in a shed or garage.

Cleaning the surface

Any well-used piece of furniture will have a layer of accumulated dirt and grease and, in some cases, wax polish which will at best make it look dowdy and lifeless and at worst will completely mask an attractively grained timber. It may also hide faults such as fine crazing of the finish, which may require further attention. The first job therefore is to clean the surface. The technique used will depend on whether the furniture is finished with a clear varnish or with paint.

A clear finish

If the furniture has a clear finish, use a mixture of four parts of white spirit to one of linseed oil. It will not lift the finish (except for wax), neither will it raise the grain nor lift veneers.
● Dampen a coarse cloth pad with oil and spirit mixture and rub it over the surface of the furniture. Quite vigorous action may be required, particularly if a heavy layer of dirt has built up. Examine the cloth as you work, turning to a clean part of the pad as required until no further dirt is transferred to it.
● If progress is slow, or if the furniture has a thick layer of wax, use very fine 000 grade wire wool. Pour a little of the mixture into a shallow dish, dip a piece of wire wool about the size of a golf ball into it and squeeze out any excess. Use light pressure only when working with wire wool or it will remove not only wax and dirt but the rest of the finish as well. Work well into mouldings where dirt accumulates.
● Finish off with a cloth dampened with white spirit, wiping the surface clean.

A paint finish

If the furniture has been painted or lacquered, dirt and grease can be wiped off with a rag dipped in warm water containing a mild detergent. It is not advisable to soak the piece as water can penetrate joints or cracks. Rub the surface dry with another soft cloth pad.

Reviving the finish

Sometimes cleaning alone is insufficient to reveal the colour of the wood; the finish looks dull and must be 'revived'.
● For any clear finish the simplest method of reviving is to use a mild liquid abrasive. Liquid metal polish or car paint cleaner work well when applied on a soft cloth. Alternatively you can use one of

the proprietary burnishing creams available from DIY shops. Follow them up with a coat of wax.

● The other method of reviving is to add a fresh coat of the original finish but this in turn depends on identifying the finish, something which may be very hard to do. Old pieces of furniture are usually finished with oil, wax or French polish, whereas more recent pieces may be covered with cellulose or a modern lacquer such as polyurethane.

● If the furniture was finished with oil or wax, the white spirit used in the cleaning process will have dislodged it.

● To test for French polish, wrap a soft cloth around your finger, dip it in methylated spirits and rub an area of the finish that does not show in use. If French polish is present it will dissolve and stain the rag.

● Cellulose can be detected in a similar way to French polish, using cellulose thinners on the rag instead of methylated spirits. Cellulose can only be successfully applied with a spray gun or aerosol (see page 17). However, you can safely revive a cellulose finish with French polish.

● If you are still unsure what the finish is, it is probably a modern lacquer. This can safely be revived with a coat of wax.

Removing blemishes

Here we are concerned with blemishes in the finish itself. For the treatment of deep scratches, dents and burns which go down into the wood, see *Surface repairs* page 18.

Water, alcohol and heat marks

Modern varnishes like polyurethane are resistant to alcohol, water and heat but older finishes such as French polish will be marked after relatively short exposure. If a drink is left on a sideboard or table, even the small amount of alcohol on the underside of the glass will dissolve the surface of the polish, leaving a white ring. The same kind of mark will often be found on a dressing table where nail varnish remover has been spilled. Water under a flower vase will produce a similar effect and a hot plate will melt the surface leaving a white patch.

● The treatment for any of these blemishes is to use a mild abrasive, such as a metal polish or car paint cleaner, on a clean damp cloth to cut back the surface to below the level of the damage. The effect is dramatic and the white mark will disappear quickly. With luck that will be the extent of the damage and the area can be repolished, but view the surface from different angles to ensure that the mark has disappeared completely. If water has permeated the finish for instance, it will still show as a dark ring and you will have to go deeper to remove it. If the end result is not satisfactory, strip the polish and refinish.

Ink stains

Try working on an ink stain with mild abrasive as described above. You can also try rubbing the stain with a cloth wrapped round your finger and dampened with meths. This can remove some drawing inks but take care as French polish will be dissolved at the same time.

● If you find that it is necessary to strip the finish locally because the stain has penetrated that deeply, bleach the stain out of the wood with a two-part bleach as described on page 10. Restrict the bleach to the area of the stain by using a small brush or stick. You will be left with a pale patch which will have to be retouched and finished to match the surrounding wood.

Scratches

These can be removed with metal polish, a paint cleaner or a commercial scratch remover. Scratches on a dark finish can be made less noticeable by rubbing shoe polish of a similar colour on to them.

● For extensive scratching, use a fine silicon carbide paper to reduce the surface initially, then one of the fine abrasives mentioned above.

● For a really deep scratch but one which has not damaged the wood itself, build up the surface using the finish as a filler. A modern varnish can be used directly but, when using French polish, pour a little into a saucer until it thickens by exposure to the air. On pale woods use a white or transparent French polish as the filled scratch tends to look darker than its surroundings.

● In the meantime rub the area of the scratch lightly with a fine abrasive paper to flush off the edges of the scratch.

● Use a fine brush to apply polish along the scratch, leaving it to harden between applications until it is proud of the surface.

● When set hard carefully scrape the polish with a very sharp knife until it is almost flush with the surface, then finish with a very fine silicon carbide paper, followed by metal polish. Apply a coat of finish.

Stripping the finish

There are several ways to strip the finish from a piece of furniture, depending on the size of the area you are working on, the type of finish, whether the piece is extensively carved or moulded and whether it is veneered or solid wood. All the methods have their advocates but it is advisable to use all or any of them as the need arises.

Scraping and sanding

You can use a sharp cabinet scraper and sandpaper to remove the finish but the method has certain disadvantages. Firstly a certain amount of skill is required to use the scraper, although this is soon acquired with practice. It will however be a very skilful craftsman who can remove just the finish and none of the wood. For large areas it can be quite hard work and it is extremely difficult on carved or moulded sections. Scraping is a good method to use on small areas which can be cleaned without spoiling adjacent ones. Unless you scrape too deeply the grain should remain filled, which will save time and produce a better finish. Take extra care on veneered surfaces to avoid exposing the groundwork.

● Use the scraper as described on page 122, working in the direction of the grain. Avoid scraping deeply in one spot or you will create a hollow which will show up when the surface is re-polished. To sharpen the scraper see page 130.

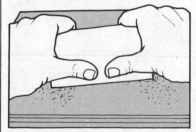

● Finish the job by sanding until the surface is smooth. 'Feather off' the surrounding polish, that is grade the sanding outwards so that you can fill in the new polish without leaving a hard edge.

Methylated spirit

Since methylated spirit dissolves French polish, some people use it to strip whole pieces of furniture but it is a slow process. It is useful for removing small areas of damaged French polish (feathering the edges as you go) but take care that you do not apply too much meths and affect a larger area than you intended.

● Apply the spirit with golf ball size pieces of fine steel wool, rubbing with the grain. Make sure all polish is removed, particularly at the edges of panels and in mouldings.

● When stripping a small patch where excess spirit might run on to surrounding areas, use a cloth dampened with spirit to soften the polish and then dry wire wool. Wipe the surface afterwards with another piece of spirit-dampened cloth.

Commercial stripper

The most efficient method of stripping a large area is to use a commercial stripper. A good one will tackle any finish without harming the surface underneath. There are two varieties of stripper generally available. One is a thick paste which is applied all over the piece of furniture and is then cleaned off after the time recommended by the manufacturers, taking the finish with it.

Unfortunately, it must be kept moist while the stripping process is taking place, usually by wrapping it in polythene. This can be quite a disadvantage when working on an intricate piece of furniture.

The other type of stripper is available as a thick fluid. This is simply painted on to the surface, left to dissolve the finish, and scraped off. In our experience this is simpler to use and is suitable for any type of furniture.

On some old pieces of painted furniture you may come across a bottom layer of paint which seems impervious to the stripper. Known as 'milk' paint, it contains casein which makes it extremely hard and it can only be stripped with ammonia, which is dangerous to handle at home. It can be scraped or sanded off but this is very hard work and you will probably find an inferior timber underneath it anyway. The best plan is to leave it alone as a good base coat and to re-paint the furniture.

Commercial strippers are dangerous. They are harmful to the eyes and skin and rapidly mark carpets, floor coverings and other furniture, so take precautions. Work outside or lay plenty of newspaper or a sheet of plastic under the furniture. Wear old clothes and vinyl gloves throughout the process. Check the manufacturer's instructions beforehand, particularly those concerned with safety. Remove all fittings before starting work, stripping them separately if necessary.

Using a liquid stripper

Paint a liberal coating of liquid stripper on the piece, using an old brush. Work it well into carvings and mouldings. Leave it until the paint or varnish begins to lift and bubble then apply a second layer of stripper, this time stippling the surface with the brush to push the first layer down on to the finish and continue working.

● Test a small area to see if the stripper has worked through to the surface of the wood, then scrape all the flat areas with a paint scraper.

- Use fine wire wool to remove the stripper and finish from carvings and mouldings, turning the ball of wool inside out as the strands become clogged. A pointed stick can be used to clean out mouldings.
- If you have to apply another layer of stripper to remove a stubborn finish, cover at least a whole panel. If you treat a small area it may show as a lighter patch.
- When scraping is complete, treat the surface with white spirit, using wire wool in the direction of the grain to ensure that the residue of stripper is washed out of the wood.

Industrial stripping

There are companies who will strip furniture for you in tanks of hot caustic soda. This is a harsh process, especially as after the finish has been stripped the furniture is vigorously scrubbed and hosed down with water to remove the caustic soda. Industrial stripping should only be considered for furniture made from solid timber. The process attacks animal glues, which may cause veneers to lift and weaken joints. It is not advisable to submit bentwood chairs (see page 44) to hot caustic soda as the components will try to straighten and the plywood seat may delaminate. If you are in any doubt about the suitability of a piece of furniture for industrial stripping, seek the advice of the company concerned first.

Some people attempt to strip furniture themselves using caustic soda. Without careful handling and rigorous precautions this is **a very dangerous substance** and is not recommended for use by amateurs.

Bleaching

Bleaching is not a process which automatically follows stripping, but if you have used industrial stripping with caustic soda or ammonia the wood may have darkened. It may also be stained unevenly and it is worth bleaching so that you can build up the colour again to your satisfaction. Bleach is also used to remove stains such as ink or wine from wood. **It is a dangerous substance so follow the manufacturer's instructions exactly.**

- Use a commercial two part bleach, applying the first solution to the wood with cheap white fibre or a nylon brush and leave it for about twenty minutes. The surface may darken at this stage but that is quite normal.
- Apply the second solution over the first and leave it for about four hours. If the wood has not bleached to your satisfaction, repeat the process after two hours.
- Wipe off any crust that may have formed with a damp rag before washing the wood with a solution of white vinegar and water. See the manufacturer's instructions for the exact proportions, but they will be approximately one teaspoonful of vinegar per pint of water.

Sanding down

Before any stain or polish is applied the surface must be perfectly smooth. Any scratches or unevenness which do not show at this stage of the work will be glaringly obvious once the finish is applied.

- Rub a cloth dampened with water over the surface of the wood and leave it to dry. This will raise the grain, which can then be san-

ded flat. If you fail to raise the grain before using a water-based stain, then the grain will rise and will have to be rubbed down subsequently, perhaps removing some of the colour. If you have washed out stripper or bleach with water then this stage is unnecessary.

- Sand in the direction of the grain using a medium grade glass paper. For flat work, wrap the paper round a cork or a softwood block.

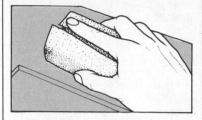

- For light sanding, or if you suspect that the surface is slightly uneven as it often is on old furniture, hold the paper as shown, applying pressure with the tips of the fingers.

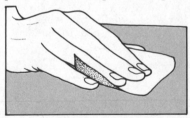

- Finish with a fine grade garnet paper in the same way, removing all the dust with a soft brush.

Power sanders

Power sanding machines make preliminary sanding easier. It is unlikely that you will require a belt sander on this type of work and you should avoid flexible disc sanders, which can damage the surface. A finishing sander, which can be bought as an attachment to a power drill or as a special purpose tool, is the ideal machine but you should still finish by hand to remove the fine 'swirl' of scratches left by the machine.

Staining

On newly made furniture, stain is applied to change or improve the colour of the wood. Furniture manufacturers are often forced to use wood from more than one batch in a piece of furniture and then stain is employed to unify its appearance. In restoration work you may need to stain a whole piece after stripping or, much more difficult, stain a repair to match the rest of the wood.

There are two types of wood stain readily available from most stockists, based on oil or water. Each has its advantages and disadvantages. Water-based stain is probably the most commonly used. It is very mobile and can be 'shaded' on wood with a damp rag, using more than one colour if you want to. Similarly, if too much stain is applied the surplus can be rapidly removed with a damp rag. Some people do not use it on old veneers in case it dissolves the animal glue underneath and of course it will raise the grain when it dries, although this can be avoided by wetting the wood and rubbing it down prior to staining, as described above. Water-based stains will happily accept any final finish – French polish, polyurethane, wax or whatever.

Oil-based stains, which strictly speaking are a mixture of white spirit and naphtha, do not raise the grain and are said to be more stable to light. On the other hand oil stains will not always accept polyurethane as a finish. They can be used to tint French polish (see page 13). This type of stain is sometimes referred to as a 'spirit' based stain due to its white spirit content. True spirit-based stains, however, contain methylated spirit and are very difficult to obtain.

There are differing opinions as to whether you should stain the work before filling the grain or vice-versa. If you stain first you run the risk of removing some of the stain when you sand down the filler. Conversely, if you grain fill first the absorption of the stain may be uneven, producing a patchy appearance. On balance it is probably best to stain first, then to apply a sealer coat of the finish. When the sealer is dry, apply grain filler and sand it down very lightly.

Grain filler may be purchased in several different shades, so you should choose one to match the stain you are using. If the match is unsatisfactory, you can mix some stain into the filler before application but make sure the two preparations are compatible, for example if the filler is oil-based use oil-based stain.

Testing for colour

Different tones or colours can be made by mixing stains together, but only within their own group. In order to see how a stain will effect the wood and to gauge its strength when covered by a polish or varnish, make a test strip beforehand using a scrap of the timber or the veneer you are using. As each coat of stain dries, apply another on top, leaving a little of the preceding coat exposed so that you can observe the graded tones. Finally apply a coat of finish over the stain.

Applying the stain

Ensure that the surface of the wood is clean, dust- and grease-free before applying any stain. Clean off any glue that may have been squeezed on to the surface as it will seal the wood against penetration. Any stain is best applied liberally in the direction of the grain and once dry should be sealed with a coat of the intended finish.

● Apply a water-based stain with a large brush or cloth pad, picking up the wet edges quickly to avoid going over an area twice. Immediately take a fresh rag and rub over the whole surface to even out the application and remove excess stain. The best way to apply water stain over a large area is to use a paint pad, a modern paint applicator with very short bristles. It is not necessary to rub over the surface with a rag as the pad distributes the stain very evenly.

● Apply an oil-based stain with a brush or a cloth. It is equally important to keep the edges wet to avoid an overlap. Leave it to dry for six hours once you have achieved an even colour.

Matching colours

Professional restorers rarely use made-up stain. Using a variety of solvents and a wide range of pigments with exotic names like lamp black, Vandyke brown and raw sienna, they make up their stains as they go. Faced with a new rail on a chair or a patch of veneer on a chest of drawers, they dab and mix away until they produce perfect match with the surrounding wood.

Skills like this are beyond the amateur, but by using commercially available stains in a trial and error fashion on several test strips, surprisingly good results can be obtained. A water-based stain is perhaps the best for the job since it is easily blended and can be removed almost completely by washing off with a wet rag.

- Apply successive coats of diluted stain to gradually build up the required colour.
- While the stain is still damp, paint in broad areas of grain with a darker stain, blending the edges with a brush or damp cloth.
- Blot the junction between old and new wood with a cloth, attempting to blend in the colour rather than stop at a straight edge.
- Small patches of veneer, or holes filled with an opaque filler, can be successfully disguised using artists' oil colours. They are easily shaded from one colour to another so they are ideal for simulating a grain pattern over a small area. A variety of browns and yellows, white and black are the most useful colours. Use a very fine artist's sable brush, such as a 00, to apply them.

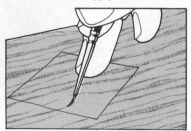

An extremely thin application of paint is essential or the repair will stand out as raised texture when finish is applied over it. Only a skilful artist will completely fool the eye but careful work will at least break

up a flat area of colour to blend better with the natural background.

- To disguise a hole patched with filler, seal the wood then mix up a colour to match the lightest background colour of the timber and, using the wood surrounding the filler as a guide, join up these areas across the patch. Use very small amounts of paint without using oil or turpentine as a medium.
- Do the same for the darker flecks of grain pattern, continuing the colour out past the edge of the repair into the natural colour of the grain.
- View the work from different angles, as what appears to be an exact match from one direction stands out from another.
- An absorbent material such as a patch of veneer can be stained with washes of oil paint and turpentine to achieve an overall colour match before applying smaller flecks of colour as described above to disguise the edges and blend in the grain.
- Leave any patch to dry thoroughly for a couple of days before carefully applying a coat of finish.

Filling the grain

In some woods, the pores of the grain are larger than in others and can be clearly seen through the finish. With some woods such as oak or teak, which can be finished with oil, this is quite acceptable but not if you want a high gloss, for example French polish on mahogany.

Having decided to fill the grain, you then have to decide how best to do it. You can apply layer upon layer of polish or varnish, rubbing down between coats with fine abrasive paper until the grain is filled up with the finish itself. This is undoubtedly the best method as you will have no problem with colour matching, but is very time consum-

ing. If you are going to paint the surface it is pointless, as you are not concerned with colour matching anyway.

Another method is to apply plaster of paris mixed with some powdered pigment to colour it. This is rubbed into the grain with a damp cloth. This is a traditional method used by French polishers from about the middle of the nineteenth century to the beginning of the twentieth, and you will often find that having stripped an old piece of furniture, the grain stands out as pale coloured flecks. This is the plaster of paris filler which was originally wiped over with linseed oil to 'kill it'. You can do the same yourself before refinishing the surface. This method of grain filling may affect the hardening of some modern finishes.

A more convenient method is to use proprietary grain fillers, which are available in a wide range of wood colours. The colour can be adjusted by adding a compatible stain to the filler, to match the wood you are working on. Mix it slightly darker than required as it will lighten as it dries.

- To use an oil-based filler, thin it to a creamy consistency with white spirit.
- Rub it on to the wood with a circular motion to push it into the grain. Use a coarse cloth like hessian to avoid pulling it out of the grain.
- Ensure that all the pores are filled then use a clean piece of hessian to wipe the filler off the surface of the wood, finishing lightly with the grain. Remove any residue of filler from mouldings or carving with a blunt pointed stick.
- Leave the filler to harden overnight, then rub it down lightly with fine glass paper. Remove all the dust with a soft brush.
- Seal the filled grain with a coat of the finish you intend to use.

Finishing the surface

Oil

Raw linseed oil is not really suitable as a complete finish for furniture. It takes up to three days to dry, picking up dust over that period. Boiled linseed oil which is heated and contains 'driers' is slightly better but can still take up to twenty-four hours to dry. It is better to use a good quality teak oil which is formulated to dry in four to eight hours.

Although it can be used on any timber, oil looks best as an open grained finish on oak, teak or any of the African or Central American hardwoods. It can be applied over grain filler as well with no problem.
• Oil is the most simple of all finishes to apply. Take a clean, soft rag and apply it liberally to the surfaces of the timber and after a few minutes wipe off the excess oil with another clean rag.
• After two to three coats of oil, the timber will acquire a slight sheen. Refresh the surface with another coat of oil as required.

Wax

On the subject of wax finishes, we enter one of the areas of controversy in furniture renovation. A traditional hard wax polish is made by melting beeswax and carnauba wax and mixing them with pure turpentine. The resulting polish is brushed on to the bare wood, allowed to set and then buffed with considerable effort to a very attractive mellow finish. Beeswax can be found fairly easily, but carnauba wax is very difficult to obtain, especially in a purified form for a white wax. There are commercially prepared waxes, both white and a dark coloured 'antique' wax, which are softer than the traditional wax polish and are therefore much easier to buff, but they are less durable. It is very difficult however, to find a ready prepared wax that does not contain silicone and it is this substance which causes most of the problems. It is added to polishes to provide more 'slip', which is why they buff to a high gloss so easily, but it can eventually penetrate the timber and it will repel other finishes should the piece ever need to be restored in the future.

On the other hand, it must be said that a pure wax finish is not especially desirable. It is a relatively soft finish which can absorb dirt and carry it in to the pores of the wood, which may take on a greyish tinge. Neither is it a particularly durable surface. Heat, alcohol and water all mark it relatively easily. For all these reasons, you should always seal the timber first, for example with shellac or polyurethane, before applying a wax polish. In this way you will have a finish which has the subtle sheen associated with wax polish, but one which is more durable. Should you wish to strip the finish for renovation at a later date, first remove the wax with white spirit (see page 7) then strip the remaining finish with a commercial stripper, which should remove any remaining traces of silicone.

French polish

French polishing was introduced to this country in the early part of the nineteenth century and became widespread throughout the Victorian period. The polish itself is made by dissolving shellac, a substance exuded by the lac insect, in alcohol.

In most hardware stores you will find a number of different French polishes. The purest shellac is reserved for *button polish*, so called because the shellac is left to cool in the form of a thin 50mm disc which can be viewed against the light to ensure that there are no impurities. Less pure shellac is produced in flake form.

Special button polish, which is rarely available today, is normal button polish which has been allowed to stand until its natural wax has settled to the bottom. The polish which is skimmed from the surface is slightly harder than normal.

White polish is produced by bleaching the normal reddish brown polish. It is used to polish light coloured woods.

Transparent polish is white polish with the natural wax removed and it is ideal for light woods or when no additional colour is required.

Garnet polish is a dark red French polish containing shellac produced by a different species of insect. It is used mainly on dark woods, especially mahogany.

All of these polishes can be dissolved by alcohol and are melted by heat (see page 8) and cannot therefore produce a particularly durable finish, especially for a table top. Whether you apply French polish to a particular piece depends on what you intend to do with it. Given that the piece was originally finished in this way, you must French polish it again if the furniture is for investment or resale. Any other finish would devalue it. On the other hand, if you intend to subject the piece to hard daily use you might well decide to use a durable finish such as polyurethane or cold cure lacquer. This may be heresy to a traditional restorer, but it makes sense for a growing family.

Making a rubber

French polish is built up by applying many thin coats with a pad of soft cloth and cotton wool known in the trade as a 'rubber'.

Ordinary cotton wool can be used to make a rubber. Some professionals prefer to use upholsterer's skin wadding (see page 83) because it makes a firmer pad which will hold a point at one end. This is useful for getting the rubber into details and corners.

- Take a good handful of cotton wool, form it into a roughly egg-shaped pad and place it in the centre of a square of clean, lint-free cloth such as a gent's handkerchief.

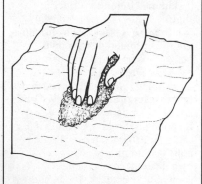

- Fold in the edges, gathering the loose fabric in the palm of the hand so that there are no wrinkles on the sole of the rubber.

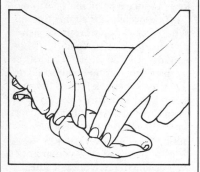

- Unfold the cloth and pour polish, a little at a time, on to the centre of the pad until it is well charged but not overflowing.

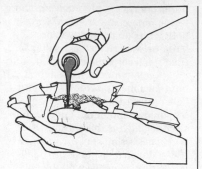

- Refold the cloth and press the rubber on to scrap wood to squeeze out excess polish and to distribute it evenly over the sole.

Applying the polish

Always work in a clean, dry and warm environment. A cold, damp atmosphere will cause the finish to 'bloom' or go cloudy. Dust should be avoided, as with any finishing process. Work in a good light, preferably in front of a window where you can glance across the surface into the light. This will enable you to see the build-up of polish and spot any blemishes. To explain the process of French polishing let us suppose that we are finishing a flat panel.

- Close the neck of a bottle of linseed oil with a finger tip and tip up the bottle to wet the finger. Dab it on to the sole of a charged rubber to lubricate it.
- Apply the polish with overlapping circular strokes, followed by sweeping figure of eight strokes. Make sure that the polish is carried right up to the edges. Very little pressure will be required on a freshly charged rubber to encourage the polish to flow but as it is used up over successive coats the pressure should be increased.
- Never allow the rubber to come to rest on a polished surface. Keep it moving throughout the sequence, sweeping on and off the surface.

If the rubber is allowed to stop on the surface it will stick, leaving a blemish. Work at a steady, even pace and apply more oil to the rubber if it starts to drag.

- Having coated the surface thinly, finish off with straight strokes along the grain and allow it to dry.
- After about fifteen to twenty minutes, the surface will be dry enough to apply another coat. Build up four or five coats a day and leave it overnight to harden before building the finish up further. The individual polisher must decide how many coats to apply, but somewhere between ten and twenty will be sufficient.
- Any blemishes, such as a rubber mark, a run or dust particles, can be rubbed down with very fine silicon carbide paper before applying further polish.
- You can adjust the colour of the furniture as you build up the finish by adding a little oil-based stain to tint the polish. Add the stain to the polish in a glass jar (not the other way round, which will result in separation of the stain and polish), applying it to the rubber in the normal way.

Spiriting off

Once you have built up the polish to your satisfaction, it should be 'spirited off' to remove linseed oil from the surface and burnish it.

- Pour a few drops of meths into the rubber, which should be virtually free of polish.
- Apply meths to the surface using the long straight strokes in the direction of the grain. As soon as the rubber begins to drag recharge it with meths.
- Leave the job for a couple of minutes before burnishing again. Finally polish with a dry soft duster.
- Put the job in a dust-free environment to harden off completely for at least a week.

A satin finish

French polish can be burnished to a very high gloss if that is what you require. If you want a more subtle sheen it can be cut back with 000 steel wool after it has hardened for a couple of days.
● Dip a ball of steel wool into wax, which acts as a lubricant, and make extremely light strokes with the grain until the surface is dull with no indications of scratching.
● Wipe the surface with a dry, clean cloth to remove any dust and apply a coat of wax polish.

Polishing small areas

Polishing furniture is never quite as simple as finishing a flat panel. Even polishing up to edges has it problems. Inevitably some polish will be squeezed out over an edge and you should pick up any runs before the polish solidifies.

Internal corners can be treated with the pointed toe of the rubber, but remember to keep it moving as for flat surfaces.

Shallow mouldings can be polished with a rubber but deep and complicated mouldings, as well as carving, can be painted with a brush. Use a soft paint brush to apply the polish, which has been diluted slightly with meths. Paint it on carefully to avoid runs and any build-up in crevices, but do not over-brush it as brush marks will show. Burnish the high points with a meths-charged rubber at the end of the process, but rub lightly to avoid removing shellac.

Cellulose varnish

Cellulose varnish was used extensively for mass produced furniture from the 1930s to the mid-1950s, mainly because it could be sprayed on and dried rapidly. Nowadays it has been completely superseded by the synthetic varnishes, such as polyurethane. It is still used in the car industry and can be obtained in aerosol cans from shops specialising in car accessories. Unfortunately these are nearly always cellulose paints containing an opaque pigment. Clear cellulose, the most useful form for furniture, is very difficult to obtain, and then is supplied in large quantity, say from five litres upwards.

French polishing kits

One of the best ways of initiating yourself into French polishing is to use one of the commercially available kits, which are specially formulated to make the job as simple as possible. The shellac polish, in a slightly thinner form than standard French polish, contains a lubricant which makes it very easy to apply without the use of linseed oil. Having built up a sufficient coat of shellac, a burnishing liquid is used to produce the final gloss. It includes a mild abrasive, similar to paint cleaner or metal polish, which removes minor blemishes from the shellac coat. This liquid can be used to revive an old French polished surface once it has been cleaned and dewaxed (see page 7).

The process of applying the polish differs sufficiently from the standard method to warrant further description.
● To start with, two brush coats of polish must be applied to the bare wood. Use as large a brush as is practicable for the size of the job so that you can flow the polish on to the surface, picking up the wet edges before they become tacky. Leave half an hour between coats without rubbing down in between. This method is employed by many professional French polishers to build up a body coat of polish quickly. An amateur is unlikely to produce a perfectly flat finish and it should therefore be sanded with the grain, using a fine abrasive paper round a block. Take care that you do not cut through the shellac to the wood.
● More polish is applied using a rubber as described on page 14, but the charged cotton wool pad is wrapped in linen which has been soaked in methylated spirit and wrung out.
● Apply the polish using circular and figure of eight strokes going over the surface about twelve times.
● Every few minutes, change the linen cloth for one which is freshly soaked in meths. Wring it out so that it is damp only and return the used one to a screw-top jar containing more meths. This will dissolve the polish on the cloth so that it can be used again.
● When the polish has set, sand the surface lightly with silicon carbide paper and re-polish as before, re-charging the rubber as required.
● Sand down again and apply one more coat with slightly less polish in the rubber.
● Let the last coat dry thoroughly, then wet one side of a cotton wool pad with the burnishing liquid contained in the kit. Burnish a small section of the surface, rubbing vigorously with the grain and covering the area about twenty-five times.
● Dry the burnished area with a soft yellow duster to put the final gloss on the surface.
● Pull off the soiled layer of cotton wool from the pad and re-charge it with burnisher. Repeat the process over the whole piece of furniture, working a small section at a time.

Cellulose is resistant to alcohol and is more resistant than French polish to heat and water, but comes nowhere near modern finishes in durability. Cellulose finish also has a tendency to 'craze', a fault which can be sometimes cured by wiping over rapidly with cellulose thinners. It is applied by aerosol or spray gun (see page 17) and when burnished to a high gloss has a curiously thin appearance which cannot compare with French polish. It does have a use in sealing new wood by wiping over on a cloth, since it dries very rapidly, and can quickly be followed by a wax polish, but unless you want to restore a 1930s piece of furniture to exactly its original appearance it has little value in modern restoration. French polish is best for a traditional finish and polyurethane or cold cure lacquer for furniture in everyday use. Bare patches in cellulose finish can safely be filled in with French polish.

Polyurethane varnish

Polyurethane varnish is an excellent finish for furniture (except oily timbers like teak or rose wood), being heated and water resistant. It dries to a hard, durable finish and is easy to apply. It tends to darken with age.

Two-pack polyurethanes are available which must be mixed before application. They have a short pot life and the adhesion between coats is sometimes not very good. They also give off fumes which can be harmful. A one-part polyurethane, which can be used straight from the tin, is preferable.

Besides the clear variety of polyurethane, you can obtain it in a range of bright transparent colours – blue, red, green and so on – and also in several wood colours such as teak, mahogany and oak. Their purpose is to avoid the necessity of applying stain to the wood before varnishing but they suffer from the disadvantage that each successive coat makes the colour darker. Also, because the colour is carried in the finish, scratches are more obvious. Polyurethanes can be obtained in gloss, semi-gloss and matt finishes. Although the matt version is visually acceptable, it does not feel as smooth as a matt finish produced by rubbing down a gloss finish with fine wire wool. The matt version is much improved by a coat of wax.

Applying polyurethane

Polyurethane varnish is painted on to furniture with normal paint brushes. Mouldings and carvings should be painted first, but pick up the wet edges so that brush marks flow out naturally.

- Leave the finish to dry overnight before rubbing down with a fine abrasive paper or wire wool. Apply a second coat of varnish. Repeat the process as necessary. Three coats are usually sufficient.
- Polyurethane can also be sprayed (see page 17).

Cold cure lacquer

Cold cure lacquer, which is very hard and durable, is capable of a high gloss finish with burnishing. The clarity will not change with age and it is used for bars, counters and the like. Before use, the lacquer is mixed with a hardener but still has a pot life of two to three days, or longer still if stored in an airtight jar. It can be bought as a clear finish or as an opaque white or black. The latter is very useful for simulating black japanned furniture.

- Paint the lacquer on to the work quite liberally, but do not over-brush it. It will flow out, leaving an even film. The first coat will be dry after two hours and another can be applied, but successive coats should be left overnight.
- Imperfections in the finish can be rubbed down with fine abrasive paper between coats.
- Leave the last coat overnight and either burnish it to a high gloss with metal polish or burnishing cream, or rub it down with fine wire wool and wax it for a satin finish.

Paint

In many ways, the modern varnishes which we have discussed so far can be considered as clear paints. The opaque paints so often used in the home have a similar chemical composition to varnish but contain pigments which colour them. It is even more important to prepare the surface well and fill the grain when using an opaque finish because there will be nothing to distract the eye from small blemishes. Even fine grain timbers can be filled using a sanding sealer which contains an inert powder which acts as a filler. Having brushed on the sanding sealer it is rubbed down prior to applying a coat of paint. For the same reason, an opaque finish is built up with a primer and an undercoat to produce a dense, even film.

Before starting to paint, you may also need to use *knotting*. This is a material used to seal in the resinous material which surrounds a knot in a piece of pine. It is not likely to be necessary on an old piece of pine furniture, but if you have added new timber during restoration the knots should be treated to prevent the resin appearing on the top surface of your paint finish.

Primer

Paint a coat of primer over the bare timber to seal it and provide an ideal surface upon which to build a good paint finish. Leave overnight before rubbing down with fine wet and dry paper in preparation for further painting.

Undercoat

Undercoat is used to build up a thickness of the paint finish, rubbing down between coats to produce a perfectly flat surface. It is always a matt finish which provides good adhesion between coats, and is either white or an approximate colour match to the top coat.

Top coat

The top coat is the final layer of the paint finish and can be matt, satin (semi-gloss) or full gloss. If there are any blemishes on the top coat, such as dust particles or runs, it can be rubbed down with wet and dry paper to produce a matt finish and repainted.

Painting with a brush

Always use a good quality brush to paint furniture. It will last a lot longer and more important, it is less likely to shed its bristles to ruin good paintwork.

- When you dip the brush into the paint, load the tip only, touching off excess paint on the lip of the can. This will not only prevent paint hardening in the roots of the bristles (which will shorten the life of the brush), but you are less likely to flood the job with too much paint.
- Start by painting mouldings or along the edge of a panel, working away from them and picking up the wet edge of the paint to prevent brush marks showing. Watch for runs and brush them out at once.

- For a flat, even coverage, apply the paint with strokes in different directions, blending the paint and finally finishing with light upward strokes to prevent runs.

Spraying

Spraying paint produces a much more even coat than is possible with a brush. It is an ideal method of painting any furniture which contains a lot of fine detail, such as carving or mouldings, which will be filled to some extent with a brush. It is also faster, although more coats will be required as they should be considerably thinner than those applied with a brush. It is essential to wear a gauze mask while spraying and to work in a well-ventilated room. Extinguish any naked flames and do not smoke. Place plenty of newspapers or old sheets under and behind the work to catch the overspray of paint.

Aerosol spray cans are suitable for small jobs but for a large piece of furniture it would be better to hire a spray gun and compressor. The paint in an aerosol is the correct consistency for spraying but you will need to thin other paints for use in a spray gun.

Using an aerosol

An aerosol should be held between 150mm (6in) and 200mm (8in) from the work to achieve the best results. If you hold it any closer, too much paint will be sprayed and runs will occur. If it is too far from the work, the paint starts to dry before it hits the surface, resulting in a powdery finish.

- Make steady parallel passes along the work, keeping the nozzle pointing directly at the surface throughout the movement. If you swing the can across in an arc you will have an uneven covering of paint.

- Make sure that the spray pattern is clear of the end of the work before releasing the button, and start spraying before each pass begins to prevent a build-up of paint at the edges. Overlap each pass for good coverage.

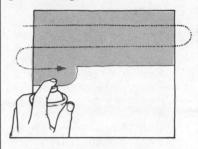

- To paint a horizontal surface, hold the nozzle at 45° to the work and work away from you, keeping the can the same distance from the surface the whole time.

Using a spray gun

A spray gun is used in the same way as an aerosol can, but as it is more powerful it should be held further from the work. Unlike an aerosol the spray pattern can be adjusted, as well as the density of spray.

An aerosol is thrown away once it is empty but do not throw it into a fire or puncture it. A spray gun must be cleaned by spraying thinners through it until it comes out clear. Dismantle the nozzle and wipe it and the inside of the paint container with a cloth dampened with thinners.

CHAPTER THREE

Surface repairs

Any old piece of furniture will have suffered some abuse. It may have been dented whilst the owner was moving house, burnt by cigarettes or crashed into by a child at play.

To some extent damage like this is part of the history of the piece and adds to its character, indeed the makers of reproduction furniture frequently 'distress' it by striking it with heavy implements to imitate this appearance.

Just how far you go in repairing holes, dents and cracks is very much a matter of individual taste, but if you do decide to give the piece a thorough repair, it should be stripped first. It is possible to disguise a dent with solid polish or varnish, but this is at best a temporary measure. Damage to solid timber surfaces is relatively straightforward to deal with but the repair of veneers is a subject in itself and is dealt with separately.

Repairing solid timber surfaces

Damage to these surfaces can be divided into dents, holes, cracks and burns.

Holes and cracks

A hole, a deep scratch, a crack or an open joint are all treated in a similar way. They have to be filled with one of a range of materials depending on their size. Wax, commercial stopper, shellac, plastic wood or household filler may all be used. Colour matching is important, so stain the piece and seal it with a coat of the eventual finish before starting the repair.

Wax

Very small holes, such as wood-worm flight holes, can be filled with wax. Beeswax, heelball (which is a shoemaker's wax) or even children's coloured wax crayons are suitable. Coloured crayons are especially useful, as they can be mixed by melting them in a heated spoon to match the colour of the wood.
- Use a knife or a chisel to press the wax into the hole, scraping it flush gently with the blade.
- Smooth the wax by burnishing with the back of abrasive paper.
- Either finish with French polish or at least seal the repair with one coat of it before finishing with a modern varnish.

Stopper

For larger holes use stopper, a thick paste sold in tubes or cans. It is sold in the usual wood colours, which can be adjusted by mixing with a stain before application. Alternatively, several coloured stoppers can be mixed together.
- Where possible, undercut the edge of the hole and press the stopper into it with a flexible blade. Leave the stopper slightly proud in case it shrinks.
- When dry, lightly sand it flush with a very fine abrasive paper.

Shellac sticks

Shellac sticks are melted into holes to produce a hard stopping. They are only available from specialist suppliers.
- Hold the stick over the hole and melt the tip with a soldering iron.

Dents

Lay a damp cloth over the area and press the tip of a heated iron or soldering iron on to the dent. The resulting steam swells the fibre locally, raising the dent.
- Alternatively, use the steam generator described for softening glue in joints (see page 28), playing the steam directly on to the dent.
- Allow the area to dry and sand it smooth with fine glasspaper.
- If the dent is too deep to be repaired in this way, treat it as you would a hole.

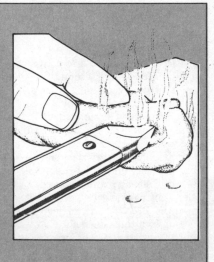

- It will set hard almost immediately and can be pared with a sharp blade until it is almost flush before sanding it smooth with a fine abrasive paper.
- A wipe over with French polish will smooth out the surface.

Plastic wood

Plastic wood is a commercial filler which is very hard when set. It is the best type of filler to use when building up a broken edge.
- Press it into the repair, shaping it to match the edge as closely as possible.
- When hard, use abrasive paper to sand the filler to shape.

Household fillers

Normal household DIY fillers, used to mend cracks in walls and so on, can be used to fill a hole and can be coloured with a water-based stain.
- Press the filler into the hole, leaving it very slightly proud, and sand it flush when set.

Burns

Firstly try abrading the damage with a burnishing cream (see page 7).
- If this does not work, scrape out the charred wood from the hole with the tip of a knife blade or a piece of abrasive paper wrapped around a pointed stick.
- Fill the hole with polish or a filler as described above. See page 11 for touching in repairs.

Veneers

A veneer is a very thin sheet of wood stuck on to a substantial wooden base called the groundwork. There are two main types of veneer – constructional (which are cheap veneers used to face blockboard and to make up plywood) and decorative. Nearly all the veneers on old furniture are decorative.

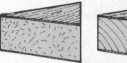

Chipboard   **Solid wood**

Blockboard   **Plywood**

One often hears the phrase 'cheap veneered furniture', implying that the piece is of second rate material hidden by veneers. Whilst this is undoubtedly true of some mass produced furniture, veneering has a very honourable history and some of the most valuable pieces of furniture in the world's museums are covered in decorative veneers. This is mainly because veneering allows elaborate pattern making based on grain patterns that could never be used with solid timber. A curl for instance, that lovely fan shape often found on door fronts, is produced by cutting veneer from an area of the tree where two main branches meet. A solid panel cut from this section would distort and split in no time. A burr veneer, which is recognised by its tiny interlocking swirls of irregular grain, is cut from a wart-like growth on the tree. Although it is perhaps the most highly prized veneer for decorative pur-

poses it would be totally useless in thicker sections, having no continuous grain.

Although veneering was known to the ancient Egyptians 3000 years ago, and later to the Greeks and Romans, it did not arrive in England until the early seventeenth century, when walnut was most often used. Later Chippendale, Sheraton and Hepplewhite veneered in mahogany and satinwood, usually on a groundwork of cheap mahogany.

Originally, veneers were cut by hand and later by huge circular saws with segmented teeth, but this practice died out in the nineteenth century. Nowadays all veneers are cut with a giant knife from logs softened by boiling or steaming. The log may be *rotary cut*, where the log is revolved against the knife, or for more decorative grain patterns, the log is sliced across the grain. It is either cut across the whole width of the tree, a process known as *crown cutting*, or the log is first quartered and the veneers sliced more or less in line with the radius of the tree, a process called *quarter cutting*. The resulting veneers are used in pairs or fours to make a variety of patterns, some of which are shown in the panel overleaf.

The groundwork in modern furniture is usually a composite board such as blockboard, plywood or chipboard. These boards make ideal groundwork, since they are relatively stable in conditions of changing temperature and humidity. In older furniture however, the groundwork is solid timber, most often softwood but sometimes a less valuable hardwood, such as cheap mahogany. It is the movement of the groundwork which causes most of the problems you will encounter with old veneered furniture. As it shrinks or swells, it breaks down the glue line between itself and the veneer, causing splits and loose veneer.

Types of veneer

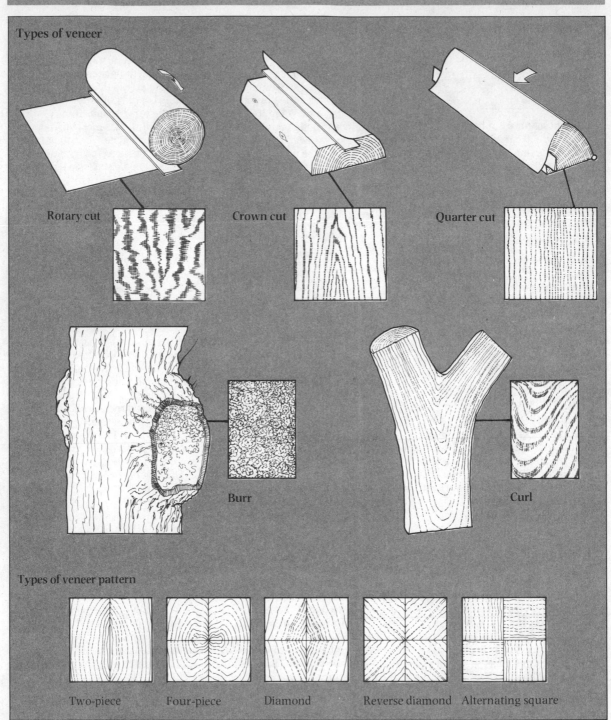

Rotary cut

Crown cut

Quarter cut

Burr

Curl

Types of veneer pattern

Two-piece

Four-piece

Diamond

Reverse diamond

Alternating square

Matching a veneer repair

Obtaining a veneer which exactly matches that of the furniture you are working on will not be easy. Strictly speaking, the old and new veneers should match in colour, grain pattern and even reflectivity, that is the appearance of the veneer as it is viewed from different angles. Without the resources of a professional, the best an amateur can hope for is a reasonably close match.

It is very much better to use old veneer if you can. This can be obtained by stripping it from an old piece of furniture which is past repairing. Having removed the finish, leave rags soaked in water in contact with the veneer overnight. With luck, this will be sufficient to lift the veneer but if not a hot iron on a damp cloth should generate enough steam to finish the job. Scrape the old glue from the surface of the veneer while it is still soft and then leave it overnight, pressed between sheets of chipboard to flatten out. Sandwich a sheet of newspaper between the veneer and chipboard to prevent any traces of glue adhering to the board.

New veneers can be bought from specialist suppliers who have considerable experience in matching veneers. They will even identify the wood for you if you are not sure what it is. The best way is to take the piece of furniture with you, or if it is too large, just a door or a drawer. Veneer shops are not all that common and you are unlikely to find one outside large towns, in which case you can use mail order. Enclose a piece of veneer to help them provide a good match. Mail-order firms also provide sheets of veneer samples from which to order, but they are no replacement for sending them a piece of your veneer. Sample sheets are mostly used by hobbyists choosing materials for marquetry.

Adhesives

On old furniture, all veneers were laid by using animal or 'Scotch' glue. It is still available as 'beads' or 'cakes' which must be melted in a heated glue pot and applied while hot and runny. Air and excess glue is squeezed out from beneath the veneer using a special tool known as a veneer hammer (see page 25). Alternatively, the veneers are clamped under heated boards known as cauls.

In many ways, animal glue is ideal for veneering because it is water soluble and is thus easily removable later, but some modern glues are more convenient for the amateur. Normal white woodworking glue (known as PVA) is suitable for small areas of veneer so long as it can be clamped. It is not really suitable for laying large sheets of veneer and is most used for marquetry.

Impact, or contact, adhesives are painted on to both the veneer and the groundwork and allowed to 'go off' for a few minutes. Then, when the two surfaces are brought together, they adhere instantly. These adhesives allow you to glue even large sheets of veneer without a press. Similarly, curved surfaces which are more difficult to cramp can be successfuly veneered with these glues. It is important to use a thixotropic impact adhesive which can be spread thinly and evenly as an uneven layer of glue will show through.

The latest adhesive, specially made for veneering, is produced as a thin film of glue on a paper backing. The film is applied to the groundwork with a warm iron and the paper backing stripped off. The veneer is then laid in position and again treated with a warm iron to give a perfect bond. The paper backing is used again to protect the veneer from the iron.

Raising dents in veneer

Dents can be raised from a veneered surface in the way described for treating those in solid timber (see page 18). However, as soon as the surface is level, apply a softening block and cramp the area of the dent to ensure that it remains glued as it cools and dries out. If the dent happens to be in the middle of a table top or a chest of drawers it can often be difficult to use a G-cramp or sash cramp. If so, try wedging a thin, flexible strip of wood between the work and the ceiling of your workshop.

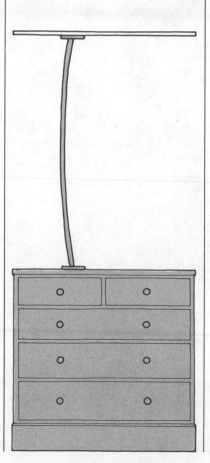

Flattening blisters

Blisters can often be found in a veneer where a patch was missed when the glue was applied, or an air bubble was left under the veneer.

● Try the simplest method first, which is to slit the blister along the grain with a sharp knife to release the trapped air. Then apply a heated iron over a damp cloth on to the blistered veneer. Do not apply too much pressure until the veneer is soft enough to flatten without cracking. If there is sufficient glue under the veneer, it will adhere successfully to the groundwork without further treatment.

● If necessary, work fresh PVA glue under the blister with a knife blade, flatten it with a veneer hammer or with a seam roller used for wall-papering and wipe excess glue from the surface.

● Stick a length of gummed paper tape over the slit to counteract any tendency for it to open up as the veneer shrinks.

Damaged veneers

One often finds small patches of bare groundwork along the edge of a panel or rail where pieces of veneer have been chipped away and lost (see **diagram a** below). Very small areas can be filled with plastic wood and coloured to match (see page 11) but a better method is to insert a small patch of veneer.

● Having selected your veneer for as close a match as possible, check its thickness against that of the veneer on the furniture. The new veneer should be marginally thicker than the old one to allow for light sanding after it has been glued. Two veneers can be glued together to make up the thickness. If you feel that sanding the double thickness will expose the glue line between them, sand the underside of the bottom veneer before positioning the patch.

● Tape a patch of veneer over the damaged area, lining up the grain pattern as closely as possible and leaving an overlap at the edge (**b**).

● Using a sharp knife and straight edge, cut a V-shaped patch through both veneers at once (**c**).

● Use a chisel and knife blade to remove the old veneer within the scored area and scrape the groundwork clean (**d**).

● The ideal method of gluing a patch is to iron a piece of glue film on to its back surface (see page 25). Position the patch, lay a piece of backing paper over it and apply an iron set at its lowest heat. When the glue has set, trim off the overhang with a sharp knife and sand the patch flush. Where possible turn the groundwork upside-down and trim the veneer from below (**e**). Any damage away from the edge of a panel, for example a burn, is repaired in the same way as chipped veneer but in this case cut a diamond or boat shaped patch (**f**).

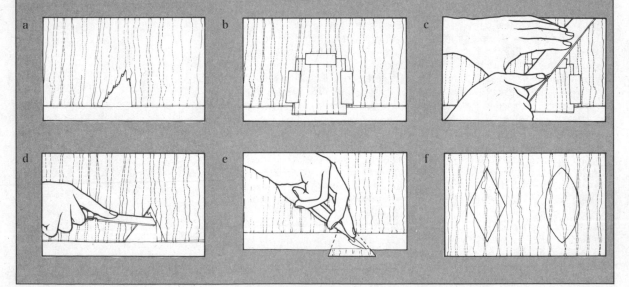

• Lay wax paper or newsprint under a softening block and cramp the work until the glue sets.

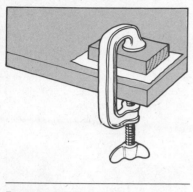

Loose veneer

A patch of loose veneer, at the corner of a table top for instance, can be re-glued in a similar way to a blister, but as dirt will have contaminated the glue scrape the groundwork and the underside of the veneer with a sharp blade to remove the old glue.
• Apply fresh glue under the veneer and cramp until set.
• Alternatively, you can peel a patch of film glue from its backing paper, slip it under the loose veneer and iron it flat.

Inlay

Inlay is the term used to describe forms of decorative pattern produced by laying different veneers together. It may be simple stringing, which is a thin line of contrasting wood running parallel to the edge of a leg or panel. Bandings are strips made up from many small pieces of veneer. Cross banding (see below) is the best known. Marquetry is the art of laying veneers to form pictorial motifs, while in parquetry the veneers are used to form geometric patterns. Marquetry motifs showing flowers, shells, vases and the like are often inlaid on old furniture.

Since they are composed of such small vulnerable pieces, inlays are frequently damaged or missing.

Loose inlays

If the inlay has loosened, scrape off the old glue as well as you can considering the fragile nature of the work and apply fresh glue to the underside of the veneer with a knife blade before pressing it back in place. Leave overnight in cramps, protecting the inlay with grease-proofed paper.

Missing inlays

Missing inlays can be replaced from a wide range of stringing, banding and motifs available from a specialist stockist or by mail order. One should attempt to conserve as much of the original inlay as possible but at times most of it may be missing. In this case it is better to remove the little that is left and to replace it with a new inlay.
• Scrape the groundwork clean of old glue and dirt with a small chisel and, using a piece of veneer, spread a thin layer of contact glue in the recess.
• Do the same on the banding and when touch dry, position the inlay.
• Alternatively, spread hot glue on to both surfaces and press the inlay into position with the cross pein of a hammer.

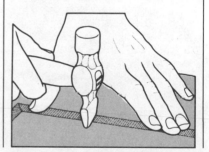

Inlay patterns

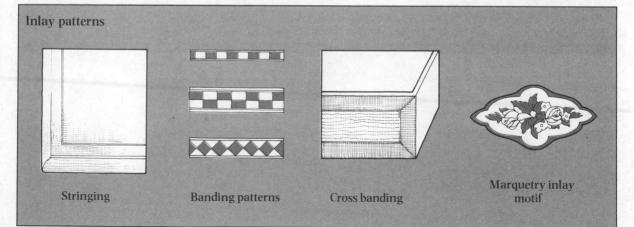

Stringing

Banding patterns

Cross banding

Marquetry inlay motif

- If a piece of veneer is missing from a marquetry motif, lay a piece of tracing paper on the work and rub over it with a wax crayon to reproduce the shape.

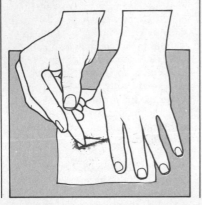

- Using carbon paper, transfer the shape on to a piece of suitable veneer or prick it through with a needle. Be careful to align the grain correctly.

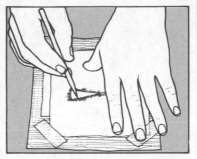

- Cut the shape out with a sharp knife, glue the veneer in place with animal glue and sand it flush.

Veneering a whole panel

If a veneered panel is so badly damaged that none of the previous repairs will restore it, soak it from the groundwork and lay a replacement veneer.

- Having scraped old glue from the groundwork, key it with coarse abrasive paper, making sure the surface is perfectly flat.

- As the veneer should be slightly larger than the panel all round, it may be necessary to join two or more sheets of veneer together, in which case lay them one on top of the other with face sides together and trim the meeting edges, using a straight edge and knife to cut through both veneers at once.
- Cramp both veneers between battens, and plane the cut edges with a sharp, finely set plane.

Shading a patch

Some traditional motifs, such as corner fans or Sheraton ovals, are made up with shaded veneers. The shaded effect is produced by dipping the veneer in hot sand. If one of these sections is missing from a motif, you will need to shade its replacement.

- Pour some fine silver sand, available from pet shops, into a metal lid or baking tray and heat it over a gas stove or electric hot plate. The exact temperature can only be gauged by experiment.
- Cut a piece of veneer larger than required and dip it partially into the hot sand using tweezers. Leave it for a few seconds and then withdraw it.
- Lightly sand the piece, then wet it to compare the result with the original shading.
- Adjust the time the veneer is in the sand to produce the required tone, then cut and fit it as described above.

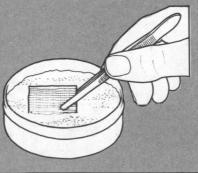

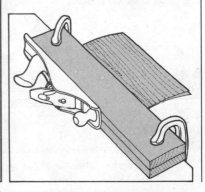

- Open the veneers like a book to reveal the face sides and butt the edges together. Secure the joint with short strips of gummed paper across it and one piece along its length. Rub the tape down to ensure that it is holding securely.

- The method of gluing depends on which adhesive you use. The methods are given below. Whichever method you use, when the glue is dry, trim the excess veneer from the edges of the groundwork with a sharp knife, soak off the paper tapes with a moist rag, sand the veneer flat and finish as desired.

Using animal glues

To use a traditional glue, heat the beads in a glue pot to the temperature recommended by the manufacturer. This will be about 120°Fahrenheit (49°C). Alternatively, you can obtain a type of Scotch glue which is heated by standing the tin of adhesive in a pan of hot water.
- Warm the groundwork with an electric iron.
- Brush an even, thin coat of hot liquid glue on to both surfaces and lay the veneer in position, taped side uppermost, smoothing it down by hand.
- Rub the veneer with a rag dampened in hot water and press down with an electric iron set to the lowest temperature.
- Take a veneer hammer and press the veneer down from the centre outwards using a series of zig-zag

strokes. This action will force air and excess glue out to the edges. Wipe off the glue before it sets.

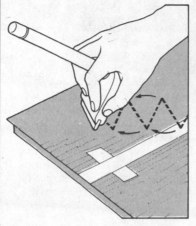

- If the glue cools before you have pressed all the veneer down, dampen and re-heat with the iron.

Using contact adhesive

To use contact adhesive, spread a thin coat on to both the veneer and the groundwork with a brush, or scrape it on with the edge of a piece of thick veneer. Allow the glue to dry.
- Lay a sheet of paper over the groundwork, except for about 50mm (2in) at one end.
- Lay the glued sheet of veneer on to the work, aligning it carefully with the edge of the panel. Press down firmly on to the 50mm strip which is in contact with the groundwork.

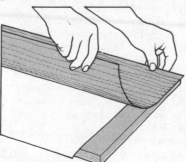

- Gradually withdraw the sheet of paper, pressing the veneer down on to the groundwork with a veneer hammer, hardwood seam roller or a block of wood.

Using glue film

To obtain the best results with glue film over a large area, first strip off the backing paper so that you have a film of glue alone. Lay this on to the groundwork. Now place the veneer on the glue and finally put the backing paper on top of the veneer.

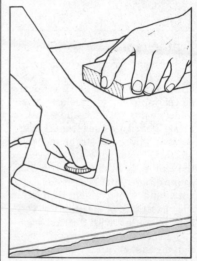

- With an electric iron on its 'rayon' setting, work slowly across the entire surface of the backing paper, heating and pressing down the veneer and following up with a block of chipboard in the other hand to ensure it is bonded firmly.
- This method is for large areas only. For small patches of veneer, lay the glue film with its backing paper intact on to the back of the veneer and press it with a heated iron. Strip off the paper and then lay the veneer as described above. The glue can be applied before the patch is cut to shape if you wish to ensure complete coverage.

CHAPTER FOUR

Structural repairs

Chairs

Our basic classification of chairs falls into four families – frame, balloon back, stick and bentwood. This is explained under *Assessing the work* (see page 6).

Frame chairs

Chairs are subjected to a good deal of wear and tear, particularly when someone tilts the chair and transfers his weight to the back legs. This imposes an enormous strain on the mortice and tenon joints between the seat rails and the back legs. A frame dining chair is designed to withstand this treatment by having the widest face of the seat rails vertically in contact with the back legs.

Some chairs of lighter construction are made with the widest face of the seat rails in line with the seat itself. In these cases, the seat frame is usually notched into the back legs and held in position by wooden pegs or screws. The front legs, which are often turned, are glued into sockets in the underside of the seat frame. Obviously this design is weaker than the dining chair, so stretcher rails are introduced to give support to the legs. These slender rails are usually morticed into the legs and may be turned to match the style of the chair. The number and position of the stretcher rails varies, but they are usually placed near the floor to counter the leverage of the leg on the seat frame. This type of chair is

often known as a bedroom chair, on the assumption that it receives less strenuous treatment in that location. Similarly, a more elegant and lightly built dining chair, incorporating stretcher rails, may be known as a drawing room chair.

Assessing chairs

The condition of the joints between the seat rails and the back legs is particularly important when buying a chair. Tilt the chair on its back legs and push down on the front of the seat. Slight movement in the joints indicates that the glue is loose, a condition which should not be too difficult to correct. On the other hand a lot of movement could mean that the joints are actually broken, which will result in a far more extensive repair.

There are lots of other clues as to whether a chair is a good buy or not. Look underneath the seat frame to see if the seat rail/back leg joints have been reinforced with metal brackets. This is a sign that the joints have been loose in the past.

In extreme cases, the joints may have been nailed. In old chairs the nails will have rusted in and are notoriously difficult to remove, a fact which may dissuade you from purchase.

Look too for wooden corner braces which were often glued and

screwed to the inside of the seat frame: they may be loose or missing. A worn stretcher rail can often be accepted as part of a chair's character, but broken ones will need to be re-glued and a missing rail may involve turning, which is not the easiest of procedures.

It is unlikely that you can repair a joint in an upholstered frame chair without first removing the upholstery. It is therefore a more complicated job so bear it in mind before deciding on a purchase.

Frame chairs

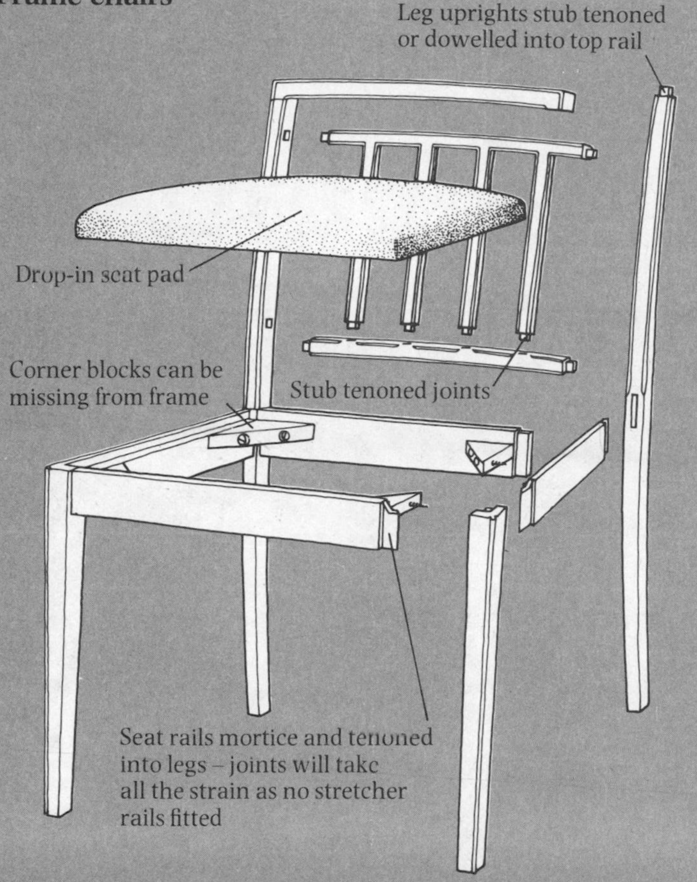

Leg uprights stub tenoned or dowelled into top rail

Drop-in seat pad

Corner blocks can be missing from frame

Stub tenoned joints

Seat rails mortice and tenoned into legs – joints will take all the strain as no stretcher rails fitted

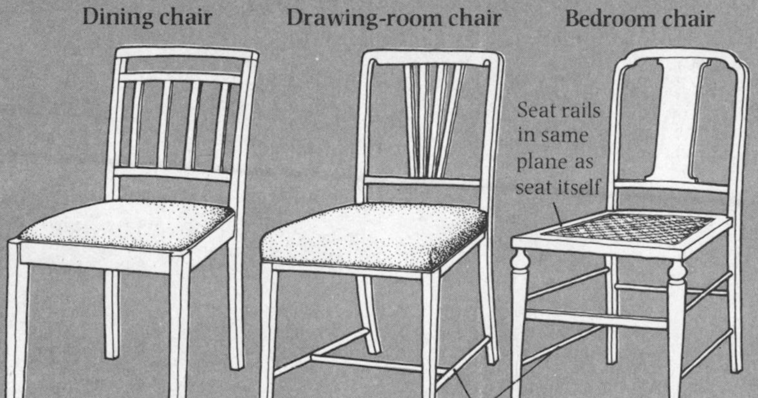

Dining chair

Drawing-room chair

Bedroom chair

Seat rails in same plane as seat itself

Stretcher rails

The back of the chair takes relatively little strain but if the chair has been picked up by the top rail alone, the joints may be damaged. This is particularly true of balloon back chairs (see page 37). The back of many frame chairs features a decorative splat which may be extensively fretted. Examine the splat for breaks across the short grain. If some of the wood is missing or a carved portion has been lost, this will again entail a lengthy repair.

Whatever the damage to the chair, always try to repair the original component rather than making a new one since matching new wood to the colour of the chair is always difficult. If you tackle the repair as soon as possible after the damage has occurred, you will have a better chance of achieving an invisible repair. If broken edges are worn they will not match perfectly and dirt in the joint may show as a dark line. Small pieces which have broken off may be lost and what started out as a simple repair turns into a much more difficult replacement job.

Repairing frame chairs

Some faults, such as a damaged splat or a broken leg, can be repaired without dismantling, but in most old chairs some or all of the joints will be loose. Loose joints are normally due to shrinking of the wood and subsequent glue failure. It is sometimes possible to inject glue directly into the joint but in most cases it is better to knock the chair apart and thoroughly clean up the joints. After any necessary repairs the joints are re-glued and the chair set up in cramps. Instructions for knocking apart are given on the following page and for reassembling the chair on page 30.

Dismantling a frame chair

When most old frame chairs were made, it was normal practice to construct the front and back frames first, leaving them to set before gluing in the side rails. If possible, follow the reverse procedure when dismantling, that is knock apart the joints at either end of the seat rail first.

Before knocking apart

Check the joints to see if they are reinforced with dowel pins or wood screws. Dowels were sometimes put through the sides of the seat rail tenons, while screws, usually covered by a plug, may be found in a joint between an arm and back frame. Drill out the pins or remove the screws as required. New pins and plugs will need to be made later.

● As mentioned above, an old chair that has been badly repaired may have nails in the joints. These must be withdrawn in the best way possible to avoid damaging the wood. Nail heads that are proud can be pulled with pincers. When the nail is below the surface, the wood will have to be trimmed away with a gouge and the head gripped with nose pliers to pull it clear.

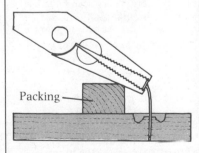

Packing

● In some cases it may be easier to cut off the head of the nail with diagonal cutting pliers and drive it through with a punch.

Knocking apart a seat frame

Before you start work, identify each joint with a patch of masking tape. Label the two parts A-A, B-B and so on, so that you will know where they go when re-assembling the chair.

● A chair with weak joints can be knocked apart with a medium weight hammer or mallet, but be sure to use a protecting block.

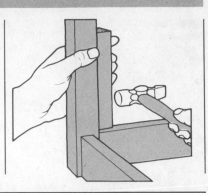

Softening the glue

It may be necessary to soften the glue before you can knock a joint apart. As most old-fashioned furniture was glued together with animal-based glues which are soluble in water, wetted rags or steam can be used to release the joint. Rags are wrapped around the joint and left until the glue has softened. Steam works faster and can be introduced into a joint with the aid of a simple applicator.

● Fit a length of small bore brass tube into a large cork that fits into a whistling kettle or a small can. The cork should be a good fit but able to release itself if the steam pressure builds up. Buy a length of silicone tubing from a model shop to fit over the brass tube. Attach one end to the kettle and fit another piece of the brass tube into the other to make a nozzle. Bind the nozzle with thick string to protect your hands from the heat or wear gloves. Fill

the kettle no more than three quarters full and never let it run dry.

● Drill a hole into the joint a little larger than the nozzle so that the steam can escape.

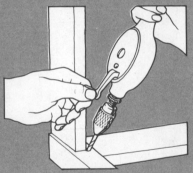

● Insert the nozzle and allow the steam to soften the glue for some minutes before knocking the joint apart.

● Note that the steam may damage the finish and some re-polishing may be necessary.

Always use a softwood block, known as *softening*, between the tool and the part being struck. When knocking a frame apart work on two joints simultaneously, tapping each out a little at a time to prevent jamming. You may find it necessary to clamp the inverted chair seat to the bench. Place pieces of carpet on the bench to prevent marking the frame.

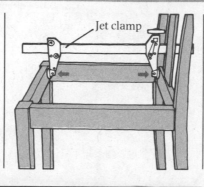

Jet clamp

● Alternatively, use a *jet clamp* to push opposing joints apart as shown in the diagram on the left.
● Loose joints fitted with wedges cannot be dismantled until the wedges have been removed. If the wedges in a through mortice and tenon joint cannot be easily extracted by pulling them out, cut them out with a chisel.

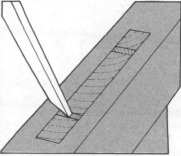

● A fox wedged mortice and tenon is more difficult to take apart as the wedges are hidden. It is necessary to cut down to the wedges with a hacksaw blade following the rail shoulder line.

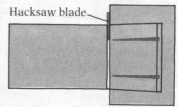

Hacksaw blade

● The weakened tenon should break away at the wedges allowing the rail to be removed.

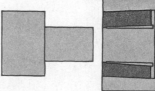

● Rebuild the tenon as described on page 31.

Dismantling a back frame

Analyse the way in which the chair back was assembled so that each component can be successfully removed – the centre splat and vertical bars or spindles that make up the backs of old wooden chairs are usually stub tenoned into the under edge of the back rail. The side uprights may be fitted in the same way, or the ends of the top rail may be tenoned into the sides of the uprights.
● Knock the joints apart, taking care not to break any short grain. A pair of hardwood wedges tapped along each shoulder line can help separate the joint.

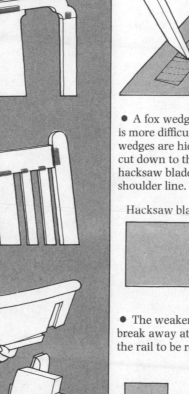

● When a single, wide back rail is used to make a back rest the side uprights may be dovetail housed into the back face. It must be knocked away parallel to the housing (see diagram on right).

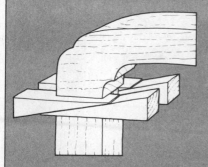

29

Re-assembling a frame chair

After the chair has been dismantled and all necessary repairs have been completed, it should be re-assembled prior to re-finishing the surface.

Gluing the joints

It is important to see that all the joints are completely free of old glue. Scrape them clean with a chisel and check that they all fit by assembling the frame without glue.

● Glue the front and back frames together using sash cramps. Check that all joints are seated properly and sight across each frame to ensure that it is not twisted. Allow the glue to set before removing the cramps.

● Next assemble the complete chair by gluing in the remaining rails. Set in sash cramps and check that the frame is symmetrical by measuring across the diagonals of the seat (see panel) and that it is not twisted by sighting across the rails.

Using a tourniquet

As an alternative to using sash cramps wrap twine around the frame, placing protective cardboard at each corner. Tighten the tourniquet with a stick.

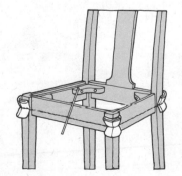

Measuring across diagonals

Cut wedge shaped points on two thick battens and hold them together to measure across the diagonal of the frame. Mark a line across the overlapping ends. Measure across the other diagonal; if the lines match the frame is symmetrical. If not, adjust the cramps or push across the longest diagonal and repeat the process. Setting the cramps at an angle will pull the frame square.

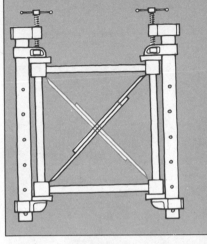
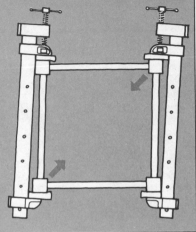

Fitting corner blocks

Brace the inside corner of the seat frame with blocks while it is in the cramps. If blocks were originally fitted and are still sound, refit them using glue and screws.

● Where blocks are missing, take a short piece of hardwood approximately 25mm (1in) thick and 60mm (2½in) wide and hold it against the underside of the rails across the corner. Mark and cut the block to the angle.

● Shape the front edge before drilling and countersinking holes for the two screws. If the block is fitted around the leg, notch the inside edge before marking and cutting the angle.

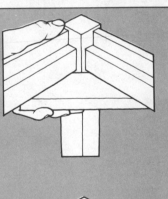
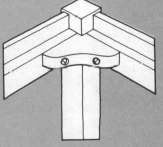

Loose mortice and tenon joints

A tenon that has been left to wear excessively will tend to reduce in size as the wood fibres crush, and at the same time cause the mortice to become over-sized at the top and bottom. There are two ways of dealing with this problem. The first is to trim the edges of the tenon and the mortice with a chisel and then to re-build them with matching wood to restore the original size (see panel right). The second is to tighten the joint with wedges (see panel below).

Rebuilding a tenon

Glue over-sized packing pieces to the tenon and into the mortice and trim to size with a plane and chisel. The grain of the new wood must follow the direction of the wood being repaired and in the case of the mortice, the exposed ends should be stained to match.

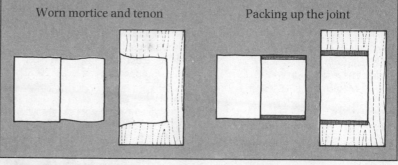

Worn mortice and tenon   Packing up the joint

Wedging a tenon

A tenon that is badly damaged and is loose because of shrinking can be tightened with wedges. A through tenon (see page 132) is wedged after assembly, but a stopped tenon (see page 132) will need to be 'fox' (or blind) wedged.

● To wedge a through tenon, first make two saw cuts in its end. Trim two thin wedges from the end of a hardwood strip to fit the saw cuts: they should be about 3mm ($\frac{1}{8}$in) thick at their widest point, depending on the amount of slack in the joint (see **diagram a**). Glue and re-assemble the joint, then drive the wedges into the saw cuts from the outside (**b**). Wipe away excess glue and trim flush when set.

● To make a fox wedged joint, insert the wedges a little way into the saw cuts before assembly (**c**). Glue and re-assemble the joint, then put it in cramps (**d**). As the cramps are tightened the wedges are forced into the end of the tenon. Fox wedging should only be attempted in straight-grained timber. It is a difficult procedure for beginners: they would be well advised to use the first method, packing the joint.

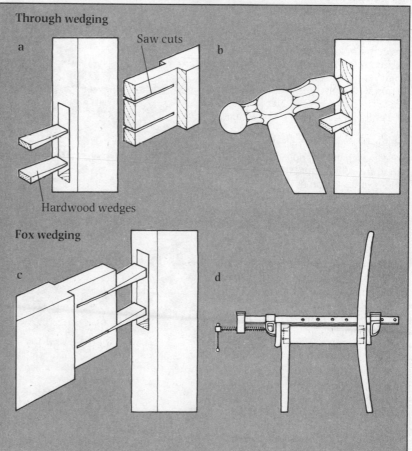

Through wedging

a

Saw cuts

b

Hardwood wedges

Fox wedging

c

d

Broken mortice and tenon joints

If excessive strain is placed on a mortice and tenon joint the tenon may break or the side of the mortice may split out. New wood can be used to rebuild the joint, removing only as much of the original component as is necessary to make a sound repair.

Repairing broken tenons

There are three ways to repair a tenon, depending on how much of it has broken away.

● If approximately one quarter of the tenon is missing (see **diagram a** in panel) or it was necessary to cut away part of the tenon in order to dismantle a chair with fox wedged joints (see page 29), rebuild the tenon with matching wood (**b**), under-cutting the shoulder to house the end of the new piece as on page 133.

● If approximately half the tenon is missing (**c**), cut a stopped housing (**d**) in the rail to equal the length and width of the tenon as on page 134. Cut a matching piece of wood to fit a little over twice the length of the tenon and glue it in place. When set trim to final size. Finish the exposed edge as required. The only trouble with this method of course, is that part of the new tenon is visible in the completed job. If the repair is in a prominent position it may be better to use an angled bridle joint as described below.

● A tenon that has broken across the shoulder line (**e**) must be completely remade. Cut an angled bridle joint (**f**) in the underside of the rail as described on page 134. Glue in a new piece of wood incorporating a tenon. On a seat rail the joint can be reinforced by dowel pegging from the inside.

Repairing a broken mortice

The side of a mortice that has been partly split away but is still attached to the leg can be re-glued and cramped back in place. Work the glue into the split with a brush.

● Where a piece that formed the side of a mortice is missing, the mortice must be re-built using a new piece of matching wood (see panel on opposite page).

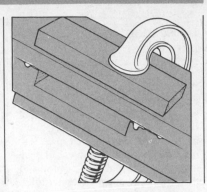

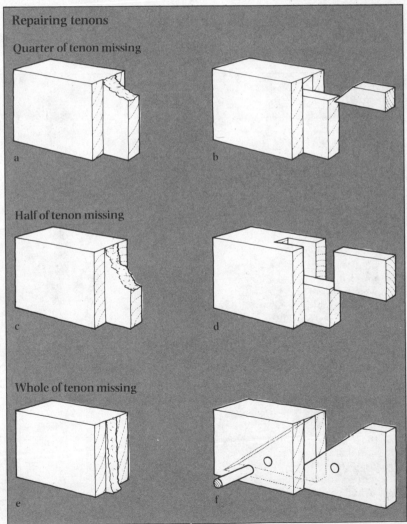

Repairing tenons

Quarter of tenon missing

a   b

Half of tenon missing

c   d

Whole of tenon missing

e   f

Rebuilding a mortice

Make a saw cut at an angle of approximately 45° at each end of the damage. The extent of the damage will determine whether a through or stopped housing is cut (see page 132).

● Remove the splintered wood with a chisel until level. Cut away only the damaged portion leaving as much of the original wood as possible.

● Cut a new piece of wood to fit the housing and glue in place. When set, plane flush all round.
● Mark and re-cut the mortice in the new piece of wood. Stain and finish the repair as required.

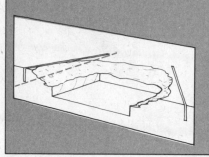
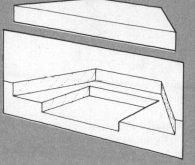
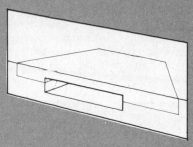

Broken legs and rails

Legs and rails are liable to break if they are infested with woodworm, if the short grain runs across them, or if their design involves excessive turning or shaping. When the break forms a natural scarf joint (see page 135), simply re-gluing the ends and setting up in G-cramps may be enough. Such a repair can be dangerous, however, if the glue fails while the chair is in use, so some sort of reinforcement is necessary, usually in the form of screws or a brace.

Reinforcing with screws

This is particularly useful for a leg which is broken across the short grain. The screws add strength to the joint and also prevent it sliding when in cramps. The screws should be counterbored (see page 111) covered with matching wooden plugs to improve the final appearance.
● First cramp the parts together without glue and drill the counterbores, which should be staggered. Then add the pilot hole and shank clearance for each screw, checking the depth carefully.
● Uncramp the joint, apply glue, insert the screws and leave in cramps until set. Use large gauge countersunk screws set at right angles to the break line, fitted from opposite sides with the thread screwed into the thickest part of the break.

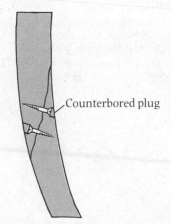

Counterbored plug

● Glue small plugs of matching wood (see page 112) into the counterbores. Plane flush when set and finish to match the surrounding wood.

Reinforcing with a brace

A break straight across a leg is best repaired by inserting a new piece of wood, preferably on the back face, where it will help to absorb the leverage. The two scarf joints so formed provide a large glue area, which again adds to the strength of the joint.
● Glue and cramp the broken ends together and when set, make a saw cut about 3mm ($\frac{1}{8}$in) deep, 100mm (4in) each side of the break line.

● If the back face is radiused, cut down to where the curve meets the side face of the leg.

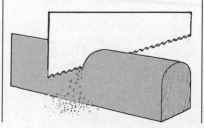

● Make a central saw cut, half of the leg's width, and join up the bottom of each saw cut with a line, making a shallow V.

● Make other saw cuts down to the line to make it easier to pare away the waste. Carefully remove the waste with a wide chisel.

● Select a new piece of wood to match the grain in the leg and mark the shape from the housing. Cut it to fit. Allow extra material on its width and thickness for trimming.

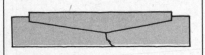

● Glue and cramp the brace into place and plane flush all round when set. Finish as required.

Adding a new section to a broken leg

A leg that is badly damaged at one end can be repaired by replacing the affected part with new wood. The wood should be selected for matching grain and colour. This technique only applies to legs which are flat in at least one plane. Legs which curve in two directions have to be shaped by hand and are probably too difficult for beginners. If you do attempt this job, you should have had some practice in the use of rasps and spokeshaves.

● Cut and plane a long taper on the old part that is to be renewed. The slope of the taper should be at a ratio of 1 to 4 approximately.

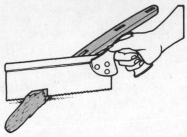

● Mark out and cut the new part of the leg using the opposite leg as a template. Leave it a little over sized for cleaning up later.

● Using the opposite leg as a guide line up the new wood with the broken leg and mark the angle of the taper. This will form the basis of a scarf joint (see page 135).

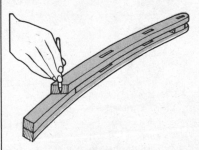

● Carefully cut the scarf joint and cramp it up dry to check the fit. When satisfactory, glue up, paying special attention to alignment as the joint will tend to slide. A sash cramp can be used to prevent the ends moving apart, while G-cramps are used across the joint.

● Many professional restorers use a shouldered scarf joint (see below) in this situation since it prevents sliding in the cramps and gives a neater finish. It is however, quite difficult to cut and fit and you should not attempt it unless you have some woodworking experience.

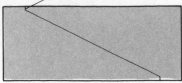

Shoulder

A broken rail

Rails which have broken across the grain are hard to repair and it is probably better to replace the broken rail altogether. One advantage of this method is that you do not have to dismantle the chair.

● Remove the broken rail, chopping out the old tenons, to leave behind clean mortices.

- Make a false tenon for each end of the rail as described on page 134, but glue them into the old mortices.
- Make a new rail with an angled bridled joint (see page 134) cut in each end, and glue it over the projecting ends of the false tenons.

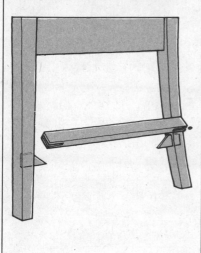

Broken turned legs

A fine turned leg is liable to break where the decorative turning has reduced its section. The feature is usually placed near the seat rail joint which means the full length of the lower leg can act as a lever, which is more likely to occur when a stretcher rail is broken or missing. The broken edges will be short as the break will tend to follow the thinnest part of the turning. This kind of break is repaired with a dowel which braces the leg from the inside. The actual method used to repair the leg depends on whether it plugs into the underside of the seat frame or whether the top of the leg is more substantial and bears the mortices for the tenons of the seat rails. In either case, the trickiest part is aligning the holes in the two parts.

Repairing 'plug-in' legs

If the break is within 25mm (1in) to 50mm (2in) from the top of a leg which plugs into the underside of the seat frame, it can be drilled down from the top. The following repair is equally suitable for a broken leg from a stick chair.

- Remove the broken end from the seat frame. Glue and cramp it to the leg, carefully matching up the break. When set, drill down with the largest bit that will pass through the narrowest part of the turning without weakening it. This will be limited by the available dowel sizes unless you turn your own. Try not to reduce the thickness around the hole below 6mm ($\frac{1}{4}$in). The hole should reach about 75mm (3in) beyond the break. Prepare the dowel as shown on page 131 and glue it into the hole.

- When the glue has set, replace the repaired leg into the chair.

Repairing morticed legs

A leg of this type cannot be repaired by drilling down from above because a substantial section of timber is present above the turning to hold the mortices for the seat rail tenons. In this case, a blind hole is drilled into both pieces of the leg.

- Drill into the upper half first, so that the hole passes beyond the turning and finishes in the wide part of the leg. The hole should be at least half the diameter of the narrowest part of the leg.

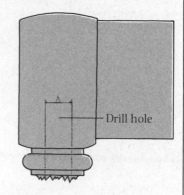

Drill hole

- Cut off the broken end with a fine dovetail or tenon saw, following the shoulder of one of the turned rings. Mark a registration line across the shoulder before cutting.

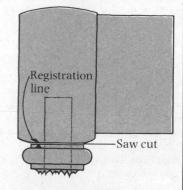

Registration line

Saw cut

- Glue the broken ends using a sash cramp to hold them together.

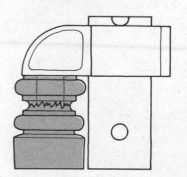

● When set, drill down the other part of the leg using the hole as a guide. Take great care when drilling, particularly if the bored end piece, which acts as the guide, is short.

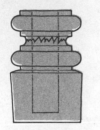

● Cut and prepare the dowel to fit the combined length of the holes. If the hole is deep it may be necessary to drill a separate air hole into the base of the drilling.

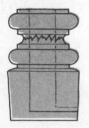

● Apply glue to the holes and dowel and press the joint together with a sash cramp, making sure the marks are aligned. The air hole should be filled with a colour-matched filler.

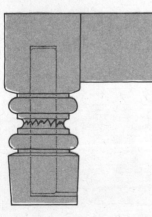

Levelling chair legs

Whatever the style of chair you will eventually come across one which stands unevenly and rocks when sat upon. This might be due to warping of a solid seat board, or a re-glued leg may have been trimmed slightly or a replacement is not quite the same length as the other legs.

● One remedy is to stand the chair on a flat surface and to pack one of the legs with small pieces of ply or hardboard until the chair stands steady and its general lines appear upright.

● Use the packing to mark the other three legs with a sharp pencil.

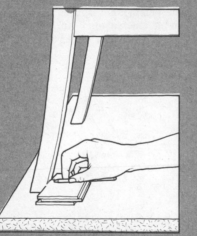

● Trim the legs to length and angle following the marked lines.

● Alternatively, place the chair on a sheet of chipboard with the longest leg overhanging the edge.

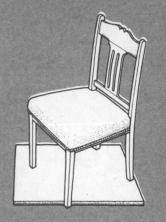

● Mark this leg from the chipboard surface and cut it down to the line.

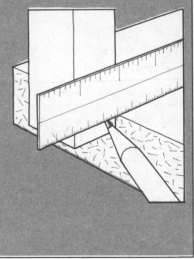

● If the leg is noticeably shorter than the others when the chair is assembled, level the leg on the other side, as described in the panel above.

● Metal rods may be used to dowel the joint, particularly where the diameter of the hole is relatively small. The end should be chamfered and a flat-filed along the side to form an air and glue escape passage. The sides of the rod can be keyed with file marks to aid glue adhesion. Use an epoxy adhesive which is thinned by heating in a foil dish to make it flow.

Balloon back chairs

These elegant chairs, with their gracefully shaped backs, are much sought after these days and you will be lucky if you can find a set which has not already been snapped up by a dealer and renovated – usually with the obligatory Dralon seats! Balloon backs, which were produced in quantity in Victorian times, are really a variant of the frame chair and they suffer the same faults as frame chairs, namely loose joints and damage to legs and rails. Most of them however, have upholstered seats, usually of the stuffed-over variety, which may obscure the condition of the seat rail/leg joints. You will also probably be involved in some degree of upholstery renovation (see page 81).

Most of the repairs to balloon back chairs have already been covered under *Frame chairs* (see page 26) but note that severe damage to the curved front legs may be too difficult for amateur repair, so that if you buy such a chair it will probably have to go to the restorer. Repairs to turned legs are described in the section on stick chairs (see page 41).

The distinctive features of the balloon back from a renovation point of view are the greater prevalence of the dowel joint and the susceptibility of that beautiful back to damage. These problems are dealt with overleaf.

Balloon back chairs

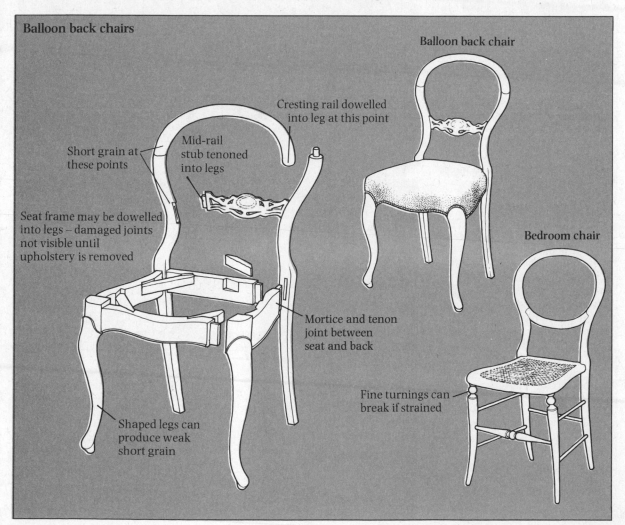

Balloon back chair

Bedroom chair

Cresting rail dowelled into leg at this point

Mid-rail stub tenoned into legs

Short grain at these points

Seat frame may be dowelled into legs – damaged joints not visible until upholstery is removed

Mortice and tenon joint between seat and back

Shaped legs can produce weak short grain

Fine turnings can break if strained

Dowel joints

Dowel joints are commonly found at the junction of the cresting rail and back legs, and in the arms of carver chairs. Dowels are also found in pegged mortice and tenon joints (see page 132) and were sometimes used instead of the mortice and tenon. Directions for making a dowel joint are given in *some basic techniques* on page 131.

Serious damage to a dowel joint usually results in shearing of the dowels close to the shoulder of the rail. The side of the joint is less likely to split away from the dowel holes because it is stronger than the conventional mortice, but if it should occur it can be repaired as described for the mortice joint. A dowel joint can be used to repair a mortice and tenon joint which has broken flush with the shoulder, and where the tenon is well fixed in the mortice.

Repairing a dowel joint

To repair the dowel joint, first remove the broken ends that project above the surface by gripping them with pincers. Twist the dowels to remove them. Do not lever sideways.
- Alternatively, cut them flush with the surface and drill down the centre with a bit somewhat smaller in diameter than the dowel itself. Cut out the remaining waste with a small gouge.
- Dowels that break off below the surface can be drilled out completely using the sides of the hole to keep the bit on centre. Keep a close check on the depth of the hole.
- If new wood is being used on one side of the joint, mark out and drill the dowel holes as shown on page 131.
- Cut, taper and groove the dowels (see page 131) and assemble the joint. Leave in cramps until set.

Damaged back

A single dowel joint is often used where a back or cresting rail is fixed to the top of the legs. Shrinkage and short grain are the major causes of failure in this joint. Avoid picking balloon back chairs up by the back rail; it is better to use both hands to grip the tops of the legs. If the chair is knocked over, the strain on these joints can cause the short grain in the rail or leg to break away around the dowel (see panel, **diagram a**).
- If the joint is otherwise sound, the broken piece can be re-glued and bound in place until set. Use waxed string to bind the setting joint. If the piece is missing, replace it as shown below.

Replacing a missing piece

Plane flat the surface on to which the new piece will be scarf jointed (**diagram b** below). Where the original dowel is missing, a temporary length of dowelling should be tack glued into the remaining part of the hole before planing flat. This will be drilled out with part of the new block which would otherwise be impossible to drill.
- Glue and bind the block to the leg. When the glue is set plane the top of the block level with the original part (**c**).

- Draw a circle on the end of the leg following the remaining part of the dowel. Mark its centre. Carefully drill the new dowel hole to ensure it follows the original angle (**d**). Measure and cut the dowels to fit as described on page 131.
- Re-assemble the joint (**e**) and set up in cramps. When the glue has set shape the new block with a gouge, spokeshave and sandpaper (**f**). Finish it to match the rest of the wood.

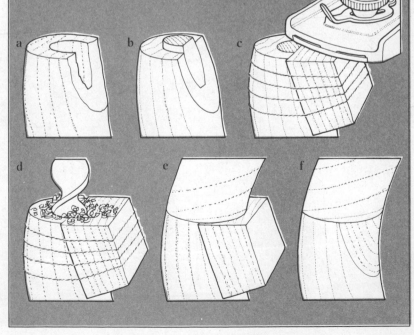

Cramping a curved back

The curved back rails of some chairs are difficult to cramp. Originally 'horns' or 'shoulders' were provided in the partly shaped wood to facilitate cramping.

These were then cut off and the rail finally shaped. When re-fitting a shaped rail an alternative method must be used.

● It is important to get the cramping force in line with and as close to the joint as possible. The rail of an oval shaped back that is comparatively flat can be pulled down using a home-made adjustable saddle. This can be made with two metal straps fitted with stout hardwood blocks bolted through at each end (see below left). The inside edge of the block should be V-grooved and faced with thick felt or carpet. A single bolt through each block allows it to pivot and follow the shape of the rail. The top corners of the block should be cut off to provide a shoulder for the sash cramps.
● If the back of your chair curves from front to back as well as from

top to bottom, the metal straps should be bent to follow the front to back curves.

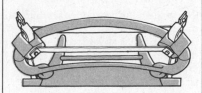

● An alternative is to make two pairs of V-blocks which are screwed together to clamp around the rail or held by G-cramps. Strong cord tourniquets looped around the blocks and lower back rail or seat rail can be used to provide pressure on the joints (below right).

Cramping a balloon back chair

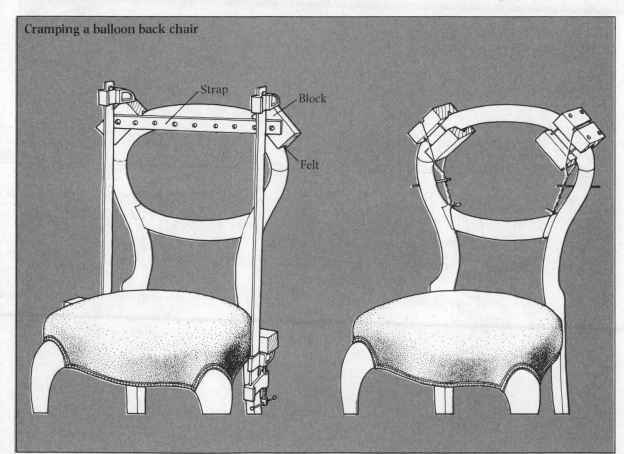

Strap
Block
Felt

Stick chairs

The majority of components which make up a typical stick chair are turned spindles glued into holes drilled in the seat board, back rail or arm. The structure derives its strength and rigidity from the multiplicity of legs, stretcher rails and back rails glued at slight angles to one another so that it is difficult to exert a straight pull on any one joint without putting a strain on another. In this way the joints reinforce each other when the chair is under load.

The ends of the spindles and holes were usually made with a slight taper so that when the spindles were driven home they were gripped tightly. Consequently, it was often unnecessary to use cramps when assembling stick chairs. Although this method of construction is relatively strong, the joints still work loose. Shrinkage causes the ends of the spindles to become oval and the glue to fail. The absence of a shoulder on the joints then allows the frame to rack until some or all of the joints need to be re-glued.

Stick chairs

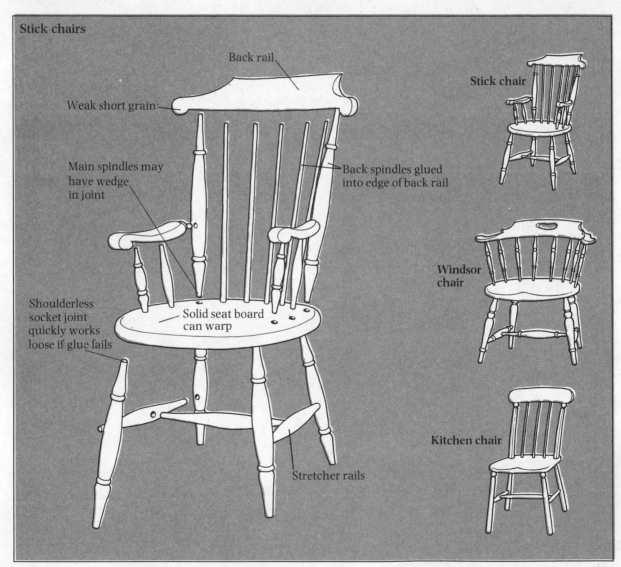

Back rail

Weak short grain

Main spindles may have wedge in joint

Shoulderless socket joint quickly works loose if glue fails

Solid seat board can warp

Back spindles glued into edge of back rail

Stretcher rails

Stick chair

Windsor chair

Kitchen chair

Dismantling a stick chair

Once a joint has loosened it allows enough movement for you to dismantle it. Remove only those components which are necessary to facilitate a repair so that as much of the framework as possible retains its original relationship. Identify dismantled joints with masking tape.

● Try to pull the frame apart either by hand or by using a cramp (see page 29). Alternatively, knock each joint apart, protecting the component with softening or use a rubber headed mallet. Soften the glue as described on page 28.

● Individual components can be twisted in their sockets or a circular motion may be applied to them until they ride out of the hole.

● Before dismantling the main back spindles, turn the chair upside down to see if the joint passes right through the seat board and is secured with a wedge. Chop the wedge out with a narrow chisel.

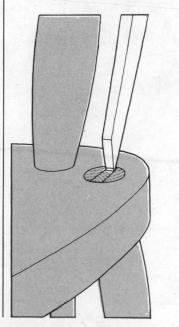

Assembling a stick chair

The re-assembly of a stick chair must follow a set pattern.

● Having scraped all the joints clean, the stretcher rails are glued together first, the legs glued to these, and then the complete leg assembly glued into the seat. The glue is then allowed to set.

● The back spindles or splats are glued into the seat and finally the shaped back rail is added.

● Arm components, when fitted, should be glued up and fitted at the same time as the back uprights.

● Components can normally be tapped into place with a mallet, but cramps can be used to ensure that each component is fitting properly and the frame is square. Stand the assembly on a flat surface, sighting across rails and legs to ensure that the frame is standing evenly.

Tightening a loose joint

The joints of a stick chair are not as susceptible to breakage as those of a frame chair but they frequently work loose. If a loose joint is not repaired promptly the hole can be enlarged and the end of the component may crush, so that the joint cannot simply be re-glued.

● When only a little wear is present, slightly trim the end of the component. The thicker portion of the tapered joint will then fit tightly into the hole.

● A badly worn joint should be fitted with a wedge to tighten it. Cut across the end of the component with a saw to form a slot. Cut the wedge from a matching hardwood. A stopped hole must be fox wedged, while a through joint is wedged after fitting (see *Wedging* page 31).

Repairing broken legs and rails

Broken legs can sometimes be repaired by gluing the parts together and reinforcing the break with a screw, as described under *Frame chairs* (see page 33), but in many cases the component is too narrow to be reinforced in this way or perhaps it has been partly destroyed by woodworm, in which case a new piece can be turned on a lathe and jointed to the remaining part of the leg or rail. The new piece may either be at the top of the leg, as in **diagram a** or at the end, as at **b**. The technique for either job is the same, but the description that follows assumes **a**.

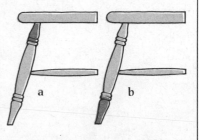

a   b

This type of repair is really only suitable for replacing pieces which do not include the stretcher rail. The hole for the stretcher rail must be drilled at precisely the correct angle and if you are doing this, you might as well remake the whole leg, as described on page 43.

The basic techniques of turning are shown starting on page 138. Note that only those jobs should be attempted which can be managed on the lathe attachment of a power drill; beyond this you will need the help of a specialist.

● Remove the broken leg from the chair frame and cut off the damaged part, preferably along the shoulder line of a turning.

● Take the lower part of the leg and mark the centre of the cut face using a centre-finding gauge (see panel right).

● Set the leg upright in a vice between V-blocks faced with hard foam or thick felt. The lining prevents the wood being bruised and should accommodate any taper or shaping in the leg.

● Drill a hole in the end of the leg at least half its diameter, using a drill press (see page 43).

● Choose a new piece of wood which matches the leg for grain and colour and square it up for turning. It should be slightly larger and wider than the finished job.

● Draw the diagonals across each end to find the centre and mark them with a centre punch.

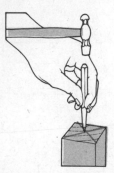

● Draw a circle that touches all four sides on each end. Plane off the corners down to the circle to produce an octagonal section.

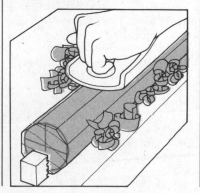

Making a centre finding gauge

You can make a gauge by accurately cutting a 90° notch in one corner of a 75mm (3in) by 75mm (3in) by 12mm (½in) piece of plywood. A blade of thin plywood or metal is then screwed to one face with its straight edge bisecting the angle.

Using a centre finding gauge

Push the end of the leg into the angle of the gauge and draw a line on it following the blade. Revolve the leg and make a second and third mark to find the centre.

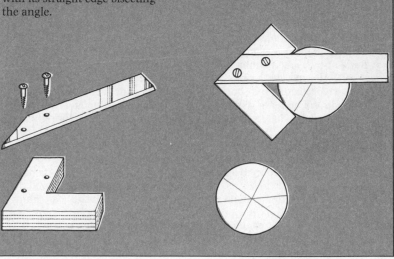

● Tap the lathe driving head centre into one end of the wood so that its teeth grip the wood.

● Fit the wood in the lathe between the head and tail stock centres. Tighten up the tail stock and check its centre is well seated in the work. The wood should revolve freely without lateral movement.

● Adjust the tool rest to within 3mm (⅛in) of the work with its top edge level with the centre line. Turn the work by hand to check that it is clear all round.

● Before beginning the work make a template, taking the shape from the other leg. An adjustable needle template can make the job easier (see *Tools of the trade* page 126). Press the needles against the shaped leg ensuring that the carrying bar is parallel with the centre line of the leg.

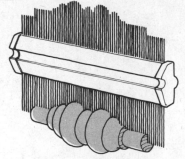

● If the shape to be turned is longer than the needle template, mark out and cut the shape from straight-edged card.

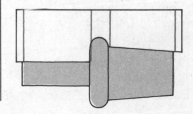

Turning a leg

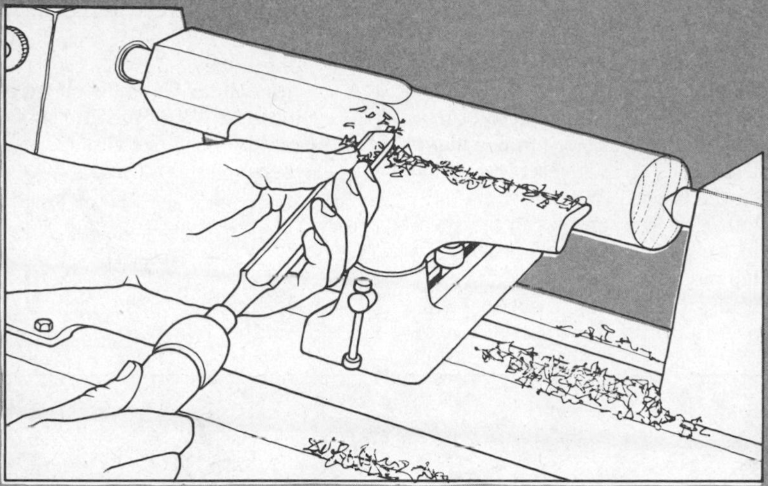

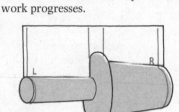

It will be necessary to measure the diameter of the turned details and their position along the turning and to construct the shape with drawing instruments. Make the construction lines clear. Cut off one side of the drawn shape to use as the template.

● Set the drill to run at a slow speed and rough turn the work down from an octagon to a cylinder, using a gouge, as shown above. Check the diameter with calipers (see page 139).

● Hold the straight edge of the template against the front of the rough-turned cylinder and mark the position of the turned detail from the construction lines. When the wood is turning these marks will show as lines.

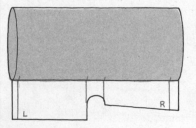

● Hold the shaped edge of the template against the back edge of the work to check the shape as the work progresses.

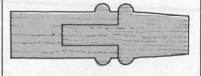

● The final shape of the turned piece should have a spigot at its lower end. This is glued into the hole drilled in the remainder of the leg. Groove the spigot as for a dowel to allow surplus glue to run out.

● The top of the turned piece should have the same diameter as the original leg. This is glued back into the chair after finishing and colour matching.

Replacing a broken leg or rail

Rather than splice together the two parts of a broken stretcher rail or leg, you may prefer to replace it with a new one. In the end, this depends on how complicated is the pattern of turnings on the piece and on how confident you are at turning. The illustration below shows a fairly typical pattern for the leg of a bedroom chair and it clearly demands a lot of work and some skill.

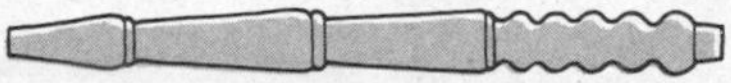

There is a further complication with legs, particularly in stick chairs, and that is that the stretcher rails probably enter the leg at an angle. This means you must drill the holes in the new leg at exactly this angle. To do this you need a drill press. Make a V-block to cradle the finished turned leg directly under the drill bit and set the leg at the required angle for drilling each hole.

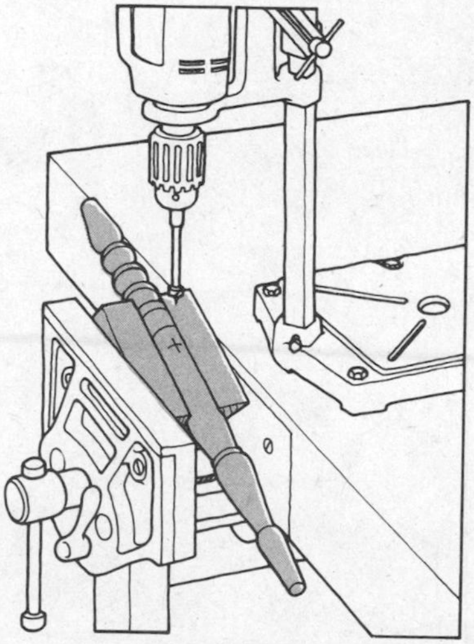

Bentwood chairs

Bentwood chairs are constructed using a specialised technique in which each component is steamed and bent from one piece of wood. This makes a bentwood chair extremely resilient, avoiding the inherently weak short grain produced by cutting components from a large piece of timber.

Most of the joints in a bentwood chair are held together with wood screws and bolts without the use of glue. Only the front legs are glued where they fit into sockets in the underside of the seat frame. The bolts which hold the back leg assembly on to the seat frame can often work loose. If unchecked the movements on these joints will put a strain on the wood screws which fix the hooped stretcher rail to all four legs. The screws can then work loose, strip their thread and finally fall out. As the rest of the chair frame weakens, the front legs will eventually become loose.

Repairing loose joints

Front leg joint

As mentioned above, the front leg is glued into a socket in the underside of the seat frame. If the glue works

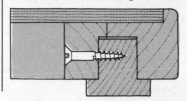

Bentwood chairs

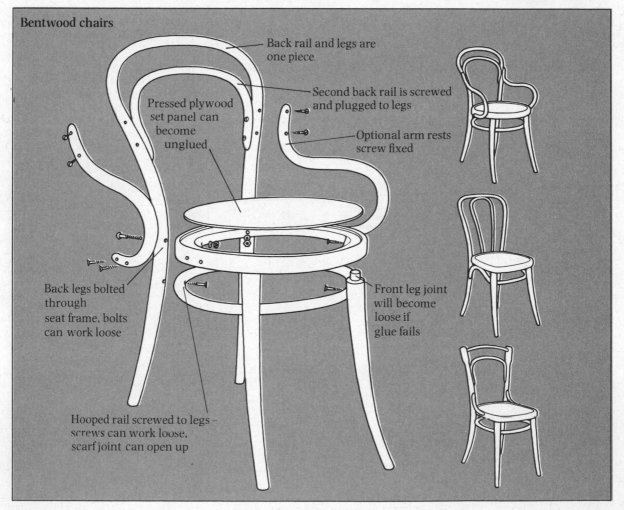

Back rail and legs are one piece

Second back rail is screwed and plugged to legs

Pressed plywood set panel can become unglued

Optional arm rests screw fixed

Back legs bolted through seat frame, bolts can work loose

Front leg joint will become loose if glue fails

Hooped rail screwed to legs – screws can work loose, scarf joint can open up loose, the joint should be repaired as for stick chairs (see page 41). Note that it is often reinforced with a screw from behind (see opposite). This is the only joint in the chair using glue; the rest use either screws or coach bolts.

Loose coach bolts

Two coach bolts are used to fix the back leg assembly to the chair seat frame. These pass right through the leg and frame. A square nut is used to clamp the joint with a large washer between it and the inside of the frame. The washer should have a locking tab to trap the nut and small spurs which grip the wood to prevent it turning.

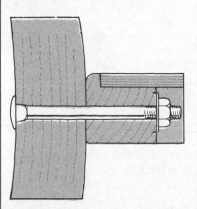

● Prise the tab away from the nut using a screwdriver and tighten the nut with a spanner. Do not apply too much force as the head of the bolt can crush the leg.
● Turn one face of the nut in line with the locking tab and bend the tab back.
● If the tab washer is missing, use a large plain washer (it should not project below the rail), and fit a second nut on the bolt to lock against the other. Use two spanners, one to hold the first nut steady as the second is tightened up.

Loose screw joints

The hooped rail is drilled through and countersunk on the inside to take wood screws which hold it to the legs.
● Simply re-tightening the screws may be sufficient to make the joint solid. If the screw has stripped, try a screw of the same length but of a larger gauge. It may be necessary to enlarge the clearance hole in the hoop and open up the countersink slightly.
● A really worn screw hole will need to be plugged and re-drilled. Take the chair apart, remembering to mark a joint to ensure that the hoop is replaced the same way round.
● Trim a tapered plug on the end of a piece of dowel so that it is slightly larger in diameter than the hole. Cut the plug from the dowelling so that it is a little longer than the hole is deep. Apply glue to the hole and drive in the plug.
● When set, trim it flush with a chisel. Drill a pilot hole for the screw in the centre of the plug and assemble the chair. Use new screws if the old ones show signs of wear.
● The back rail, the seat to back reinforcing piece and the arm are also screw fixed.

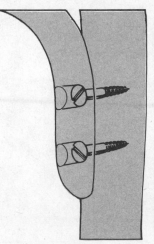

● Exposed screws can be simply dealt with but in some cases the screws holding these parts are hidden below the surface by flush wooden plugs. More care is needed when repairing this fixing to avoid damaging the surrounding wood.
● The plugs can be cut out using a small, sharp gouge or drilled out with a twist bit. A small centering hole should be made with a bradawl or drill to prevent the tip of the larger bit from slipping.
● Re-tighten the screw fixings and make new plugs cut from beech with the grain running across their face. A plug cutting bit fitted into a power drill can make this simpler. Glue in the plugs with the grain following the surrounding wood.
● Trim flush when set, stain and finish as required.

Loose scarf joints

Due to their method of construction, components of a bentwood chair are rarely broken. The hooped stretcher rail however is usually joined with a scarf joint. If this joint should open up, it can be re-glued simply.

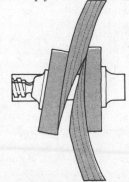

● Clean up the joint and clamp the ends with G-clamps and softening blocks, or bind with waxed string. The projecting end may need to be held over a steaming kettle so that you can bend it back into place before applying the glue.

Tables

The structure of a table offers a designer much more freedom than a chair. There can be one leg or four, the top can be square, round, oval or semicircular and flaps or drawers may be added. The top may be veneered or inlaid and castors may be added to the feet. As a result there is a bewildering array of tables and in a short book like this we cannot hope to mention every problem that you are likely to encounter. However, using our four table families – basic frame, draw-leaf, drop-leaf and pedestal – we can include all the more important techniques and you should be able to modify one or other of them to suit your own purposes.

Basic frame tables

A frame table is just what it says it is – two side rails and two end rails jointed into legs at the corners and surmounted by a top. The joints may be mortice and tenons or dowels. This basic form of construction may be used for simple work tables and a variety of side or coffee tables.

Frame tables are often modified by the inclusion of drawers – at the ends in kitchen tables or on the side rails in simple desks. A Victorian washstand is merely a frame table with drawers at the front, a marble top and a wooden screen at the back to protect the wall from splashes.

In these pieces of furniture the rail construction has to be modified to accommodate a drawer within the depth of the rail. The end rail for instance is turned on its side and is dovetailed into the top of the leg

and part of the side rail. A second rail is added beneath the drawer and this is stub tenoned or dowelled into the legs.

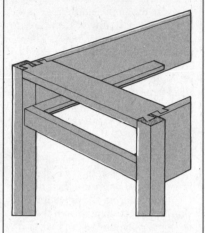

If you want to dismantle this type of table frame, the top rail must be removed first by tapping it upwards with a hammer and a softening block before the lower rail can be removed by tapping the leg sideways. A desk or kitchen table with two front drawers will have a similar rail construction with the addition of an upright post to support the lower rail in the middle. This will be removed as the top rail is dismantled.

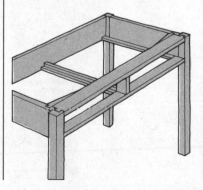

The problems of drawers, and the runners and guides which surround them, are described on the section on cabinets (see page 74).

The tops of most old tables are made of solid timber which may or may not be veneered.

Beware of veneered tables which show extensive splitting of the top: you may have to strip off the veneer to effect the repair, then lay it again afterwards. A top which is warped is another pitfall. Various methods of correcting warping have been described, usually involving steam and pressure, but they do not always work and the fault often returns. To avoid warping the top was nearly always originally made of several narrow pieces glued together side-to-side. These joints may open up or the top may split along the grain due to shrinkage. The repair of split table tops is discussed on page 48.

Loose and broken underframe joints

Although a table is not usually put under so much strain as a chair the joints can work loose and can even be broken. To test the joints put your weight on the top of the table and push it sideways to see if there is any movement at the joints. If there is, the table must be dismantled and the joints repaired in exactly the same way as for frame chairs on page 31. Broken or damaged legs are also repaired in the same way as frame chairs. However, being somewhat larger, tables require longer cramps and it helps to have an assistant on hand when gluing up a table frame.

Basic frame tables

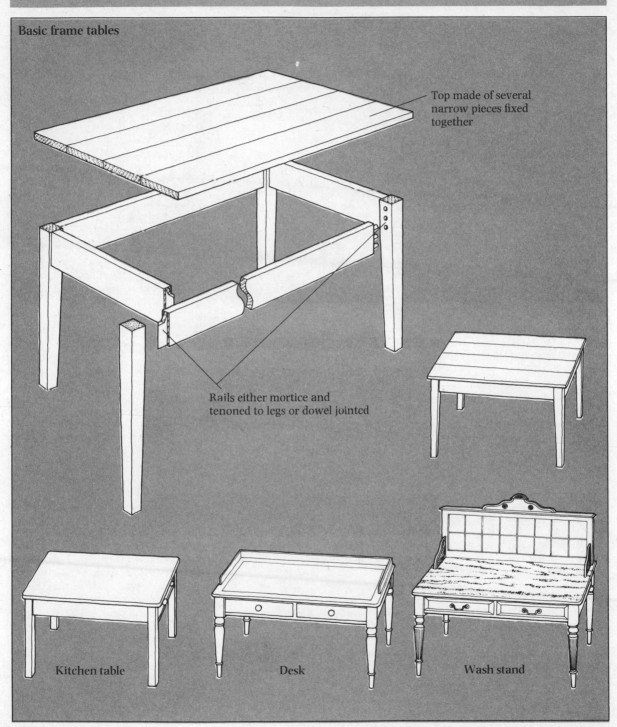

Top made of several
narrow pieces fixed
together

Rails either mortice and
tenoned to legs or dowel jointed

Kitchen table

Desk

Wash stand

47

Split table top

Small shrinkage cracks in an old table top are often acceptable as they add to the table's character. More severe ones can be packed with pieces of veneer or filled with a small hardwood lath, as described for split cabinet panels on page 70. Loose joints, on the other hand, will involve the dismantling of the top, a job which is complicated by the fact that one of several types of joint may have been used in the original construction.

Dismantling the top

Turn the table upside-down and re-move any screws holding the top in place. Alternatively, it may have been glued to the frame using small blocks of wood rub jointed into place. Tap a chisel behind them to lever them off.

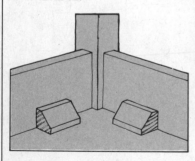

Types of table top joint

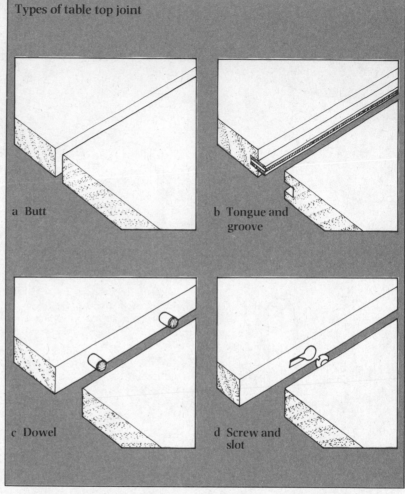

a Butt

b Tongue and groove

c Dowel

d Screw and slot

● If the top is made up using a glued butt joint, it will fall into two or more pieces (see **diagram a** in panel above).
● A tongue of plywood may be glued into a groove in the edge of each piece of timber (**b**) . If you can see light through the joint no tongue is present. It may show on the end of the top but not if the groove runs out before the end.
● Try passing a thin blade or a metal feeler gauge through the gap. If you feel an obstruction all along

the joint try shocking the glue line by hitting the end of one side of the joint while clamping the other side to the bench. Protect the top with softening blocks. In addition play steam along the joint to soften the glue as described for chair joints on page 28.
● If you find that the gauge passes through the joints but comes up against obstructions at regular in-tervals, the joint is probably dowel-led (**c**) or joined with hidden metal screws (**d**). The dowels can either be pulled apart having softened the

glue or sawn through with a hack-saw blade.
● The screws are inserted in one edge of the joint leaving counter-sunk heads protruding so that they fit into dovetailed slots in the other. When the joint was assembled holes at the end of the slots were dropped over the screw heads and the slotted piece of wood tapped sideways. The screw heads bit into the grain pull-ing the joint together. A sharp tap in each direction will soon deter-mine which way to dismantle the joint.

Re-assembling the top

Clean old glue from a butt joint by scraping with a sharp chisel or scraper. Take care to keep the blade flat on the surface to avoid damaging the edges.

● If the joint will not close up properly when assembled dry, it will have to be trued up with a plane. Hold the two pieces together and the jointing edges flush. Clamp long boards to the side of the bench. With a very finely set plane take off as little wood as possible to ensure a snug joint. Use a long straight edge to ensure that you are not planing a hollow or a bump along the joint.

● If the work is square across the joint so much the better, but an angled face will not prevent the boards lying flat when rejoined.

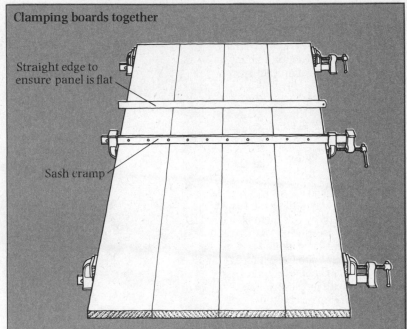

Clamping boards together

Straight edge to ensure panel is flat

Sash cramp

● When gluing a flat panel together, use at least three sash cramps, two below and one above, to even out the force (see panel).

● Make softening blocks to protect mouldings along the edge of the top and to lift the work off the sash cramp bars.

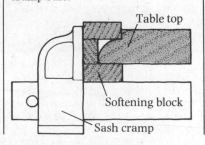

Table top

Softening block

Sash cramp

● Paint woodworking glue on both edges of the joint and rub them together. Place the job in the cramps and put light pressure on it to squeeze out excess glue and allow you to check the alignment of the joint. Slight adjustments can be made by placing a block across the joint and tapping with a hammer.

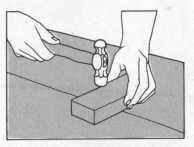

● Put final pressure on the cramps, wipe off excess glue with a damp cloth and check that the top is flat with a straight edge. Move the cramps down or up to make any adjustments.

● Dowels or plywood tongues can be replaced and the joint re-glued as above (see page 131 for gluing dowel joints).

● To clamp sections of a round table top together make up two 'cradles' from scrap timber to position the cramps and spread the load.

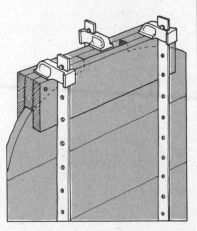

Replacing the top

A top which has split was probably originally fixed to the underframe by pocket screws which hold the top rigidly and prevent movement due to water loss.

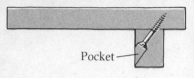

Pocket

● Since the wood has done its shrinking it may well be satisfactory to refix the top by this method, but if the wood does shrink further, fresh splits will appear and it is preferable to use a fitment which allows the wood to move. This can be achieved with metal shrinkage plates or hardwood buttons.

● Shrinkage plates (see panel, **diagram a**) are right-angled pieces of metal with screw holes on one side and two slots at 90° on the other. The side with holes is screwed rigidly to the frame of the table, then the top is screwed on through one of the slots using the one which runs across the grain. If the wood moves the screw simply moves up and down the slot.

● 'Buttons' are small hardwood blocks about 37mm (1½in) by 25mm (1in) by 18mm (¾in) in which a rebate has been cut. The rebate fits into a slot cut in the inside of the frame (**b**).

● The buttons should be cut from a hardwood strip with a tenon saw in the direction shown, so that the grain runs across the rebate, not along it.

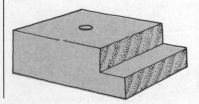

Methods of attaching table tops

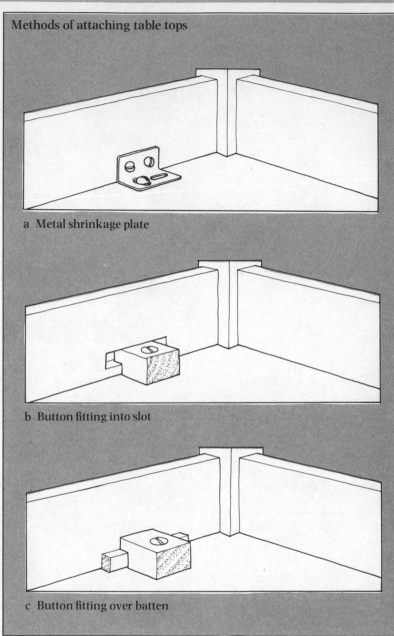

a Metal shrinkage plate

b Button fitting into slot

c Button fitting over batten

● Slots for the buttons can be bored out with a power drill, then cleaned up with a mortice chisel. This traditional method of top fixing involves a lot of work in cutting the slots.

An alternative method (**c**) is to fix a hardwood batten on the inside of the table frame. This lies in the rebate of the buttons, which are screwed to the underside of the table top.

Draw-leaf tables

A draw-leaf table is simply a frame table in which the top has been modified to allow extension of its length when needed. At other times it can be closed to save space in the room. The two extensions, or leaves, are carried on wooden bearers which lie side-by-side inside the frame when the table is closed. When it is opened, the top, which is loose, falls down between the two leaves.

The underframe suffers the usual problems of loose joints or broken components, which should be dealt with as described under *Frame chairs*, page 26. The extra problems are to do with the leaves, which may stick, over-extend, drop down or become scratched.

Draw-leaf tables

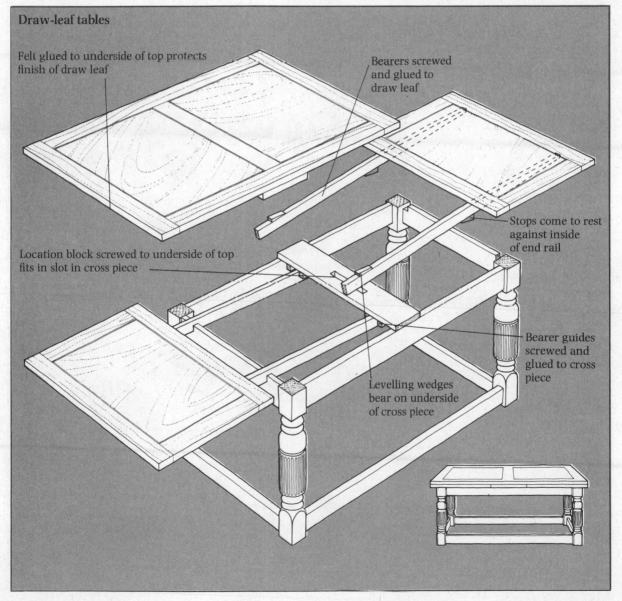

Felt glued to underside of top protects finish of draw leaf

Bearers screwed and glued to draw leaf

Location block screwed to underside of top fits in slot in cross piece

Stops come to rest against inside of end rail

Bearer guides screwed and glued to cross piece

Levelling wedges bear on underside of cross piece

A sticking leaf

Check that the bearer guide blocks are screwed securely to the underside of the cross pieces and that there is sufficient clearance for both leaves to operate.
● Sight along the bearers themselves to ensure that they are not warped and therefore binding against the guides or each other. If they are warped you should make a replacement bearer out of a hardwood strip.

Replacing a bearer

Unscrew the bearer from the leaf, clamp it flat against the hardwood strip and draw round it to cut out a replacement. Ensure that the grain is straight along the bearer.

● Clamp the blank and original bearer together and mark and drill the screw centres. Stain the bearer to match the table before screwing it to the leaf.
● Finally lubricate the bearers with candle wax for smooth running.

A scratched leaf

If a draw-leaf table is badly scratched, the surface finish must be repaired (see page 8) but it is essential to remedy the cause of the damage first.
● Remove the main top and inspect the underside where it comes into contact with the leaf as it is extended. There should be a protective strip of felt glued to the underside of the top along each edge. If it is missing, there may be a gritty residue of glue which is scoring the surface of the leaf or, even worse, projecting panel pins which have been used to hold down the baize when it started to peel. Remove these with pincers.
● The table top itself consists of a frame enclosing a number of panels. Scrape out the gap between the panels and the frame to make sure there are no foreign bodies which could be scratching the leaf.
● Scrape the old glue from the underside of the top with a sharp chisel and glue a strip of felt to it using PVA glue. Re-finish the surface of the leaf.

An over-extending leaf

There should be stops glued to the underside of each bearer which come to rest against the inside of the end rail. If these are missing, the leaf can be drawn too far out. The bearers come out of their guides and they are difficult to relocate without taking off the top.
● If the stops are missing, extend the leaf until the top just drops into position and use the inner face of the end rail to mark a line on the bearers.

● Rub joint wooden blocks up to this line on the underside of each bearer and check the position with the leaf in place. When the glue has set, secure them with panel pins.

A drooping leaf

If a leaf droops when fully extended ensure that the bearers are screwed securely to it, then support it temporarily in the required position. Inspect the clearance between the bearers and the underside of the cross piece.

● If there is a gap, the simplest solution is to cut small hardwood wedges which should be glued and rub jointed to the top of the bearer while it is still in position.

● When the glue is set, carefully remove the leaf and secure the wedges with panel pins.

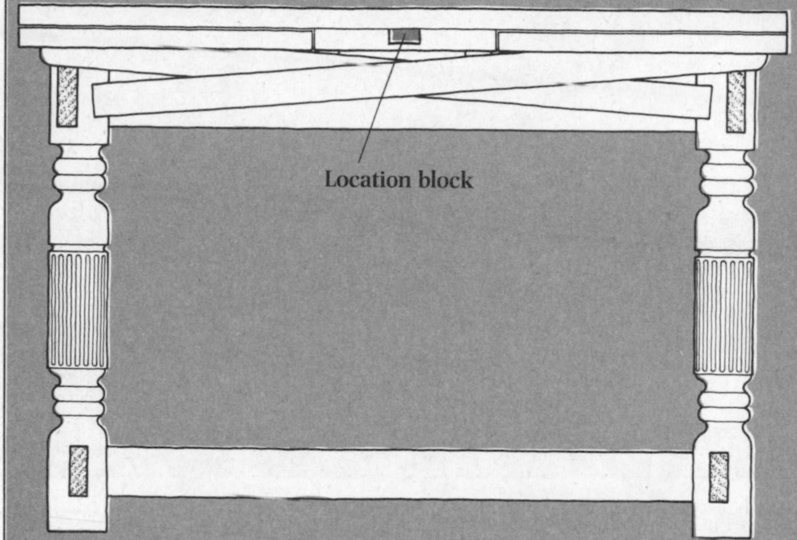

A badly fitting top

The top must be lifted in order to re-place the leaf, but it should be prevented from moving sideways by a block screwed to the underside, which locates in a slot in the cross piece. Tighten the screws or make a replacement if it is missing.

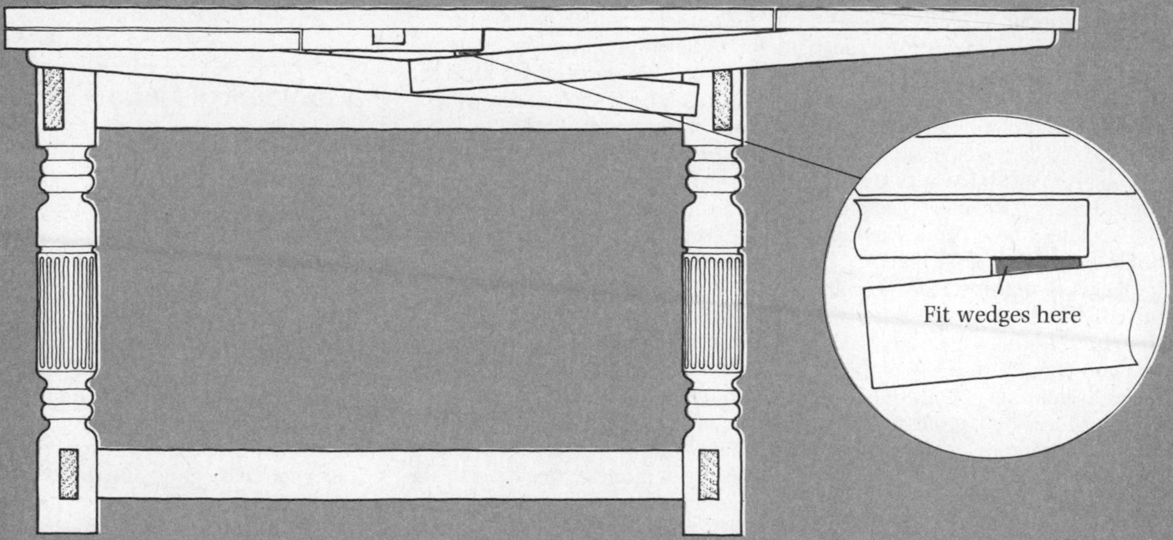

Location block

Fit wedges here

Drop-leaf tables

Drop-leaf tables are an alternative method of increasing the area of the table top without increasing the size of the underframe. On draw-leaf tables the leaves are stowed underneath the loose top; with drop-leaf tables they hang down parallel to the underframe. Drop-leaf tables are quite often narrow when closed and hence take up very little space in a room.

There are two methods of supporting a drop-leaf, either a bracket as in Pembroke tables, or an extra leg which folds out from the underframe as in gate-leg tables.

Pembroke tables

Said to have been designed originally by the ninth Earl of Pembroke in the mid-eighteenth century, these tables have a drop flap parallel to each side rail. When open, the flaps are supported by fly support brackets which fold out from the side of the underframe on knuckle joints (see panel). Between the leaf and the main table top, a rule joint is normally used (see panel).

The breakfast table of the eighteenth century is constructed on similar lines to the Pembroke table but it has a lower shelf enclosed by lattice work on three sides. A sofa table has its flaps at the ends rather than at the sides.

If you come across any of these tables as genuine old antiques, have them restored by a professional unless you are totally confident of your own ability.

All of these tables have drawers, repairs to which are shown from page 74 onwards. Similarly, underframe problems such as loose joints

Joints on a Pembroke table

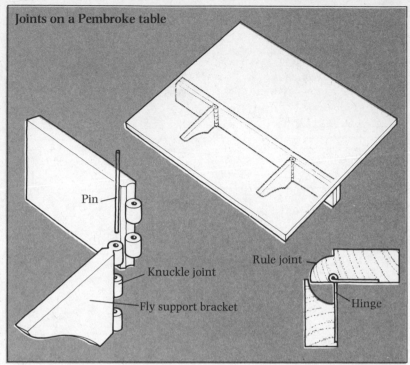

Pin

Knuckle joint

Fly support bracket

Rule joint

Hinge

or broken components should be dealt with as described for frame chairs (see page 31).

The problem of warping is particularly relevant to drop-flap tables as their flaps are not securely fixed to a frame. Methods such as screwing a stout batten to the underside of the flap to take out the curve are really too crude and unless the bowing is excessive it may be best to accept it as part of the natural ageing of the furniture. If the bowing is excessive it is best not to purchase the piece in the first place. The same goes for Pembroke tables with one flap missing – quite a common find. There is so much work in making a new flap, planing it flat and then staining it to match the rest of the table, that the game really isn't worth the candle.

The rule and knuckle joints on these tables have their own peculiar problems and are dealt with below.

Most Pembroke and sofa tables bear castors which are described in *Hardware*, on page 115.

A broken rule joint

The rule joint on a drop-flap table performs two functions. Firstly it supports the weight of the flap when it is in the raised position and thus reduces the strain on the hinge. Secondly it produces a neat moulded detail to the edges of the fixed top when the table is folded.

Drop-leaf tables come in for a good deal of wear and the moulding of the rule joint is frequently broken. It is repaired by gluing on a piece of matching timber which is shaped when the glue has hardened (see repair of mouldings on cabinets, page 71).

Pembroke tables

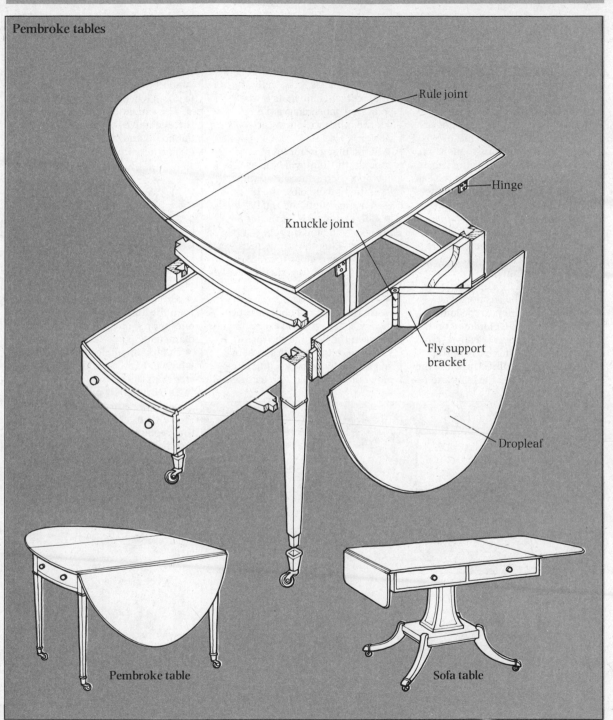

Rule joint

Hinge

Knuckle joint

Fly support bracket

Dropleaf

Pembroke table

Sofa table

A binding rule joint

If you have a rule joint that binds as the flap is operated, try rubbing a little candle grease along the quadrant of the joint.

● If this simple solution is not enough to cure the problem, the wood may have swollen due to moisture. Keep the table in a dry atmosphere for a while, preferably with the flaps removed, and held between battens under cramps to ensure that they do not warp.

● Another possible cause for the rule joint binding is inaccurately fitted hinges. The hinge has an extra long leaf on one side which screws to the flap. The knuckle of the joint must be positioned accurately in relation to the joint in order for the cove moulding on the flap to move concentrically around the quadrant. The centre of the knuckle must be directly below the square shoulder of the joint and re-

cessed so that both leaves are flush with the undersides of flap and fixed top. If this is not so, various problems may arise.

● If the hinge is set in too deep, so that the knuckle is too high, the rule joint will bind at its lowest point (see panel, **diagram a**). Pack out the hinge with thin card or veneer.

● If the hinge is not set in far enough, the joint will bind as the flap approaches horizontal (**b**). Pare the timber below the hinge with a chisel until the leaf lies flush.

● If the knuckle is set too far back the joint will bind throughout its travel (**c**). Plug the screw holes (see page 114) and move the hinge slightly forward, wedging a piece of veneer behind the leaf.

● If the knuckle is set too far forward, the joint will not bind but there will always be an excessive gap between the flap and the top (**d**). If you wish, plug the holes as above and set the hinge back a little, chopping out the timber with a chisel.

A worn knuckle joint

A badly-worn knuckle joint on a fly support bracket will cause the flap to droop when in the raised position.

● The simplest solution is to cramp the two halves of the bracket to a flat board and stand it on the jaws of an open vice.

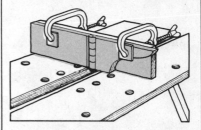

● Drive out the central steel pin from the joint with a punch and another pin of a slightly smaller diameter.

● Enlarge the hole with a twist drill which is 1mm ($\frac{1}{16}$in) larger in diameter than the original pin.

● Drive in a new pin which is the same diameter as the drill.

● If the knuckle joint is so worn that replacement of the pin is insufficient, take it apart and pare away the worn parts of the knuckles. Build them up with thin slips of veneer until the joint again fits snugly, then rebore as described above.

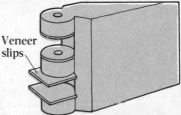

Veneer slips

● The complete remaking of a knuckle joint from new wood is a difficult job. It should only be attempted by amateurs with a great deal of woodworking experience, or by a restorer.

Positioning of hinge

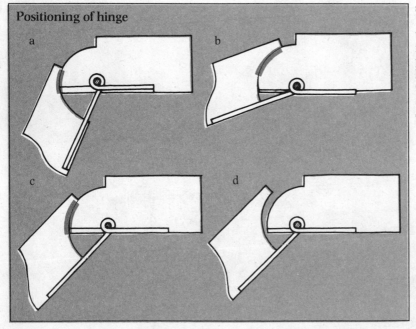

a

b

c

d

Gate-leg tables

Many early card and tea tables had a gate-leg, often on a knuckle joint, but by far the most common form of this table is the double-flapped dining table, usually made of oak or stained beech, which has become a firm favourite in sale rooms over the last few years.

Here the gate pivots on two dowels located in the side rail and stretcher rail. On very old tables they become slack due to wear or they may have been broken by careless handling. In most cases the repair will be fairly straightforward.

Another characteristic feature of the gate is the halving joint cut into the lower part of the long leg which enables the gate to lie flush with the stretcher rail. There is an obvious

weakness at this point which could promote a split in the leg. It is worth examining this detail before buying a table to determine how much work is involved.

Although it is a minor point, check that the stop of the gate is screwed to the underside of the flap. This is essential to ensure that the leg is in the optimum position to support the flap and avoid straining the hinges.

Gate-leg tables

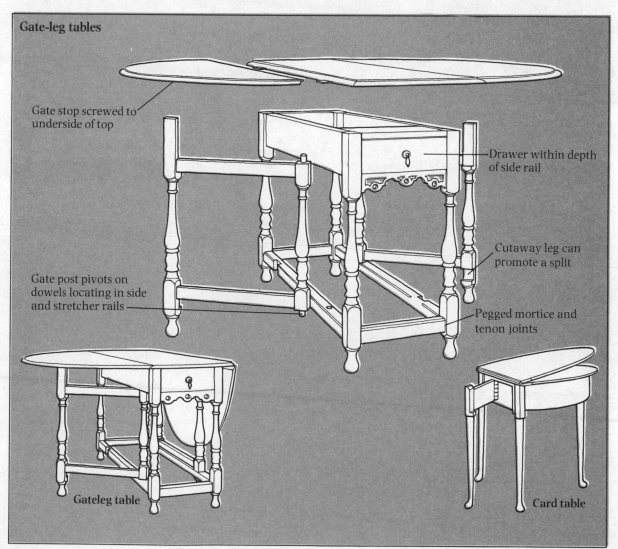

Gate stop screwed to underside of top

Drawer within depth of side rail

Cutaway leg can promote a split

Gate post pivots on dowels locating in side and stretcher rails

Pegged mortice and tenon joints

Gateleg table

Card table

A broken leg at the halving joint

Careless transportation or handling could result in a split in the halving joint on a gate leg. If the grain is relatively short at that point, the leg might actually be broken in two pieces and should be repaired as described for broken chair legs (see page 41).

● To repair a partial split, work glue into it with a blade, flexing the leg to encourage the glue to penetrate as deeply as possible. Clamp, and leave the glue to set.

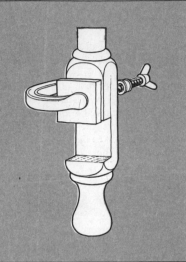

A missing gate stop

The leg of the gate should come to rest against a wooden stop fixed to the underside of the flap. If it is missing, gauge its size and position from the discolouring of the surface finish.

● Cut a block from a piece of hardwood which matches the table top and bevel three edges.
● Screw and glue the block to the underside of the flap, using the leg to gauge its position exactly.

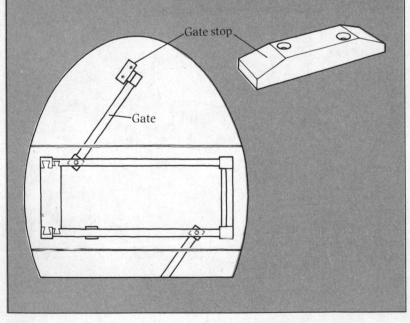

Gate stop

Gate

A loose gate

The dowels on which the gate pivots may be worn or broken. They may be repaired in one of two ways depending on the original construction.

Screwed block

On some tables the dowel at the base of the gate post plugs into a hole in the stretcher rail while the dowel in the upper end is held in a recess in the side rail by a screwed block (see panel on next page, **diagram a**). Remove the block to lift out the gate, fit new dowels in each end of the gate post and replace it.

Integral dowels

Both dowels may have been located in the main table frame when it was assembled (**b**). Use a hacksaw blade to cut through them.

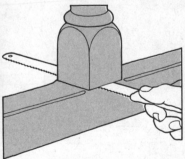

● Plane the ends of the gate post flush. At the bottom end, drill a hole in the centre to take a 19mm ($\frac{3}{4}$in) dowel, if possible using a drill press (see *some basic techniques* page 131). Rub a small piece of candle wax around the inside of this hole to lubricate it.
● Use a brace and bit to drill right through the stretcher rail using the original pivot hole as a guide.

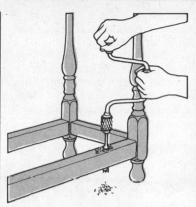

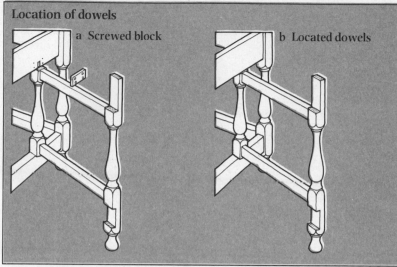

Location of dowels

a Screwed block   b Located dowels

• Drill in the centre of the top end of the gate post to take a 6mm (¼in) diameter metal pin. Glue it in position with an epoxy glue.

• Fit a 3mm (⅛in) thick metal plate into a stopped housing (see page 132) in the underside of the top rail, over the original pivot hole. Use two screw fixings (see panel on right).

• Drill a hole in the plate, centred on the rail to take the metal pin.

• Remove the plate and cut a small notch with saw and chisel in the back of the rail to allow a clearance for the metal pin.

• Drop the plate over the pin and position the gate post between the two rails. Screw the plate to the top rail.

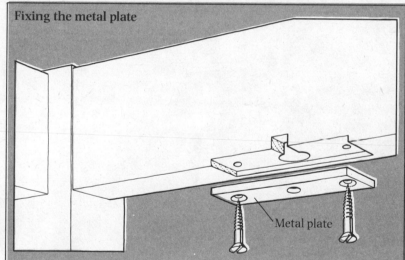

Fixing the metal plate

Metal plate

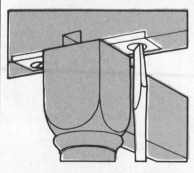

• Ensure that the gate lies flush with the frame, then tap a wooden dowel through the stretcher rail

into the bottom of the gate post. The top of the dowel should be chamfered and a saw cut should be made across the other end.

• Test the movement of the gate before driving a glued hardwood wedge into the dowel. When the glue has set, plane the dowel flush with the rail. Plug the notch in the table side rail with a small piece of matching hardwood.

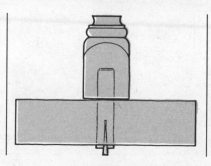

Pedestal tables

In this group of tables the underframe has been abandoned altogether in favour of a central pillar or pedestal, supported on three legs at the base. Most of these tables are small and elegant, being used to serve tea or wine. They are light enough to be portable, with a circular top which very often pivots upwards to a vertical position, so that they can be stood against the wall when not in use.

Pedestal dining tables are usually larger and of much heavier construction. Their top is circular (or less commonly rectangular) and the central pedestal support provides plenty of leg room all round. The top can be pivoted or de-mounted for easy transportation.

Pedestal tables come in a variety of designs, depending on their size and function.

Wine tables

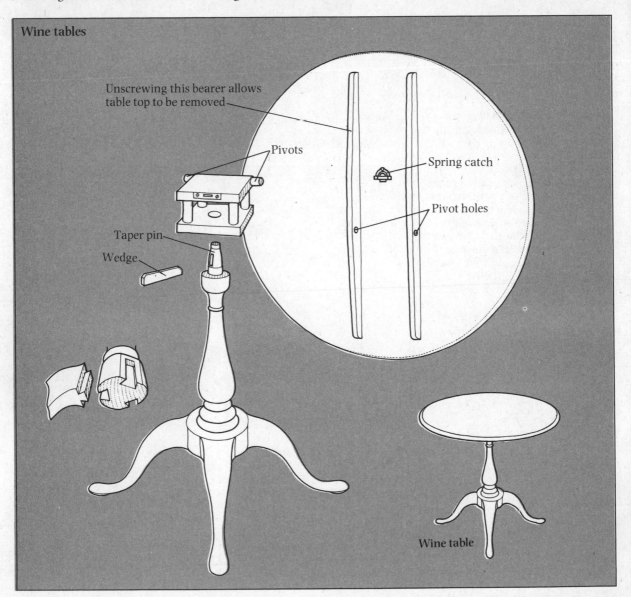

Unscrewing this bearer allows table top to be removed

Pivots

Spring catch

Pivot holes

Taper pin

Wedge

Wine table

The base

In wine tables, the legs are dovetailed into the column to produce the tripod base. You may find that the dovetail joints are loose or that the wood at the column base is split or broken. Because the legs are curved they are prone to fracture across the short grain.

As the size of the table increases, a more robust construction is called for. Heavier versions of the wine table design have to be reinforced with metal plates under the legs. More often the problem of the increasing weight is solved by changing the design of the table. The tripod becomes a flattened, sturdy structure made of framed softwood veneered in an exotic wood. The feet, which are usually turned from solid timber, are screwed to the underside of the base and fitted with castors.

Dining tables

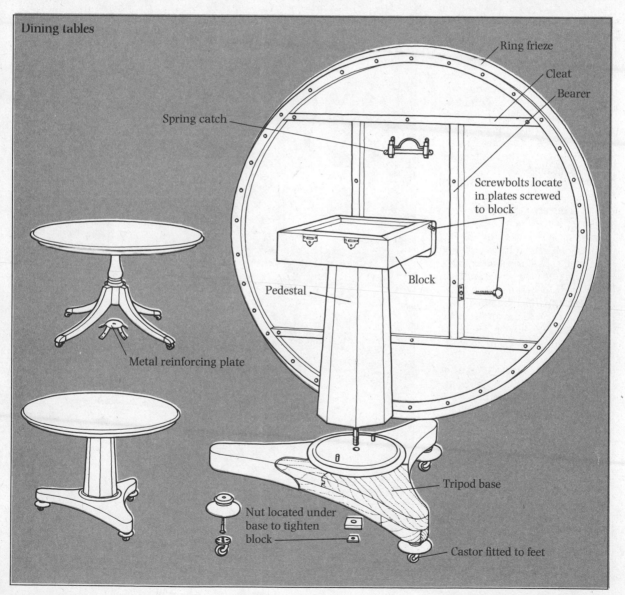

Ring frieze

Cleat

Bearer

Spring catch

Screwbolts locate in plates screwed to block

Block

Pedestal

Metal reinforcing plate

Nut located under base to tighten block

Tripod base

Castor fitted to feet

The column and its fixings

On some small tables the top of the column is threaded and screws into a hole in the centre of a wooden block (see panel **diagram a**). In most cases the block is fixed to the top with wood screws or glue and thus has no tip-up action. Avoid a table where this thread has stripped or is broken. Making a replacement thread is an extremely difficult job.

In most cases the top pivots on the block and here the block may be fitted to the column in a number of ways. In the simpler version the column is morticed into the block and is secured by wedges which spread the end of the column (see panel **diagram b**).

On a more sophisticated table the top can revolve as well as pivot. The block is replaced by an open wooden cage or 'gallery' which fits over a turned post on top of the column. A wedge is driven through a slot in the post to hold the gallery in position (see panel **diagram c**). If you own a pedestal table with a gallery, it is worth having it valued. Some of these tables are worth a great deal of money and should only be repaired by a professional restorer.

Small tables always have a solid turned column but on some dining tables the weight is reduced by making the column as a hollow box. These dining tables use a block again but this time it is framed up like the rest of the table but in hardwood for extra strength. It is fixed to the top of the column by a bolt which passes through the length of the column to a nut on the underside of the flattened base (see panel **diagram d**). Dining tables with a heavier version of the traditional solid tripod base have a solid block fitted with wedges to the top of the column.

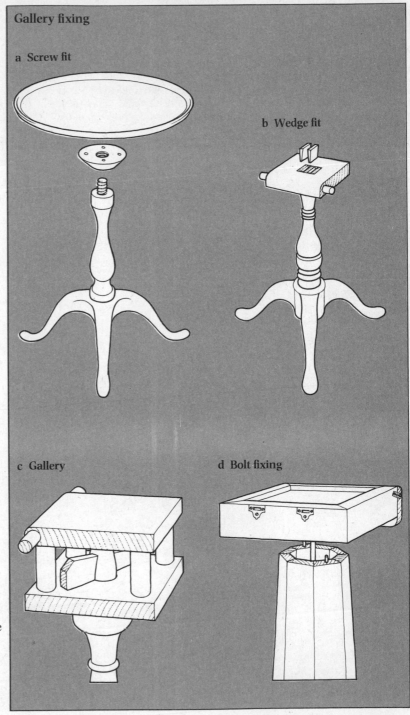

Gallery fixing

a **Screw fit**

b **Wedge fit**

c **Gallery**

d **Bolt fixing**

The pivot mechanism

On small tip-up tables, two wooden pegs project from the block and fit into holes drilled in two bearers screwed to the underside of the top (see panel below, **diagram a**). It is this simple mechanism which enables the top to pivot. As the top comes to rest in a horizontal position on the block it is held down by a spring catch, which should operate automatically. If it does not, oil it lightly.

Those tables fitted with a gallery work in exactly the same way, the top section of the gallery forming the block with projecting pegs.

Even large dining tables sometimes employ this type of pivot but more often they will be fitted with two brass screw bolts which pass through the framing of the table top into threaded plates screwed to the side of the block (**b**). The top pivots on the bolts.

Because the whole weight of the top is concentrated on the central column rather than on a leg at each corner, wear of the pivot mechanism in pedestal tables is very common, usually resulting in a loose top. This makes the table very inconvenient to use, so tackle the job as soon as possible, following the instructions overleaf.

Top construction

In older wine or tea tables, the top was sometimes made from one solid piece of timber, which can warp catastrophically when subjected to a centrally heated interior. Most tops, however, will have been made from two or three pieces of solid timber glued side-to-side (see page 48).

The edge of the top on small tables is usually slightly raised to form a moulding to contain spillage (see panel below, **diagram a**), or it might take the form of a carved 'pie crust' edge (**b**) to perform the same function. These edges frequently become chipped or broken and should be repaired as described under cabinet mouldings (see page 71). The pie crust version, however, will require some wood carving and this is perhaps best done by a professional restorer.

Normally, the two hardwood bearers screwed to the underside of small table tops are sufficient to prevent warping. In the case of dining tables the top is of greater area and is usually thicker, so more safeguards against warping must be built in. These usually take the form of a ring frieze of softwood plus cleats and bearers, all screwed into the top from below (see page 61). Where the softwood shows, on the outside of the ring frieze, it is veneered to match the top, usually in a crossband pattern (see page 23).

As in other tables, the commonest fault in pedestal table tops is shrinkage across the grain, leaving splits between the boards. The top should be knocked apart and re-glued as described for frame tables (see page 48). Note the methods for cramping a round top on page 49.

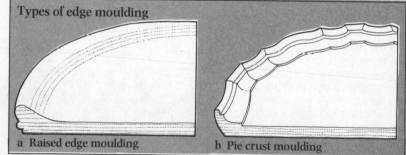

Types of edge moulding

a Raised edge moulding

b Pie crust moulding

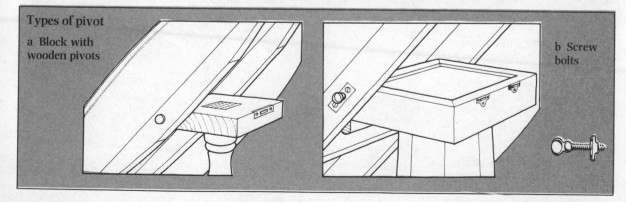

Types of pivot

a Block with wooden pivots

b Screw bolts

A loose top

There are several factors which may make a top loose on a pedestal table. Remove the top from the column and inspect the pivoting mechanism.

Removing the top

On those small tables where the top pivots on wooden pegs, unscrew one bearer so that the top can be removed.
- If a gallery is fitted the top is removed simply by tapping out the wedge that holds the gallery to the column.
- On dining tables, the brass screw bolt which holds the top frame to the block should be withdrawn from both sides to remove the top.

Fixing of block/gallery to the column

The joint between the block or gallery and the column may be loose, so that the table top will rock when in use.
- In tables where the block is fixed by a wedged mortice, check whether the wedges are loose. If they are, chisel them out, re-glue the joint and tap in new hardwood or plywood wedges.
- If a gallery is present, check that the upright posts are firmly glued into the top and bottom blocks. If not, tap the gallery apart and re-glue them. When you replace the gallery on the column make sure that the fixing wedge is tapped home to take up any movement at this point.
- On large tables it may only be necessary to tighten the nut on the underside of the base in order to pull the block on to the column. Put a little penetrating oil in the thread beforehand.

Wear on the pivots

It is unlikely that there will be much wear on the metal screw bolts of a dining table but if one is missing or another fitting of the wrong size had been substituted, you should replace both bolts. You can find them in specialist ironmongers or obtain them by mail order. You will have to fit the plates and fill screw holes as described on page 114 under *Protruding screw heads*.
- The wooden pins on the small tables are more likely to wear. As long as the wear is not too extensive it may be possible to trim them in order to glue a brass tube over them. Details of this job are given in the panel below.

Fitting a brass tube

To ensure a snug fit, make a cutter from the same brass tubing. Cut across the end and file down the metal between the cuts into crude saw teeth. Run a file around the inside to ensure that there are no burrs which would cut the pins too small.

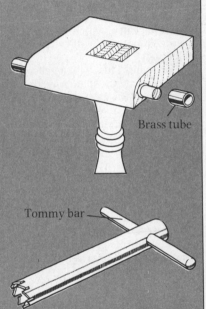

Brass tube

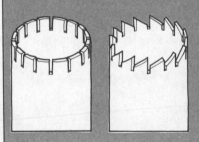

Tommy bar

- Bore a hole across the other end of the tube for a 'tommy bar'.
- Fit the cutter over the worn pins and gradually cut them to size, withdrawing the cutter periodically to clean out the teeth.

- If necessary enlarge the holes in the bearers to fit the tubing but try to use tubing which fits the original holes.

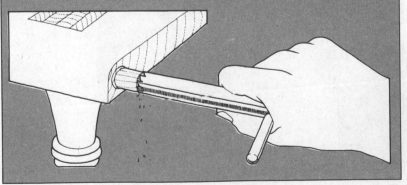

Damage to the column and tripod

The projecting feet of a tripod base are easily damaged especially if they belong to a small wine table of delicate proportions. Those of a dining table will have been subjected to kicks from the feet of guests (or of owners for that matter!) and to blows from carelessly replaced dining chairs. It is rare to find such a table that has been in continuous use for a long time which does not show dents, deep scratches and chipped veneer around its base, and there is little point in trying to restore it to its original condition. Parts which are broken or missing however detract from the table's appearance and should be repaired if at all possible.

Complete fractures of the wooden column can be repaired using an integral dowel, as described for stick chairs on page 41, whereas splits or fractures in the tripod legs should be repaired as described for chair legs on page 33.

A peculiar problem of pedestal tables is that since the weight is all centred on the column, the base of the column between the dovetail joints may become split or broken.

A split column base

Work glue into the split with a knife blade and bind the tripod with a tourniquet as shown in the panel below, **diagram a**. To prevent the tourniquet riding up the leg, use three blocks which are notched to fit over the bottoms of the feet.

A broken column base

If the leg and part of the base have broken away completely, it is a difficult job to hold them in the correct position whilst the glue sets.
- Make a block to fit over the leg from a piece of ply, as shown in **diagram b**, and another to fit against the column on the opposite side.
- Glue up the joint, hold the blocks in position, then set the job up in sash cramps whilst the glue dries.

A broken foot

Solid feet which are screwed to the underside of a dining table base may be broken where they have split along the grain. The central fixing screw can usually be located by first removing the castor.
- Plane the broken surface of the foot to a flat face.
- Plane a similar angle on a block of matching timber and glue it to the foot.
- Before shaping the foot, the repair can be reinforced with a slim dowel passing at an angle through the underside of the block into the original foot.

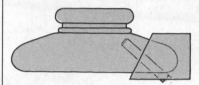

- Cut the block roughly to the diameter of the foot with a saw and use a rasp, wood files and abrasive paper for the shaping.
- Finally, stain and finish the repair to match the rest.

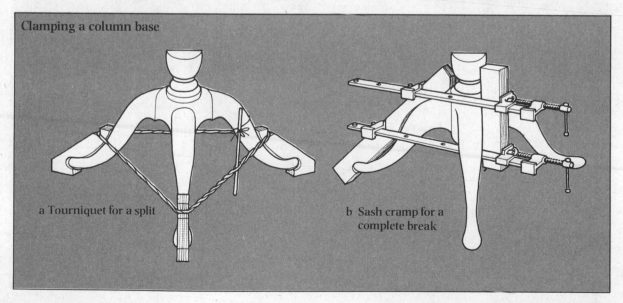

Clamping a column base

a Tourniquet for a split

b Sash cramp for a complete break

Cabinets

Types of cabinet

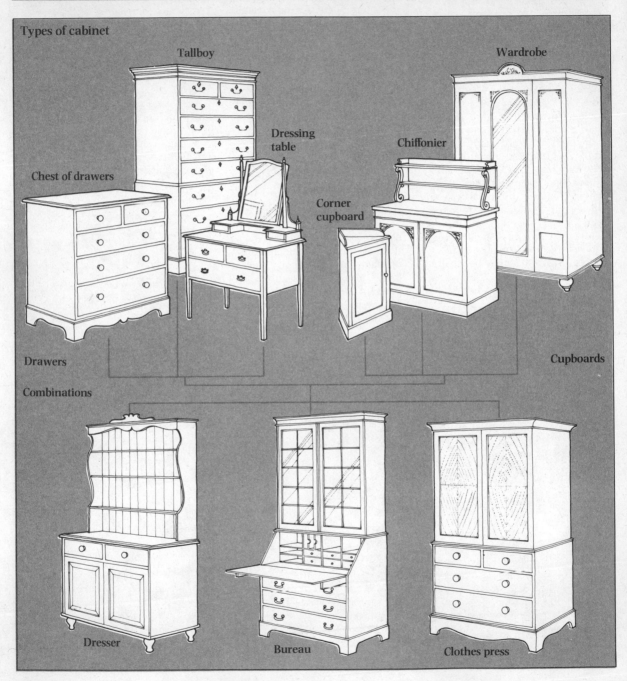

Tallboy

Wardrobe

Dressing table

Chiffonier

Chest of drawers

Corner cupboard

Drawers

Cupboards

Combinations

Dresser

Bureau

Clothes press

Pieces of furniture designed for storage exist in many forms – wardrobe, bureau, clothes-press and so on – but in fact they are all made up from two basic units, a chest of drawers and a cupboard. An apparent exception to this rule is an open shelf unit, such as the top section of a kitchen dresser, but that is only a narrow cupboard without doors and indeed there are many examples of similar constructions, albeit more elegant, which are fitted with glass doors and become bookcases. From the point of view of repairing old pieces of furniture we can therefore consider cabinets in three categories – the *carcase*, which is the basic 'box', *drawers* with their attendant runners and guides, and *cupboard doors*.

Most carcase problems will be the result of shrinkage or of excessive wear. The sides, for example may have split from top to bottom because drawer runners have been glued across the inside, preventing the natural movement of the wood. Mouldings may be broken or missing and of course, it is always worth looking for the tell-tale holes of woodworm (see panel) especially in the unpolished parts of the cabinet such as the back.

It is rare to find a cabinet with loose joints unless the back, which keeps the carcase rigid, is missing or badly damaged, or unless the furniture has been subjected to industrial stripping with hot caustic soda, which sometimes weakens the glue. Rack the cabinet by pressing on a top corner to see if there is any movement in the joints.

Remove any drawers to inspect the running surfaces. Deep grooves will often be found in the drawer runners coupled with corresponding wear on the bottom edge of the drawer sides. If this has been ignored for some time the drawer bottom may show signs of running on the stops attached to the transverse drawer rails. In addition, the bottom may have become detached from the back of the drawer, allowing it to move in its retaining grooves and to eventually spring out of them altogether. This may in turn loosen the corner joints of the drawer, particularly if shrinkage has caused the glue line to fail. Dust boards, which are fitted into grooves in the edge of the drawer runners, are often missing. They are intended primarily to protect the contents of the drawer and should be replaced.

If a door will not close the hinges are probably faulty (see page 114) but check also the clearance between the door and the cabinet. Framed doors should be examined to ensure that the joints are sound and that the panel has not split.

Woodworm

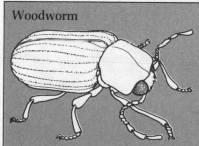

Most woods used in furniture construction can be attacked by the furniture beetle, commonly known as woodworm. It prefers to lay its eggs in crevices and cracks in unfinished surfaces where the grubs can hatch out and burrow into the timber, emerging several years later as adult beetles, producing the familiar flight holes. These holes, about 1mm ($\frac{1}{16}$in) in diameter, are only the outward sign of a network of interconnecting chambers inside the wood which can reduce its strength considerably.

● Press a knife blade into the timber in the area of the flight holes to test the consistency of the wood. Badly infested timber will be very soft, offering little resistance to the blade. Look for fine powder in the vicinity of the holes which indicates recent activity. In addition the inside of a fresh hole will be clean and light in colour, whereas a darker hole will probably have been made some time ago and may even have been treated previously.

● Unless furniture is very seriously affected by woodworm, it can be treated without professional help by using a proprietary woodworm-killing fluid. Treat the flight holes first, using special injector bottles or aerosol sprays. Insert the nozzle into a hole every 50mm (2in), squirting fluid into the interconnecting chambers.

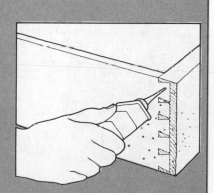

● Follow this treatment by brushing fluid over all unfinished surfaces, particularly the insides of cabinets, backs, drawers and the underside of wooden feet.
● When the furniture has dried out completely, fill visible flight holes with a wood filler.
● Regular treatment with special insecticidal polish will prevent reinfestation.

The carcase

Basic construction

Understanding the basic construction of the cabinet will help you to decide on the best way to dismantle it and to carry out any repairs with confidence.

There are many varieties of construction but for convenience we will consider two categories: a carcase with solid end panels and a frame and panel carcase. You will find both methods used for building cupboards and chests of drawers, depending on the material used, the overall size and weight of the piece, and the whims of the designer.

A carcase with solid end panels

As its name implies, this type of carcase has end panels (and often a bottom) made of solid timber. The top may be another solid panel dovetailed to the ends, but more often two top rails with triangular fillets are used and the top is screwed on from underneath.

The back, which may be made from several pieces of solid timber, locates in rebates or grooves in the top, sides and bottom.

The cabinet is usually raised off the floor on a separate frame known as a plinth, or legs are screwed on to the underside. A cupboard will have doors screwed inside the cabinet, flush with the outer edges, or

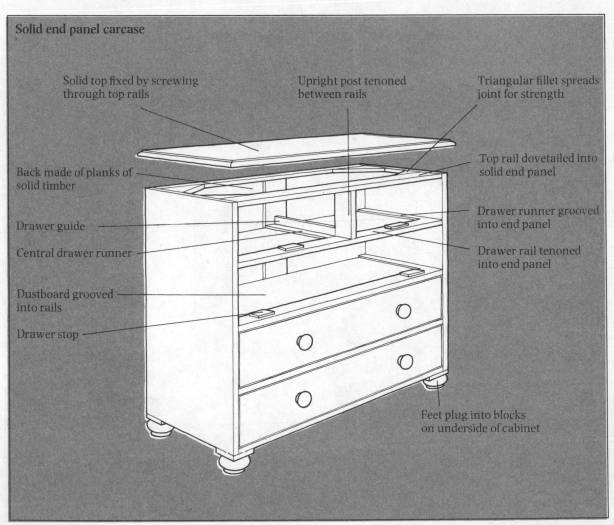

Solid end panel carcase

Solid top fixed by screwing through top rails

Upright post tenoned between rails

Triangular fillet spreads joint for strength

Back made of planks of solid timber

Top rail dovetailed into solid end panel

Drawer guide

Drawer runner grooved into end panel

Central drawer runner

Drawer rail tenoned into end panel

Dustboard grooved into rails

Drawer stop

Feet plug into blocks on underside of cabinet

they will be face mounted which means that the doors actually cover the front edges of the panels.

If the carcase is to contain drawers it will be fitted out with a number of rails. There are drawer runners on the sides of the cabinet upon which the drawers slide. Each drawer is supported by a drawer rail which runs across the front of the cabinet. Short drawers are separated by an upright post tenoned between the drawer rails and they slide on central runners which are fixed front to back. As there is no panel in the middle to stop the drawer slipping sideways, it will also require a drawer guide. Dust boards are also fitted between drawers to keep the contents clean and secure.

A frame and panel carcase

This type of carcase avoids the problem of warping timber by using a framework which is grooved, or in some cases rebated, to take a separate panel of timber or plywood.

Apart from that basic difference, it is constructed in much the same way as the cabinet described above. It is often used for larger pieces of furniture in order to reduce weight, or it may be used to build cheaper items which are covered with more attractive veneers.

Doors and drawers will be fitted as described for a solid end panel but because the end panel is set inside a frame, drawer guides will be required in all cases.

Frame and panel carcase

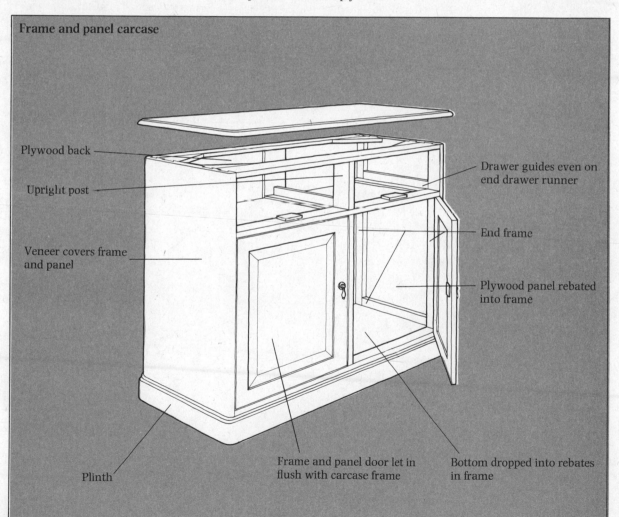

Plywood back

Upright post

Veneer covers frame and panel

Plinth

Drawer guides even on end drawer runner

End frame

Plywood panel rebated into frame

Frame and panel door let in flush with carcase frame

Bottom dropped into rebates in frame

Dismantling and re-gluing a carcase

Fortunately it will hardly ever be necessary to dismantle a carcase completely. Not that the job is particularly difficult but there are usually a great many components which must be re-assembled in the correct order. Study the construction of your particular carcase, using the diagrams of typical construction as a guide, so that you can work out in advance the way a joint should be dismantled. Identify each component and label the joints with pieces of masking tape so that the carcase can be re-assembled without confusion. Knock the joints

apart carefully using softening blocks and a hammer, and take care with solid panels which could easily split if too much force is applied.
● Re-assemble the carcase in reverse order and make a dry run before gluing up to ensure that you are completely familiar with the construction. Check for square at each stage of re-assembly.

A split end panel

The solid end panel of a cabinet may have split along the grain or an original butt joint between two pieces of timber may have parted. Depending on the circumstances, the cabinet could be dismantled and the split glued up before re-assembling the furniture as for a split table top (see page 48). However, it would be unwise to break perfectly sound joints in order to repair the split, especially if the panel is likely to be subjected to the same conditions which caused the damage in the first place. In this case, repair the split with a tapered lath, as in the panel below.

Repairing a split end panel

Clean out the split with a wood chisel or make yourself a tapered scraping tool from a steel strip.

If necessary increase the gap to take a tapered lath cut with a power saw from a piece of timber selected to match the original wood.
● Hold the lath between bench stops to smooth it with a plane.
● If the split itself is tapered from top to bottom, the lath may need to be shaped to fit.
● Apply glue and tap the lath into the crack with a hammer and wipe excess glue from the surface.
● When set, plane and sand the lath flush with the panel. Stain and polish to match the original finish.

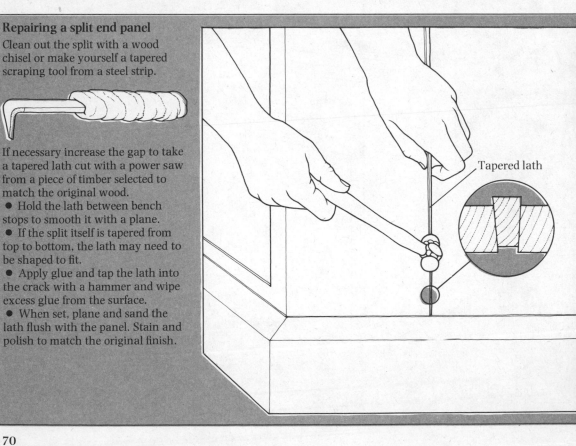

Tapered lath

A broken edge moulding

The moulded edge of a cabinet top normally projects somewhat from the rest of the cabinet and can be damaged by careless handling, or accidental knocks. If you have managed to retain the piece which has broken away, glue it back immediately before further damage makes a good joint impossible. More often the piece will have been lost for ever and you will have to use a piece of matching timber to remake the damaged edge.

● A corner, which is particularly vulnerable, should be planed to produce a squared edge to the moulding.

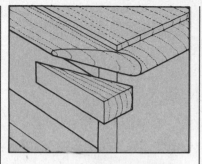

● Cut a piece of wood to follow the grain direction of the top, leaving it slightly larger than its intended shape. Rub joint the timber in place and hold it in position with a sash cramp across the cabinet top. Fix a stop block to the end of the wedge with a G-cramp to prevent it from sliding sideways.

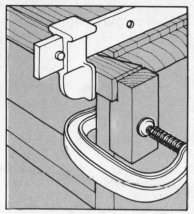

● Use a moulding plane, files, shaped scrapers or sanding blocks to shape the repair to the moulding.
● Stain and polish the new wood to match the original finish.

Patching a drawer rail

The groove worn by the bottom edge of the drawer will extend across the drawer rail, showing as a shallow notch at the front edge.

● Before fitting new drawer runners, cut out the damaged section of rail. To start, use a try square and knife to mark a line below the damage on the front edge of the rail.

● Make a 60° angled cut straight across the rail with a fine saw before chiselling down to the line with a bevelled edge chisel. Shape and cut a patch of matching hardwood to fit in the notch.

● Fit the drawer runner and tap in the glued patch from the front of the drawer rail until it fits snugly against the runner and hold it with a small G-cramp.
● Use a block plane to flush off the front edge of the patch and pare down the top surface with a chisel or a chisel plane.

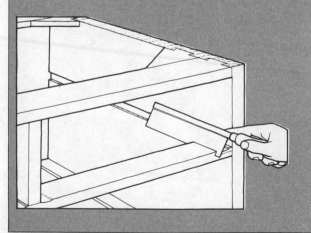

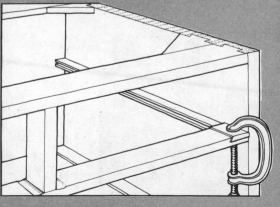

Worn drawer runners

Solid end panel carcase

In carcases built with solid end panels, the drawer runner fits into a housing cut across the inside of the end panel. A stub tenon on the front of the runner locates in the dust panel groove along the back edge of the drawer rail (see **diagram a**). This groove continues along the inside edge of the runner itself. With the dust board in place, the runner is held securely in the housing. You may find that it has been glued in place, although this is bad practice (see *Split end panel* page 70). It may however be glued at one end only or better still, located at the back with a single screw in a slot (see **diagram b**).

Where two small drawers lie side-by-side, separated by an upright post, the central drawer runner is wide enough to support both drawers. On top of it is a drawer guide to keep the two drawers apart (see **diagram a**).

● If a deep groove has been worn in the top edge of the runner, the simplest solution is to swap it with its partner on the other end of the cabinet, turning it over so that the wear is on the other side. This is only possible if the runner is truly symmetrical and each runner has been made sufficiently well to fit in any of the housings. To remove a glued runner, tap a chisel under the back edge.

● Another solution is to make new runners from a suitable hardwood. The hardwood need not be the same as before unless you wish to restore the cabinet to its original condition. Take the dimensions from the old runner and other components of the cabinet.

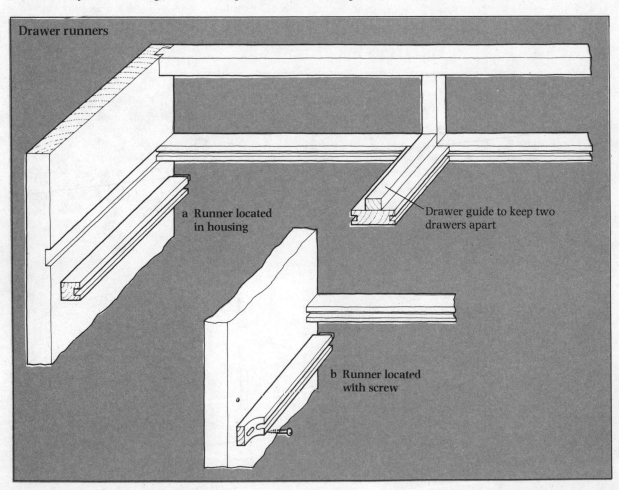

Drawer runners

a Runner located in housing

Drawer guide to keep two drawers apart

b Runner located with screw

Frame and panel carcase

Here the drawer runner does not lie in a housing but lies flat against the end panel. It is stub tenoned into the front post of the side frame and bears a groove for the dustboard on its inner face. A drawer guide is screwed on to the top of it to prevent the drawer moving sideways. Sometimes it is held in position by the dustboard but most often it has a slotted screw at its back end. In carcases with plywood end panels, the runner can be safely glued to the panel because plywood does not 'move' like solid timber.

● The best method of repair in these cabinets is to replace the worn drawer runner with a new one

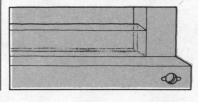

made of hardwood, not forgetting to replace the drawer guide as well. It should be screwed and glued to the top of the new runner, flush with the inside of the front post.

● In all replacements it is best to fit a slotted screw at the back end, making sure the screw can move freely in the slot to allow for timber movement.

Missing dustboards

Dustboards protect the contents of a drawer from airborne dust, as well as that produced by the action of the drawer itself. They also serve to hold the drawer runner securely in its housing and provide a means of security to a locked drawer, which could otherwise be tampered with by removing the drawer above.

● Dustboards in old chests of drawers were made of thin sheets of solid timber but a plywood panel is a simpler and more efficient substitute. Normally a 4mm ($\frac{1}{8}$in) panel will be suitable but measure the groove first. If necessary, plane a bevel on the edge of the plywood to

fit a narrow groove. Sand the edges well to allow it to slide in the grooves.

● The original dustboards were placed in the grooves before the back of the cabinet was fixed. New boards can be fitted in the same way. If, however, it is inconvenient to remove the back, cut a plywood panel which is about 25mm (1in) shorter from front to back, so that it can be sprung into the side runners before pulling it into the groove in the drawer rail. This will leave a small gap in the back of the cabinet which will hardly affect the efficiency of the dustboard.

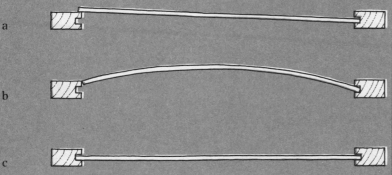

a

b

c

Drawer stops

The front of a drawer should come to rest against the drawer stops fitted to the top face of the drawer rail. This ensures that the face of the cabinet is flush. Often these stops, originally made from solid timber, have been broken and lost.

● Cut two new stops per drawer from 6mm ($\frac{1}{4}$in) plywood approximately 50mm by 35mm (2 x 1$\frac{1}{2}$in).

● Mark a line on the drawer rail with a marking gauge set to the thickness of the drawer front. Allow for any beading or moulding, which should project slightly from the face of the cabinet. Each stop should be about 75mm (3in) from the end.

● Rub joint the stops up to the gauged line, wipe off excess glue, then before it sets, position each drawer to locate the stops exactly.

● Carefully drive two panel pins into each stop to hold it securely.

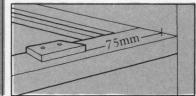

Traditional drawer construction

Drawers found in older cabinets are normally constructed as shown in the exploded diagram below. The sides are dovetailed into the front and back and a thin sheet of solid wood, usually bevelled at the edges, slides in grooves in the front and sides to form a bottom. Once it is fixed to the underside of the back, the bottom holds the structure square and rigid. The top of the back is rounded to prevent damage to the contents should they become trapped between it and the drawer rail. The back corner of each side is chamfered to help locate the drawer in its opening. Some drawer fronts are left plain; in others a scratch moulding is applied round the edges, or a cock bead is added. A common method for attaching cock beading is shown in the diagram.

Traditional drawer construction

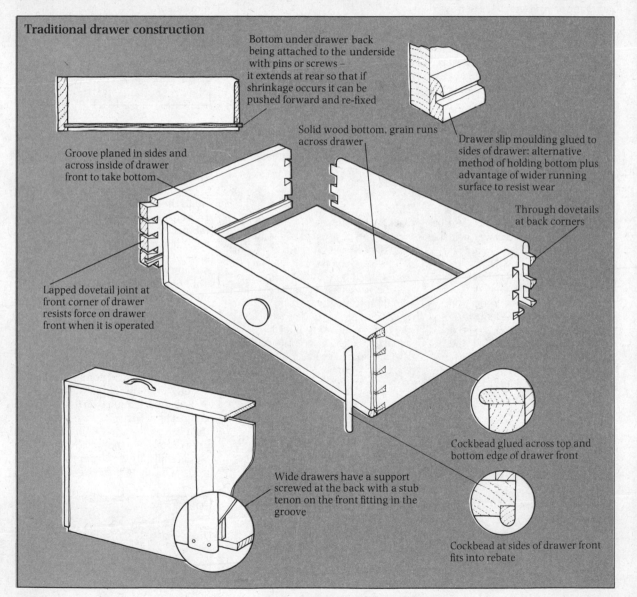

Bottom under drawer back being attached to the underside with pins or screws – it extends at rear so that if shrinkage occurs it can be pushed forward and re-fixed

Solid wood bottom, grain runs across drawer

Groove planed in sides and across inside of drawer front to take bottom

Drawer slip moulding glued to sides of drawer: alternative method of holding bottom plus advantage of wider running surface to resist wear

Through dovetails at back corners

Lapped dovetail joint at front corner of drawer resists force on drawer front when it is operated

Wide drawers have a support screwed at the back with a stub tenon on the front fitting in the groove

Cockbead glued across top and bottom edge of drawer front

Cockbead at sides of drawer front fits into rebate

Re-gluing loose joints

Dismantle a loose-jointed drawer by first unscrewing the drawer bottom and sliding it clear of its groove.

● Place softening blocks inside the corners and apply sharp blows with a hammer. Work your way around the corners, tapping the joints apart little by little to avoid putting a strain on any one of them. Keep the force in direct line with the dovetails. Alternatively, use jet cramps to prise the joints apart (page 29).

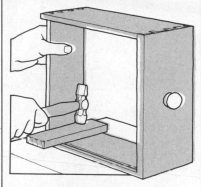

● Use a sharp chisel to scrape old glue from all the joints.

● Re-glue each joint, tapping the sides in place with a hammer and softening blocks. Wipe off excess glue with a damp cloth.

● Use two sash cramps parallel with the front and back of the drawer, with softening blocks as close to the joints as is practicable. Use stout blocks and make sure they extend across the full width of the side (see panel right). Wipe off excess glue. Ensure the joints are flush.

● Measure the diagonals to ensure that the drawer is square and sight across the drawer from both sides to see that it is not twisted. It is advisable to slide the bottom in place carefully to ensure that it fits and check for square and 'wind' once again (see checking for square in *Re-assembling chairs* page 30).

Repairing or replacing a drawer bottom

A well-fitted drawer bottom should remain in good condition but if it has split, due to misuse, or because it has been fixed in its grooves so that the wood cannot move, it can be either repaired or replaced.

● To repair the bottom, remove it carefully and, having glued both edges of the crack, set it up between G-cramps and battens on both sides of the panel. Wax the battens, or place paper between them and the job, to protect them from glue.

● Pull the crack together with a sash cramp, adjusting its position to ensure that the board is kept flat.

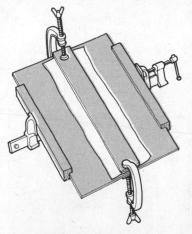

● Having cleaned up the glued job, the crack can be reinforced by gluing a strip of canvas to the underside of the drawer bottom. Paint glue along the crack and rub the canvas well down into it.

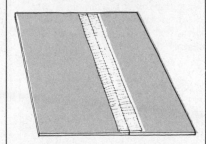

● Alternatively, replace the bottom with one of plywood. Match the thickness to the width of the groove if possible or plane a shallow bevel on the edges of a thicker board.

● With the bottom in position, mark screw centres across the back edge to fix to the underside of the drawer back. Drill and countersink the screws.

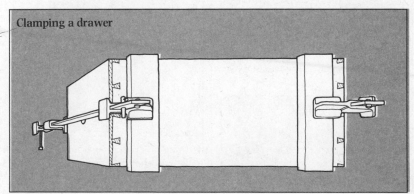

Clamping a drawer

Broken cock beads

If a cock bead along the top or bottom edge of a drawer front is broken away, it is a simple matter to insert a patch. To ensure that the action of the drawer does not disturb the repair, dovetail the patch into the remaining beading.

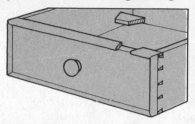

- From a piece of matching wood slightly thicker than the original moulding, cut a patch which is tapered from back to front and is large enough to cover the damaged section. Make it slightly deeper from front to back to allow for flushing off after it is fitted.
- Lay the patch in place on the damaged area and mark both ends with a knife.

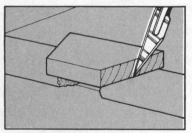

- Cut on the inside of both lines to the depth of the beading with a fine saw and pare down the waste with a chisel.

Worn drawer sides

The action of the drawer over many years not only wears a groove in the runners but also wears away the bottom edge of the drawer side.
- Turn the drawer upside-down and plane the bottom edges of the sides, sloping down from the front to back edge until the damaged section is removed.

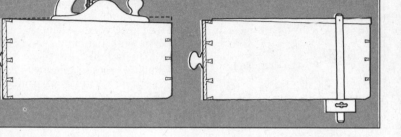

- Cut a wedge from matching timber for each side. Glue it to the drawer side flush with the inner face but proud elsewhere.
- When the glue has set, plane the outer surfaces flush on each side. Use a marking gauge to mark a line parallel to the top edge and aligned with the bottom edge of the drawer front. Plane down to this line on both sides.

- Glue the patch and recess and tap the patch in from the back to fit snugly in the dovetail. If necessary, hold it with a G-cramp until the glue sets.

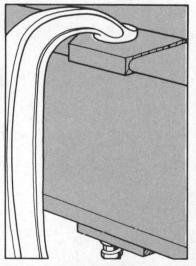

- Plane the patch flush, top and back, and shape the rounded front as closely as possible to the existing bead with a chisel, finishing with a scratch moulding tool (see page 122). Use a fine abrasive paper before staining and polishing the patch.
- Cock beads at the sides of the drawer front are often fitted into small rebates. If the timber has shrunk across the width of the drawer front, this moulding will sometimes have worked loose.

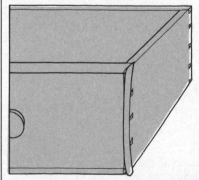

- Trim the mitres at both ends until the beading fits and re-glue it, using the original pins to secure it. In some cases these are made of hardwood. Wrap adhesive tape around the corner until the glue sets.

A sticking drawer

If a cabinet is subjected to damp conditions, it will take up moisture. The timber will expand and the drawers will bind. Storing such a piece in a dry environment is all that is required to solve the problem. If on the other hand you know that this is not the case, examine the running surfaces of the drawer and cabinet, noting shiny areas which indicate that they are rubbing. The drawer sides can also be at fault, as can the top edges, particularly if the drawer is twisted.

● Rub any suspected areas with candle wax and treat all running surfaces at the same time.

● If this is insufficient to cure the fault, use a finely set plane to skim a few shavings from the trouble spots.

● Check that there are no protruding nails or screws, splits or dried glue on the runners and drawer guides which may be contributing to the problem.

Doors

The most common problem with doors is that they will not close properly. This is dealt with under *Hinges* (see page 114). Most of the doors on old furniture consist of a panel enclosed in a frame. The panel may have split or the joints of the frame may be loose.

Repairing a split panel

The split wooden panel can be repaired in exactly the same way as a split end panel in a carcase (see page 70) or, if it can be removed from the frame, re-glue it in a similar way to the method described for repairing a drawer bottom (see page 75).

● A panel which is held in the frame by a strip of beading can be removed by prising off the beading with an old chisel.

● If the panel is held in a groove in the frame itself, it can only be removed by dismantling the frame. This is a simple procedure if the joints happen to be loose anyway but if not, try softening them with steam as described on page 28. Do not use steam on panels made of veneered plywood. Check beforehand that the tenons are not secured with dowel pegs.

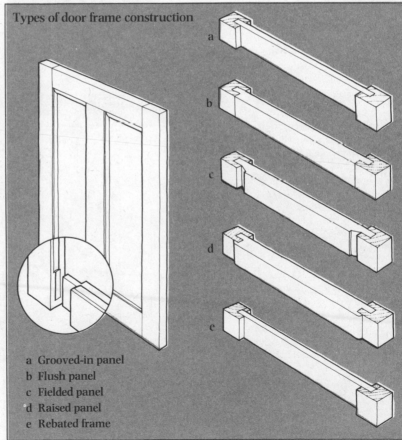

Types of door frame construction

a Grooved-in panel
b Flush panel
c Fielded panel
d Raised panel
e Rebated frame

● Once the glue is softened, lay the door face down on a flat surface and place softening against the inside of the frame, as close to the joint as possible. Tap the softening with a hammer or mallet, sliding the hammer head on the panel to avoid denting it with a badly aimed blow. A sheet of paper placed on the panel will stop the hammer head scratching the finish.

● When re-assembling the door, ensure that glue does not squeeze out of the joints into the groove in which the panel locates. Put the frame in sash cramps and check that it is square, as described on page 30.

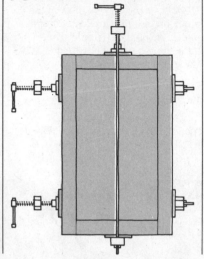

A sticking door

Cupboard doors which are stubborn to open usually show one of two faults. Either the hinges are worn or wrongly positioned, or else the woodwork has split allowing the door to drop and bind against its neighbour or against the frame of the cabinet (see page 114).
● If the cabinet has been stored in damp conditions, allow it to dry out slowly.
● Ensure that it is not standing on an uneven floor, which could cause the whole cabinet to become twisted.
● Inspect the edges of the door for signs of abrasion. This can be verified by passing a thin piece of paper between the door and frame, noting where it catches. If the door is of solid timber, sand or finely plane these areas. If it is edge-veneered, plane down the hinge side or bottom of the door.

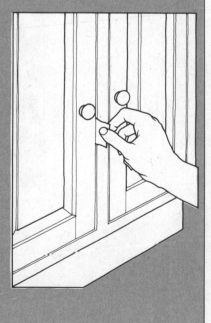

Re-glazing a cabinet

Many old cabinets have glazed doors, often made up of several small panes fitted into extremely fine wooden ribs called *glazing bars*.
● To remove a broken pane, inspect the inside of the door to determine how the glass is held in its rebate. If a wooden bead is used it may be screwed or pinned in place, sometimes with the addition of glue (see panel opposite, **diagram a**). Remove the beading carefully, if necessary prising it off gently with a knife blade. Having fitted new glass, replace the beading.
● Putty, which is shaped into a bevel on the inside, will have to be removed using an old chisel (**b**).
● Old putty will probably have been mixed with gold size to accelerate drying and reduce shrinkage. When removing it, there is a risk of damage to the fine framing and more glass may be broken, so soften it first. Use a soldering iron, warming a small section of putty at a time and scraping it away with a chisel. Small headless nails called *sprigs* may have been used to secure a large pane of glass, but smaller ones will be held in by putty alone.
● Wearing protective gloves, remove any pieces of broken glass.

Holding the glass in its rebate

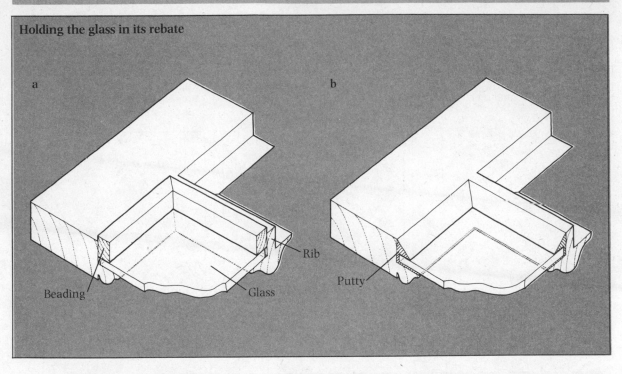

a

b

Beading

Glass

Rib

Putty

● Measure the distance between rebates, reducing both dimensions by 1mm ($\frac{1}{16}$in). Cut a cardboard template and fit it between the glazing bars to check the dimensions. This is important since not all panes are rectangular. Measure the thickness of the glass from one of the remaining fragments and have a glazier cut a matching pane, using your template as a guide. It may be useful to take a fragment of the glass with you to ensure a good match.

● If you wish to reproduce the original hard putty make a shallow dish of putty in which to pour a little gold size. Knead the putty care-

fully to absorb the size. A coloured putty is an advantage when matching the colour of certain woods.

● Use your fingers to press a little putty along the rebates, pressing the glass into it. Scrape excess putty from the outside with a putty knife.

● Press enough putty on the inside to fill the rebates all round, shaping it to a bevel with the knife.

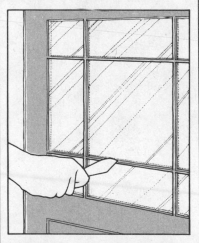

● Clean the glass with methylated spirit to remove finger marks and leave the putty to harden thoroughly before painting the bevel to match the inside of the door.

79

Leaded lights

Book cases often have glazed doors consisting of panes of square or diamond-shaped glass, held in a lattice of lead strips. Each strip is H-shaped in section and is called a *came*.

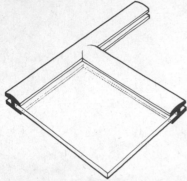

• To remove a broken pane, first cut through the corner of the cames on the inside of the door with a knife, tapping the blade with a small hammer if necessary. Avoid outward pressure or the whole lead framework could be distorted.

• Use an old chisel to prise back the edges of the cames to remove the broken glass and clean out dry putty in the grooves.

• Make a template for the glass by holding a stout piece of paper against the empty cames and rubbing with a wax crayon. Test the template and have the replacement pane cut by a glazier.

• Add putty to the cames and press the glass in place. Fold the cames back in place with your fingers and scrape off excess putty before smoothing the cames with the rounded handle of a screwdriver.

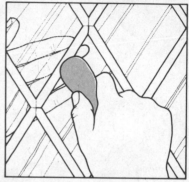

• Finally rub the cut corners with a medium grade glass paper and solder them.

Replacing curved glass

It may be necessary to replace a piece of curved glass in a bow-fronted cabinet. If the piece of furniture is sufficiently valuable to warrant the expense of such a highly specialised job, measure exactly the height of the pane between rebates and the straight measurement across the rebates, ignoring the curve.

• Make a cardboard template which fits in the curved rebate. Take your measurements to a glazier who can have a piece of glass cut and bent by a firm that specialises in such work, but ask for a quotation beforehand.

• Alternatively, contact the Glass and Glazing Federation (6 Mount Row, London W1, telephone 01-629 8334) who will put you in touch with a specialist. Some glaziers will take over the whole job for you, including fitting the glass.

• If the cabinet is not worth the expense of re-glazing, try springing a sheet of thin acetate into the rebate. This is a glass-clear plastic available from many model or hobby suppliers. Alternatively, a clean crack may be repaired using a proprietary glass adhesive.

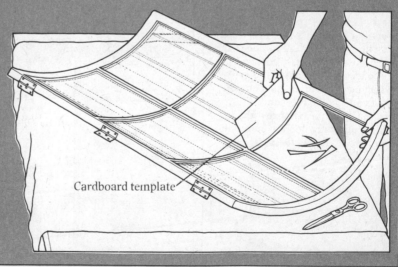

Cardboard template

CHAPTER FIVE

Simple upholstery

Upholstery differs in one basic respect from all the other skills we have discussed so far. When you are repairing a broken or damaged component on wooden furniture, you normally have a similar component in sound condition which you can use for comparison, or else the shape of the repair can be inferred from the surrounding material. With upholstery, once you have stripped away the old materials, there is nothing left to act as a guide for reproducing the shape of the original piece, except for perhaps a photograph, and probably the furniture was already in poor condition when the photograph was taken. In other words, to renovate the piece

properly you have to be as skilful as the upholsterer who built the furniture in the first place, and that is a tall order when faced with something as sophisticated as a deep buttoned Chesterfield sofa or a Victorian spoonback chair. Of course, amateurs can and do renovate furniture of this kind, but it requires a great deal of experience and far more space than is available in this book to explain the techniques adequately. What is more, the renovation of a large upholstered piece takes a long time and many evening classes are elephants' graveyards of pieces which have been deserted because their owners ran out of either skill or patience.

For all these reasons, we would prefer to describe the techniques which will enable you to re-upholster a limited range of furniture, but to do it well. We have concentrated primarily on the type of upholstery you will find on various kinds of dining chair, from a simple drop-in seat pad to a stuffed-over seat with coiled springs. Even these simple pieces contain all the basic techniques and materials used for more complicated jobs and will serve as an ideal introduction to upholstery methods in general. We have also included a few simple tips for the care and repair of upholstery which are relevant to any upholstered furniture, old or new.

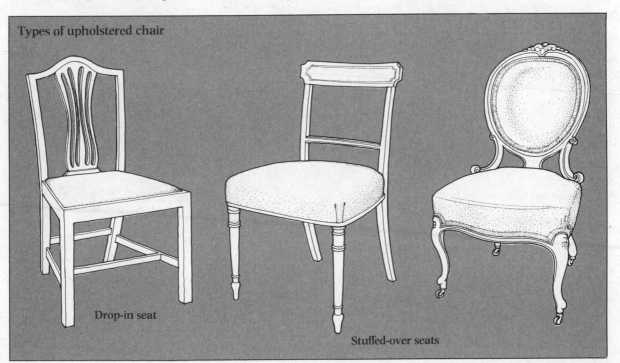

Types of upholstered chair

Drop-in seat

Stuffed-over seats

Upholstery tools and materials

Tools

You may already have many of the tools required for upholstery work, such as a screwdriver, pliers, pincers, a fairly large pair of scissors, a sharp knife and a mallet. In addition there are certain specialised tools which you will need in order to carry out even simple upholstery. In some cases we have suggested alternative tools which you can make yourself, or ways of using tools which you already possess.

Upholstery hammer

The upholstery hammer is a special tool with a narrow head between 12mm and 15mm ($\frac{1}{2}$in and $\frac{5}{8}$in) in diameter. Some of these hammers are magnetic so that they can pick up tacks and a claw may also be incorporated for removing them. Alternatively, use a pin hammer.

Ripping chisel

A professional upholsterer's tool, used to remove old tacks and upholstery. You can use an old screwdriver to do the same job. Either tool should be struck with a wooden mallet only.

Skewers

Upholstery skewers are used to hold a cover in position temporarily.

Staple gun

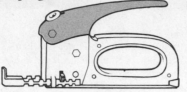

While traditional tacks will be required for temporary fixing of fabrics, the staple gun offers a neat way of permanently fixing the top cover and lining. It is particularly useful when working close to a show wood edge. Most staple guns are hand operated, but electrically powered versions ease the job.

Regulator

The point is used to adjust or spread the stuffing easily through a calico or hessian cover. The flat end is used to tuck under turnings and pleats.

Needles

Certain specialised needles are required for upholstery.

The mattress needle is double-pointed with an eye at one end. It is used for stitching right through upholstery and for sewing a firm edge to a seat. Half-circle needles are available in a range of sizes. They have rounded or bayonet points and can be double ended. They are essential in upholstery work because you quite often meet situations where it is not possible to use a straight needle. The spring needle is a specially strong curved needle with a bayonet point used for sewing springs to webbing.

Webbing stretcher

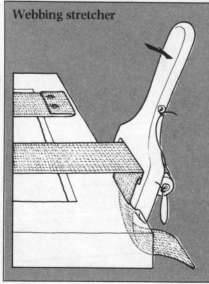

An essential tool to ensure that webbing is strained as tightly as possible on to the frame. You can buy one or make a simpler version from a block of wood, as shown below.

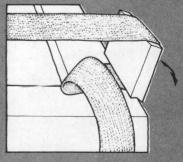

Materials

Webbing

Fifty millimetre (2in) webbing is widely available and made from black and white cotton, recognised by its herring-bone pattern, or jute, which is sandy brown in colour. The black and white webbing is strong and best suited for seat work. Jute webbing can be used for seats but it is more suitable for chair backs. Webbing is tacked to the chair frame and used to support springs or stuffings. It is sold in rolls and can be bought by the metre. Rubber webbing is not suitable for use on old furniture.

Springs

The traditional coil spring is made of spring steel wire coiled into an 'hour glass' or 'double cone' shape. It is available in various gauges of wire and in sizes from 100mm (4in) to 300mm (12in) long in 25mm (1in) increments.

Hessian

Hessian is a coarse woven fabric made of jute, which is available in various weights. The heaviest grades, either 456 grams (16oz) or 366 grams (12oz) are used for covering springs, or for the base platform for stuffing. Medium weight, or 305 grams (10oz), is used for covering the first stuffing. Lightweight, or 229 grams ($7\frac{1}{2}$oz), is used for covering the second stuffing, or as a light panel under the seat.

Hair

Horsehair was traditionally used for the main stuffing in upholstered furniture and is considered to be superior to other types of material. The best, and most sought after, is the long hair from the horse's mane and tail. This has more resilience or 'spring' and also more body than other types of hair stuffings, which may be a mixture of short horse hair and other animal hair. Hair will generally outlast other types of stuffing and can be re-used once cleaned and teased out.

Fibre

Vegetable fibres are a good alternative to short hair stuffings and cost about one third of the price. The most common types are Algerian fibre, a sort of coarse grass, and coconut or coir fibre. Algerian fibre is often dark grey or black in colour, the dye being used to kill bacteria. Coir stuffing is recognised by its light brown colour. Both coir and Algerian fibre are coarser in texture than hair but provide a good stuffing for most work and are particularly economical when stuffing a large piece such as a settee. They can be re-used after beating the dust out and teasing, providing they are still resilient. If they show signs of breaking up it is better to renew them.

Cotton felt

Cotton felt is a type of coarse cotton wool which is supplied in rolled sheets about 25mm (1in) thick. Suppliers sell it by the metre. A sheet of paper separates the layers in the roll and this is removed before the felt is placed on the chair. It is used as the final top stuffing, or on its own for a small pad such as a chair back. More than one layer can be used to build up the shape.

Wadding

A fine cotton wadding, sometimes referred to as skin wadding, which is supplied in thicknesses between 6mm ($\frac{1}{4}$in) and 12mm ($\frac{1}{2}$in). A thin soft paper protects both faces of the wadding and is an integral part of the material It is horsehair-proof and used as a top layer to prevent the hair working through the cover. It also gives the superficial soft feel to the upholstery and provides an even layer to complete the shape of the padding.

Calico

A woven fabric of unbleached cotton available in a range of weights, including an upholstery grade. It is used as an under cover over the second stuffing for traditional upholstery, and as a lining for cushions. It is also used over foam padding to help pull the foam down into shape. When a piled fabric is to be used, a calico lining should be fitted to prevent friction from the foam pulling the pile back through the fabric.

Cambric

A thin inexpensive fabric used on the underside of seat frames as a dust cover.

Tacks

Upholsterer's tacks have very sharp points with large flat heads. They are available as 'fine' or 'improved'. For upholstery work, fine tacks are used for fixing lining and top covers. Ten millimetre ($\frac{3}{8}$in) or 12mm ($\frac{1}{2}$in) will be suitable for most jobs. Sixteen millimetre ($\frac{5}{8}$in) improved tacks are used for fixing webbings, hessian and for temporary tacking.

83

Gimp pins

These are small-headed tacks used for fixing gimp or braid and are available with coloured heads. They can also be used to fix the back panel on some chairs.

Chair nails

Large dome-headed decorative nails used to finish the edges of leather and leather cloth coverings. They are available in various colours, in a brass finish or covered with fabric.

Buttons

Buttons are available in a range of sizes and can usually be covered with your own material by your local supplier. Buttons used for tying through the stuffing have a wire loop or fabric tuft on the back for stitching through. Button nails are also made. These are driven into thin stuffings over a firm base, such as when covering a padded arm.

Edge binding tape

Available in a range of sizes with a plain or self-adhesive back, edge binding tape is used to hold the edges of foam to the frame. A strip of calico can be used in the same way, with an upholstery adhesive to bond it to the foam.

Adhesives

Special adhesives are available for bonding latex and polyurethane foam. They are available in cans and are applied with a spreader. An aerosol adhesive is also available which can bond both types of foam.

Latex adhesives, which are white in colour but dry clear, are used for attaching gimp or braid.

Foam

Most modern upholstered furniture is padded with a foam material, which may be latex or polyurethane. You can use foam when re-upholstering an old chair but this has its pros and cons. Foam is easier to use than loose stuffings such as horse hair and since it is so resilient it can often be used to replace springs. It does not suit all chairs however since it will not always reproduce the shape of the original. More important, the polyurethane variety will produce poisonous fumes if you are unfortunate enough to have a fire. Latex does not have this disadvantage, but it is harder to get hold of, comes in a smaller range of thicknesses and is more expensive than polyurethane.

All foam consists of millions of minute interconnected air cells, which produce its softness and resilience whilst making it self-ventilating. Both latex and polyurethane are produced in sheet form in a range of thicknesses, polyurethane having the larger range –

6mm ($\frac{1}{4}$in) to 100mm (4in).
A choice of density is available, soft, medium and firm, although not in all thicknesses. Polyurethane is also supplied in a 'chip' or 'crumble' form for stuffing loose cushions.

As a rule, a medium to firm density is used for seats of chairs and soft to medium density for backs. A composite pad can be made by bonding layers of foam together, with the softest used as a thin layer on the top. This will give the initial soft feel which makes upholstery comfortable, while the firmer base gives the necessary support to prevent 'bottoming'. Bottoming occurs when the foam compresses so much that the frame is felt through it.

When testing the density of foam, press it with the full width of the hand, not simply by pinching it with the fingertips, as this gives a false impression. Should foam be used over a solid base such as plywood, and covered with a relatively non-ventilating material such as leather or leather cloth, then holes must be drilled in the base to allow the foam to recover its shape.

Cutting foam

Foam can be sawn with an ordinary bread knife. However, an electric carving knife will cut foam almost as well as a professional foam cutter. It will cut through even thick foam with one pass and is particularly useful for making angled cuts. Mark any guide lines on the foam with a felt tipped pen or ballpoint pen.

● To cut an angled edge, lay the foam sheet on a table flush with the edge. Holding the knife at the required angle, make the cut, using the edge of the table to guide the knife.

● A square cut is made in a similar way, holding the knife upright.

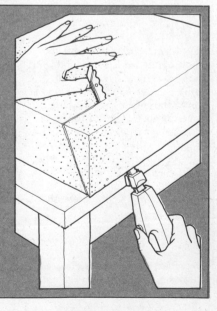

Twine

Twine may be made from hemp, jute, flax, cotton, nylon or polypropylene, in various sizes. Nylon and polypropylene are stronger and are best used for buttoning, but they are more expensive. The thickest twine, sometimes known as No. 1, is used for tying springs to webbing and making ties through stuffing. Thinner twine is used for stitching edges and rolls. A dressing of wax, applied by pulling the twine through a block of beeswax, makes it lie straighter and helps it to hold knots.

Piping cord

Cotton piping cord is available in three sizes: thin 3mm ($\frac{1}{8}$in), medium 5mm ($\frac{3}{16}$in) and thick 6mm ($\frac{1}{4}$in). It is sewn into a folded strip of covering fabric for fitting into a seam.

Threads

Coloured threads are used for finishing seams, sewing in piping and for attaching grimp.

Laid cord

A thick, strong cord used to lace traditional coil springs together and tie them down to the seat frame (see pages 98 and 99).

Knots

Slip knot

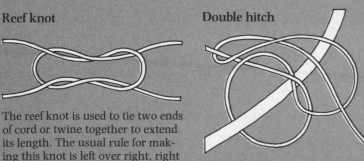

The slip knot is used in upholstery to secure the end of cords or twine at the beginning of a run of lacing or stitching and for tying in buttons.

Reef knot

The reef knot is used to tie two ends of cord or twine together to extend its length. The usual rule for making this knot is left over right, right over left.

Half hitch

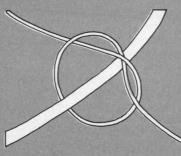

The half hitch is a simple knot which is widely used as the first knot when lacing springs. This knot makes a secure fixing but can be released easily for making adjustments.

Double hitch

The double hitch is used to make a permanent fixing, as on the second tie when lacing springs.

French knot

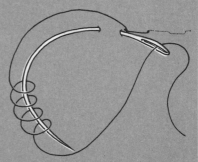

In upholstery the French knot is used to finish a row of ladder stitching. The same knot is used in embroidery. A small stitch is made at the end of a row of stitches and the thread is looped three or four times over the needle before it is pulled through. The loops tighten and lock the stitch when pulled up. A long stitch is made back along the row and the thread cut where it exits.

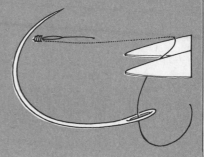

Care of upholstery

Fabric coverings protect the underlying materials from the wear and tear of normal use, as well as enhancing the appearance of the furniture. Regular care and attention is required to keep the fabric in good condition. Brush down or preferably vacuum clean the furniture, using the appropriate attachments to extract dust and dirt from crevices and folds. Brush and beat feather-filled cushions however, as vacuum cleaning can pull the feathers through the cover.

Stains should be dealt with promptly as not only are they more difficult to remove at a later date but the cleaned spot may show up as a lighter patch which is little better than the original mark. If this should happen, the fabric as a whole should be cleaned.

Strong sunlight may cause some fabrics to fade and the fibres may even deteriorate over a period of time. Avoid placing furniture by an unshaded window, or at least move it periodically to reduce the effect of light.

Cleaning upholstery

Any fabric on old furniture will have dulled, due to a combination of dirt and fading, and will often be improved by cleaning. A fabric that is badly worn, however, should be replaced, as its condition will not justify thorough cleaning. There may be exceptions, such as when a pleasing design is no longer available, in which case cleaning the fabric may restore some of its original quality.

Some fabrics are washable but, generally speaking, dry cleaning is preferable. Loose covers can be sent away for cleaning but fixed covers must be treated *in situ*. There are cleaning companies who will carry out this work for you.

● If you feel that dry cleaning will be too expensive do the job yourself with upholstery shampoo, but be sure that it is suitable for your fabric and follow the manufacturer's instructions carefully. It is never particularly easy to identify a fabric but in general old pieces of furniture are likely to be covered in natural fibres such as wool, cotton, linen, or on rare occasions, silk. These fabrics are still available but they are now usually blended with man-made fibres.

● Always test the shampoo on an inconspicuous piece of fabric to check its colour fastness before cleaning the whole piece. Work on small areas at a time, moving progressively from clean to dirty areas. Do not soak the fabric, for it is the foam generated by working with the sponge or brush which actually cleans the covering. When the covering is thoroughly dry, brush or vacuum the surface.

Cleaning leather furniture

Leather and plastic coverings can be cleaned with normal upholstery shampoo but it should be wiped off before it is dry.

● Saddle soap is made specifically for cleaning and treating leather. It is applied with a damp sponge and the foam is worked into the surface. The surplus is removed with a clean, barely damp, sponge and when dry the leather is rubbed over with a soft dry cloth.

● Treat leather with a nourishing cream such as 'hide food' once or twice a year. Do not apply a wax polish to leather as it causes it to dry out.

Removing stains

A fresh, light stain caused by spilt foodstuffs can usually be lifted by sponging with clean water. If this is unsatisfactory, use a commercial cleaning fluid, but always check its suitability first on an area where it will not show.

● Stains from tea, coffee, fruit juice or beer can be lifted with upholstery shampoo. Use a sponge to work the foam into the stain. When dry, brush or vacuum clean the area. Try repeating the process on persistent stains. Stains caused by substances with a high sugar content such as syrup or sweets can be treated in the same way.

● Spots that remain after treatment may be due to a residue of grease. For these, and other grease marks, such as butter, soup, shoe polish, lipstick and so on, use a commercial cleaning fluid or dry cleaner. Apply the fluid with a clean cloth wrapped around a finger, wiping towards the grease mark so as not to spread it. Sponge the spot with clean water after treating.

● A deep stain can be lifted by mixing some cleaning fluid and an absorbant such as Fullers' Earth to make a paste. This is applied over the spot and then brushed off when it is dry.

● Dry cleaners are available in aerosol cans. When the solvent has evaporated, an absorbent powder is left which is simply brushed off.

Small repairs

Mending a tear

Tears in woven fabric should be repaired promptly to prevent the weave fraying.
- Cut a patch larger than the tear from a strong but thin fabric. Tuck it under the tear with the handle of a spoon.
- Hold the tear open and apply a latex fabric adhesive between the patch and the underside of the torn fabric with a brush. Take care not to get any on the surface.

- Press the fabric together while still wet, using skewers to take the tension out of the covering. Adjust the edges of the tear to make a neat, butted joint.

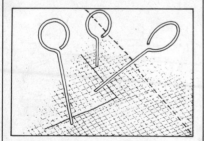

- For thin fabrics, apply the adhesive and keep the tear open with pins while it becomes touch dry. When dry, unpin and press the tear together. Care must be taken to ensure that the edges meet first time as they will stick on contact.

Renewing a button

The button is pulled into the stuffing with a loop of nylon tufting twine on a mattress needle. Local upholsterers will usually cover a button for you. With luck you may find a spare piece of matching fabric tucked inside the frame.

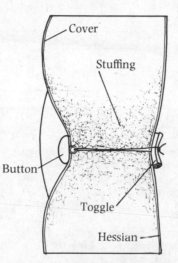

Cover

Stuffing

Button

Toggle

Hessian

- Remove the outer back covering of the chair. Pass the needle through the stuffing and out at the front. Thread it through the wire loop or leather tuft on the back of the button, then push the needle back through the stuffing again.
- Remove the needle and tie a slip knot in the ends of the twine. Partially tension the twine, then place under the knot either a tuft made from a small patch of leather or a toggle of rolled fabric.
- Adjust the folds on the front covering with a regulator, then tighten the slip knot to give the correct depth and tie it off. Replace the back cover, using slip stitching.

Re-sewing a piped edge

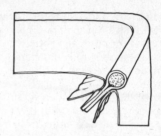

Piping is used to make a feature of a seam in the covering material. It is usually machine stitched into the seam as the cover is made up. In some cases it is hand stitched into the seam using a half circle needle and it is this method that is used to make a repair.

The raised edge formed by the piping is subjected to more wear than the surrounding fabric. Worn piping can be replaced without removing the rest of the covering, providing a matching fabric is available. In the absence of a matching fabric, try using one which will blend or contrast with the rest of the covering.

Making piping

Mark and cut 38mm ($1\frac{1}{2}$in) strips diagonally from the fabric. If the length of piping you need is longer than you can manage from one strip of fabric, shorter pieces can be cut and machined together to make up the length. It is important to keep the strips the same way round, as they are cut to ensure that the weave follows through when they are sewn together. This is done simply by making a chalk mark on the back of each strip at the bottom edge. Stack the strips in the same order as they were cut from the piece.

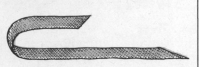

● Pin the second strip at 90° to the first with its bottom end overlapping the top of the other and pattern sides facing each other. Machine stitch across the centre of the overlap.

● Turn the face of the second strip uppermost and repeat with the third strip, and so on as required.

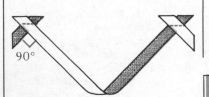

90°

● Cut off the waste to within 12mm (½in) of the seam. Open up and iron the seam flat.

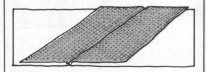

● Buy cotton piping cord of the same diameter as the one you are replacing. Fold the fabric over the cord and line up its edges. Machine through both thicknesses of material close to the cord, using a piping foot.

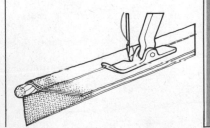

Making the repair

Strip out the old piping by carefully cutting the stitching along the seam. A dressmaker's thread cutter may make the job easier. Upholsterer's skewers pinned into the stuffing will hold the cover in place. Note how the ends of the piping are fitted, for future reference.

● A slip (or ladder) stitch is used to fit the piping and to close the seam invisibly. This is a very useful stitch generally used in upholstery for bringing two edges together, for example in closing a cushion cover. The basic idea of the stitch is that the needle is stuck into the fabric slightly *behind* the point where it has just emerged – the principle of 'back and in'. When the line of stitching is completed and the thread is pulled, the two edges come together very tightly.

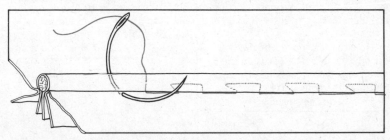

Slip (or ladder) stitch

Using a 65–75mm (2½–3in) curved needle, attach a thread to the end of the upper hem, using an upholsterer's slip knot (see page 85).

● Place the flange of the piping inside the seam, then stick the needle through the flange close to, and behind, the cord, avoiding the lower hem (see **diagram a**).

● Pull the thread gently through, then insert the needle into the lower hem, 2mm ($\frac{1}{16}$in) *behind* the level of the knot. Make a stitch *forwards* about 10mm ($\frac{3}{8}$in) long (**b**).

● Pull the thread through again, pass the needle up through the flange, then stick the needle into the upper hem about 2mm *behind* the stitch on the lower hem. Again make a 10mm stitch forwards (**c**).

● Continue in this way, pulling the seam closed after each six stitches.

● Cut the piping to length and tuck it in, or secure it with a tack, and complete the seam. Finish off with a French knot.

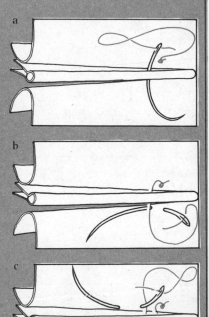

a

b

c

Upholstering dining chairs

As explained in the introduction to this chapter, we shall be confining ourselves to three basic tasks in upholstery – first the re-upholstery of a simple drop-in chair pad, which is an ideal first project for a beginner; next a stuffed-over seat, in which the covering is carried over on to the front surfaces of the seat rails, using either foam or stuffing; and finally traditional upholstery using tied-down springs.

Removing old upholstery

Before re-upholstering a piece of furniture, it is obviously necessary to get rid of the old upholstery, a process known as 'ripping off'. This can be a dirty job, especially when removing old horse hair or fibre stuffings, so spread sheets of newspaper around the work area to make the job of clearing up easier. In addition it is advisable to wear a gauze face mask to avoid inhaling the dust. The process is basically the same for any upholstered piece, but to explain the methods we will assume we are stripping a dining chair with a sprung seat and a padded back.

Ripping off the seat pad

Start by removing the hessian covering tacked to the underside of the seat, using a ripping chisel (see *Upholstery tools* page 82) or an old screwdriver. With the chair supported upside-down on the bench, place the tip of the chisel under the edge of the hessian immediately under the head of the central tack in the seat rail. Holding the chisel in line with the grain to prevent the wood splitting, drive the tool with a mallet, using a levering action at the same time. Work along the rail in both directions, driving out each tack in turn.

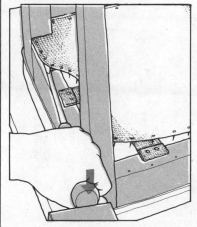

● The webs supporting the springs will now be exposed. Before removing them, note the number of webs, their position and the method of tying the springs. It is worth making a sketch, or even taking a series of photographs to serve as a reference when you re-upholster the chair. Cut the twine holding the springs and remove the webbing tacks with the ripping chisel.

● Turn the chair on its side to inspect the gimp or braid edging. If it is sewn in place, cut the threads to release it and remove any tacks. If there are no apparent threads or tacks, it is probably glued in place and can be ripped off to expose the tacks securing the top cover.
● Remove these tacks with care to avoid damaging the show wood which forms the tack line rebate. Use a tack lifter or a pair of pliers, taking special care around the front legs to avoid splitting the wood. Remove the cover in one piece if you can, using it as a guide when cutting the replacement.

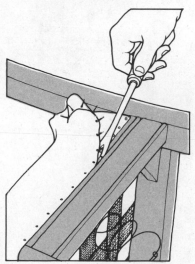

● If the top cover is tacked under the seat rail, the tacks can be removed safely with a ripping chisel.
● Lift off the thin wadding below the top cover and remove the tacks holding the calico lining.
● The second layer of wadding and hair will now be exposed and can be lifted off. Below this, the next layer of hessian may be stitched through with twine. Cut through the twine

and remove the fixing tacks, then lift off the hessian to expose the horse hair or fibre stuffing. Remove the hair carefully, as this is likely to be the dirtiest part of the procedure, and lay it aside for cleaning and possible re-use.

● You are now down to the last layer, the heavyweight hessian covering the springs, which are still attached with twine. Cut the twine to release the springs and remove the tacks holding the hessian.

Inspecting the frame

When all the soft materials have been removed examine the chair frame carefully for loose joints, damage to the back and so on. Repair these as described under *Structural repairs: chairs* (see page 26). You should also do any re-finishing of the show wood on the frame before starting to re-upholster.

● One repair which is often necessary on an upholstered chair is the strengthening of a rail which has splintered, due to the repeated insertion of upholstery tacks.

● Coat the splintered rail with PVA glue, working it well down into the damaged wood.

● Lay a piece of hessian over the rail and paint glue on to it, brushing well down into the material, then press the hessian down firmly with a block of wood.

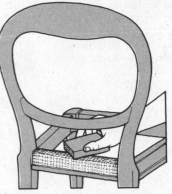

Re-using old materials

Most of the materials originally used in the upholstery will not be of any use when re-upholstering the chair. The webbing, hessian and calico should not be used even if they appear sound, as they will have stretched unevenly and will not last as long as new material. The wadding may be too compressed for re-use and will probably be full of dust.

● It is worth while trying to re-use the horse hair stuffing however, so long as it retains its original resilience. Working in the garden, shake out the loose dust and remove any lengths of twine used for stuffing ties. Wash the hair in mild detergent and leave it to dry before teasing it apart by hand to restore its resilience.

● The springs may be usable if they are not distorted and spring back readily when compressed between your hands. Check that they are all still of the correct height.

Ripping off the back pad

Because the back of most chairs is an open frame, the upholstery is visible from both sides, so it is covered front and back. The back frame is rebated front and back to receive the upholstery tacks. The padding is placed on the front surface of the chair back, whereas the back surface merely has covering material. Webbing is only found on chair backs with a large area of upholstery.

● Rip off the front layers first, as far as the webbing, if present, then turn the chair round and remove the back layers. Finally remove the webbing. Take great care when removing tacks or nails to avoid splitting the back across its short grain.

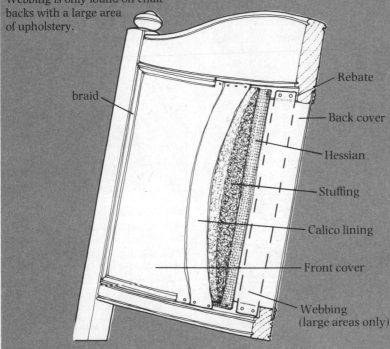

braid

Rebate

Back cover

Hessian

Stuffing

Calico lining

Front cover

Webbing
(large areas only)

Re-covering a drop-in seat

The simplest form of upholstered dining chair has a separate seat pad which is supported on rebates on the inside of the seat rails. The upholstery of the pad is supported on an open wooden frame, which is either webbed or filled in with a plywood panel. Plywood panels are found only on relatively modern chairs, or on old chairs which have been unsympthetically repaired. The pad itself is traditionally stuffed with hair and wadding but modern polyurethane or latex foam can be used successfully and is a lot simpler to apply.

If the new top covering fabric is thicker than the original, the edges of the pad frame may have to be planed down to fit in the chair frame rebates.

Stripping off the seat pad

The tools and techniques described on page 89 can be used to strip the old upholstery from a drop-in seat pad, but because the pad is so light either clamp it to the bench or support it in a vice.

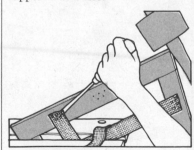

If staples have been used to hold the fabric prise them free and lift off the fabric and stuffing. Take out any partially removed staples from the seat frame with pincers.

Drop-in seat pads

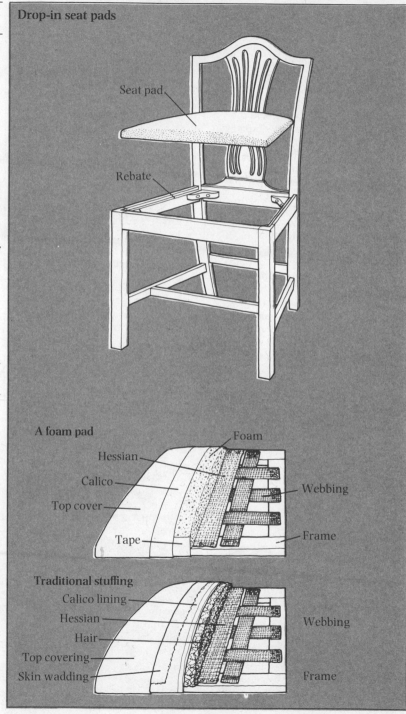

Seat pad

Rebate

A foam pad

Foam

Hessian

Calico

Top cover

Webbing

Tape

Frame

Traditional stuffing

Calico lining

Hessian

Hair

Top covering

Skin wadding

Webbing

Frame

Re-webbing the seat frame

Webbing is the foundation for all the subsequent upholstery and must be taut and securely fixed. You can gauge the spacing of the webbing from the position of the tack marks, but if in any doubt fix the webs about 12mm to 25mm ($\frac{1}{2}$in to 1in) apart. For the type of drop-in seat we are describing here, the webs are placed on top of the frame but in old seat pads, coil springs are included in the upholstery. In this case the webs will be fixed under the frame and the springs attached (see page 98).

● Before the webbing is fixed, inspect the inside edges of the frame to ensure that they are not damaged or too sharp, which could cause the webbing to wear locally. Smooth them with a rasp and glass paper if necessary. Clamp the frame to the bench in preparation.

Fixing the webbing

Leaving the webbing in one length, fold over one end about 38mm (1$\frac{1}{2}$in) and tack it to the back rail approximately 12mm ($\frac{1}{2}$in) from the outer edge. Use five 15mm ($\frac{5}{8}$in) improved tacks spaced as indicated. They are staggered to avoid splitting the wood of the rails.

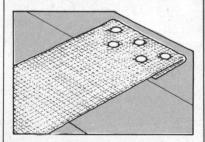

● Using a webbing stretcher (see page 82), tension the webbing across the frame and fix it with three tacks. The amount of tension

can only be judged with experience, but the web should not be so taut that excessive strain is put on the tacks.

● Cut the webbing 38mm (1$\frac{1}{2}$in) beyond the tacks, fold over the end and fix with two more tacks.

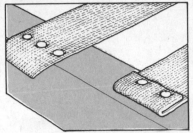

● Fix the other front-to-back webs in the same way, then interlace and fix the cross webs.

Fixing the hessian panel

Lay the webbed frame on to heavyweight hessian, draw round it with a felt tip pen and cut it about 18mm ($\frac{3}{4}$in) larger all around.

● Fold back 25mm (1in) along the front edge and tack it to the front rail of the frame with improved tacks spaced 25mm (1in) apart. The folded edge should be 6mm ($\frac{1}{4}$in) from the front edge of the frame. Keep the weave square across the frame.

● Pull the hessian taut over the back of the frame and tack it to the frame in the centre. Work in both

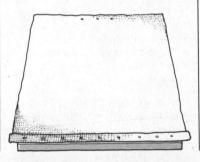

A collapsed chair seat

On some chairs you will find that the webbing has stretched or broken, although the rest of the upholstery is still perfectly sound. New webbing can be fitted without removing the rest of the upholstery.

● First strip off the dust cover and old webbing (see page 89).

● Fit new webbing from front to back. Push the springs aside as you work, allowing them to project above the webs at this stage.

● Fit the cross webs one at a time, tucking the springs back and tying them to the webs as one row (see page 98).

● Finally tack a new dust cover to the underside of the seat frame (see page 95).

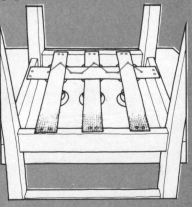

directions along the back of the frame, pulling the hessian taut and driving in tacks every 50mm (2in), about 6mm ($\frac{1}{4}$in) from the edge.

● Fold back the edge of the hessian over the line of tacks and fix with another row of tacks spaced between the first.

● Tack the hessian to the sides of the seat frame in the same way.

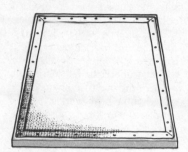

● At this stage in the operation you can either proceed with traditional hair or fibre stuffing or you can use foam for the upholstery.

Using foam upholstery

Use a 25mm (1in) thick, firm density foam. Place the seat frame on the surface of the foam and mark its outline with a felt tip pen. Cut 12mm ($\frac{1}{2}$in) larger all round (see page 97).

● To form the domed shape which is typical of this type of seat, cut a piece of 12mm ($\frac{1}{2}$in) thick foam, 60mm ($2\frac{1}{2}$in) smaller all round than the thicker pad. Cut a shallow bevel on its edges (see page 84) and bond it centrally to the *underside* of the thicker pad.

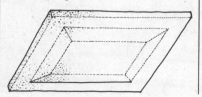

● Cut approximately 75mm (3in) wide strips of calico and glue them to the top face of the foam pad. Each strip of calico should overlap the edge of the foam by about half its width. Alternatively, use a self adhesive cotton tape which is produced for the purpose and is available in various widths.

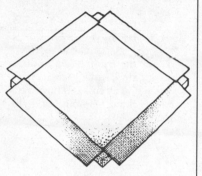

● Lay the foam pad in place on the frame, then position the frame on the bench so that it overhangs the edge. Hold the foam down with your left forearm and with the other hand pull the tape down, tucking the edge of the foam under at the same time.

● Hold the tape in position with the left hand while temporarily tacking it to the frame with a single tack in the centre. Leave the head protruding so that it can be removed later.

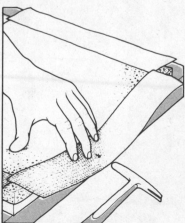

● Holding the foam down, spin the frame around and repeat the operation at the other end and both sides.

● Hold the frame vertically, resting one corner on the bench with the foam to your left. Pull the tape over the centre of the top edge that faces away from you and temporarily fix with three or four tacks on the underside. This operation is not so awkward as it sounds. You will find that the tacks are so sharp that you can push them into position while you pick up the hammer. Nestle the frame well into your body to absorb the force of the hammer blows. Turning the frame, repeat on the opposite edge then on the sides.

● With the frame on its edge, smooth the edge of the foam into an even curve, tucking it under as you go. Work in both directions from the centre, holding the tape down with temporary tacks. When you are satisfied that the edge is perfectly even, drive a row of closely spaced fine 10mm ($\frac{3}{8}$in) tacks outside the line of temporary tacks. Remove the temporary tacks.

Stuffing with hair

The first stage in preparation for a traditional hair stuffing is to make a series of 'stuffing ties' or 'bridle ties' to hold the hair to the hessian.

● Using a large half circle needle threaded with No 1 twine, start at one edge of the frame with a slip knot (see page 85), Make a series of loops across the hessian as shown, finishing off with a double hitch (see page 85). The loops should be large enough for you to pass two fingers under them. Make three or four rows of ties across the seat.

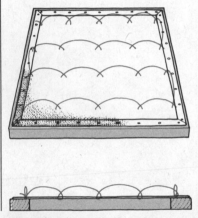

● Push handfuls of stuffing under the ties to make even ribs across the seat.

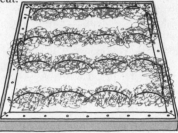

● Fill up the spaces between the ribs with more stuffing, then continue adding it until you have an even pile about 150mm (6in) high at the centre.

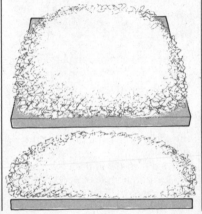

Fitting the calico lining

Whether the pad is stuffed with hair or covered with foam, it should now be covered with a calico lining, allowing an extra 50mm to 75mm (2in to 3in) all round for tensioning. The lining is attached to the frame following the same procedure as described for tacking the foam layer, as far as the point where it is held with three or four temporary tacks (see page 93).

● Now smooth the fabric from the centre of the pad to each opposite corner, pulling the fabric evenly. Temporarily tack the calico to the underside of the corner.

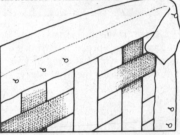

● Starting at one side, remove the temporary tacks and ease the fabric over the edge with the flat of the left hand. Keep the tension on the fabric

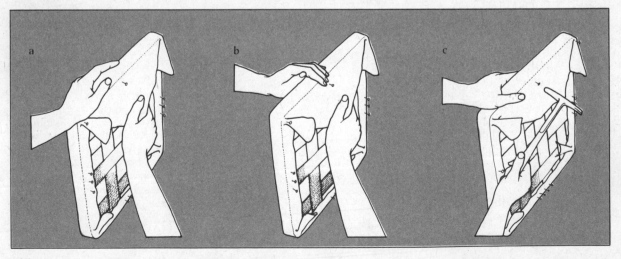

a

b

c

with the other hand, gripping it with your thumb held against the frame as shown in **diagrams a** and **b** opposite. Simply holding the fabric between forefinger and thumb will produce uneven tension, showing as depressions where the cloth is held with tacks.

• Hold the fabric in place with the left hand while you drive temporary tacks along the entire underedge, working from the centre towards each end and stopping short at the corners (**c**).

• Proceed with the opposite side of the frame, then the back and front.

• Remove the temporary tack at one corner, take up the slack in the fabric and drive home a single tack (**d**). Make neat pleats to lose the extra fabric and hold them with temporary tacks (**e**). Proceed similarly with the other three corners.

• Check that the shape of the pad is perfectly even all round before finally fixing the fabric with closely spaced fine tacks or staples. If the shape appears slightly uneven with a hair stuffing, use a regulator to reposition some of the stuffing.

• Remove the temporary tacks and trim the fabric close to the tack line with a craft knife to complete the first covering.

Including wadding

Before fitting the top cover over a traditionally stuffed pad, a layer of thin wadding (see page 83) must be laid over the seat to prevent the hair working through the covering. It must be cut to the exact size and shape of the seat, as any overlapping at the edges may prevent the pad fitting into the rebates.

Fitting the top covering

Mark the centre of each side of the seat pad with a felt tipped pen.

• Measure the pad and cut the top covering fabric 50mm (2in) larger all round. Cut small notches in the fabric at the centre of each side.

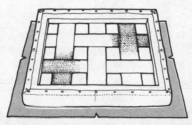

• Lay the fabric over the pad with the notches lining up with the edge marks. Turn the fabric under and follow the tacking procedure described for fitting the calico lining.

• At the corners, cut away some of the spare fabric before making the final pleats.

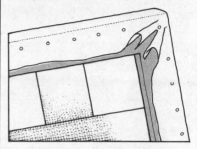

• Turn the cut edges under and tack the fabric down to produce neat flat pleats.

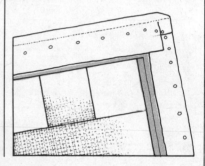

Fitting a dust panel

To neaten the underside of the seat pad, cover it with a panel of cotton fabric or lightweight hessian.

• Turn the edge under and fix it to the underside of the frame with fine tacks. The dust panel should just cover the tacks holding the top cover and its edge should be parallel with the edge of the seat pad.

• Fix the opposite side of the panel, turning under and tensioning as you go, working from the centre in both directions. Continue with the other two sides.

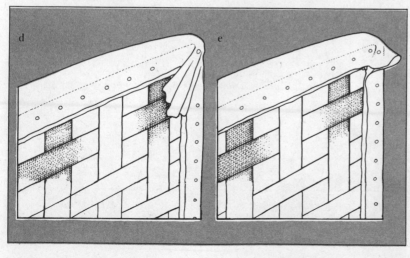

Re-covering stuffed-over seats

On many chairs the upholstery wraps over the seat frame. Either the cover is tacked underneath, obscuring the seat joints, or it may be tacked to the side of the rails, leaving decorative show wood along the lower edge. Both types of upholstery are referred to as 'stuffed-over'. Coil springs, in conjunction with hair or fibre stuffing, are used to upholster a stuffed-over seat, but once again these can be replaced with foam. A seat which has been re-upholstered with foam will tend to be somewhat softer at the edges than traditional upholstery and you will have to decide whether this is compatible with the style of chair you are working on. In the details which follow, we show a foam seat with the cover tacked underneath the seat rail and a sprung seat incorporating a show wood edging. However, both methods are interchangeable.

Stuffed-over seats

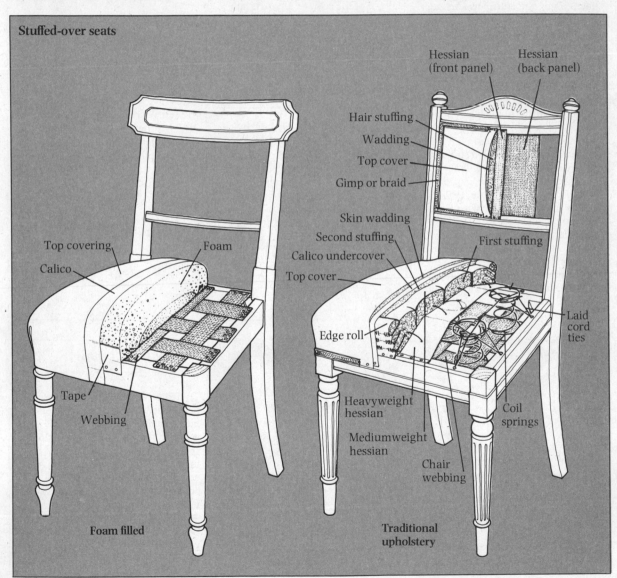

Hessian (front panel)

Hessian (back panel)

Hair stuffing

Wadding

Top cover

Gimp or braid

Skin wadding

Second stuffing

Calico undercover

Top cover

First stuffing

Laid cord ties

Top covering

Calico

Foam

Edge roll

Coil springs

Heavyweight hessian

Tape

Webbing

Mediumweight hessian

Chair webbing

Foam filled

Traditional upholstery

Using foam

Webbing the frame

The seat frame is webbed using those methods described for webbing a drop-in seat pad. As no coil springs are to be used, the webs are tacked to the top of the seat frame. It is also covered with a hessian panel, as previously described.

Fitting the foam

Make a paper pattern from the seat frame and lay it on a slab of 50mm (2in) medium density foam. Mark out the shape with a felt tipped pen, carefully marking the recesses for the back legs. Cut it 12mm ($\frac{1}{2}$in) oversize all round.

- Cut a piece of 25mm (1in) medium density foam 60mm (2$\frac{1}{2}$in) smaller all round. Trim the edges to a shallow bevel and glue it to the *underside* of the larger pad. Leave square edges on the thicker foam to produce a firm edge to the cushion.

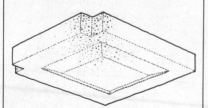

- Glue calico strips or self-adhesive cotton tapes to the top face of the pad all round (see page 93).

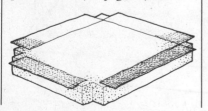

- Attach the foam pad to the seat frame using upholstery tacks, as described for fitting drop-in seat pad (see page 93).

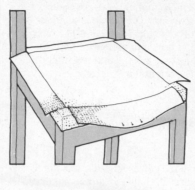

Fitting a calico lining

Proceed with fitting a calico lining as described for a drop-in seat pad, but turn back the rear corners and make a diagonal cut from the corner of each flap towards the leg, stopping 9mm ($\frac{3}{8}$in) short.

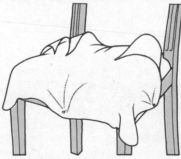

- Cut excess material from the flaps, fold under the edges and fit them to the line of the back legs.

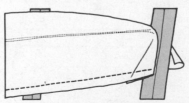

- The management of the material at the front corners depends on whether you want a soft curve or a sharp angle.
- To finish a front corner with a soft curve, pull the corner of the calico diagonally across the frame, fold back the cut edge of the material and tack the folded edge to both faces of the leg, in line with the seat rails.

- Cut away the spare fabric and fold under the cut edges to make neat pleats.

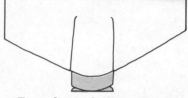

- To produce a sharper corner, first make two short cuts in the fabric corresponding to the outer lines of the leg. Fold under the excess and pull the fabric round the corner, tacking it to the side rail.

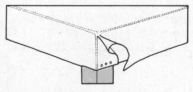

- Cut away excess fabric from the inner fold and make a single pleat to follow the line of the corner and tack it in place.

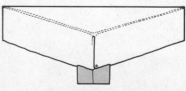

- Tack the rest of the material to the underside of the seat rails.

Fitting the top covering

Follow the same procedure as for fitting the lining, but take into consideration a few points regarding the thickness of the fabric.

• A thin fabric is easy to fold and 'lose' at the corners but it should also be folded back along cut edges to take the tacks. For this reason, leave excess fabric when tacking temporarily and fold the fabric under as the tacks are finally replaced.

• Thick fabrics can be tacked to the frame leaving a single thickness, so long as a dust panel is fitted (see page 95). When working the corners, cut away as much excess as possible, without leaving short turnings which could fray. Use a hammer to flatten thick folds to a crisp edge and to reduce the effect of the double thickness.

• When finishing off corners, do not allow tacks to show. Any gaps in the material should be closed with slip stitching (see page 88). On softly curved corners where several pleats have to be made, you can often smooth the material round the front of the leg and tack off under the seat rails, but with the sharper corner slip stitching will nearly always be necessary.

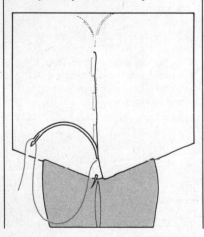

Using springs

Traditional upholstery requires some practice before a beginner can become totally efficient, it is worth the time and patience to produce the exact shape and feel intended by the original upholsterer.

Webbing the frame

When coil springs are to be included, the webs should be tacked to the underside of the frame and they should be spaced so that the intersections correspond with the position of each spring. The webbing is fitted as on page 92. No hessian cover is required, as the springs are sewn directly to the webbing.

Fitting springs

Dining chairs normally have four or five coiled springs. If you are using five springs, place one centrally, with the twisted end of the top coil facing the front of the seat. Space the other four springs around the central one with their twisted ends facing inwards. This will ensure that all the springs exert equal pressure.

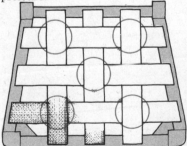

• Each spring is stitched to the webbing with No 1 twine as described below, using a curved spring needle. Lay the chair on its back so that you can hold the spring reasonably conveniently while stitching from beneath the chair.

• Starting with the central spring, pass the needle up through the webbing, close to the outside of the bottom coil, then back down again on the inside. Pull the thread through and fasten it with a slip knot (see page 85).

• Do not cut the thread but make two half hitches (see page 85) evenly spaced around the coil.

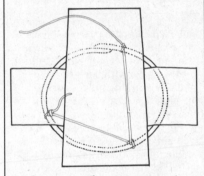

• Carry on to the next spring, tie three half hitches, and so on until all five springs are stitched to the webbing, finishing with a double hitch (see page 85) on the last spring.

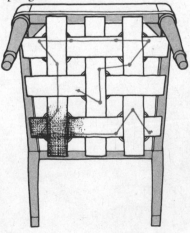

Tying the springs

Stand the chair upright, so that you can tie the tops of the springs together using laid cord (see page 85). The cord also serves to anchor the springs to the frame at the required compression, position and angle.

- Drive 15mm (⅝in) improved tacks part way into the rails of the seat frame in line with each spring (see panel, **diagram a**).
- Cut the cord into lengths about twice the depth and width of the seat frame.

- Knot one cord around the central tack in the back rail and drive the tack in fully to hold the cord.
- Compress the central spring by about 50mm (2in) and tie the cord across the top coil with two half hitches. Tie the cord to the tack in the front rail and drive it home (**b**).
- To provide extra support to the outer springs, they are tied in a slightly different way. Tie a cord to the tack in the back rail but leave about 225mm (9in) hanging free.
- Compress the spring, then make your first knot on the second coil down, followed by another on the top coil (**c**).

- Compress the next spring, tie a knot in its top coil, then in its second coil. Finally tie off the cord on the appropriate tack in the front rail (**d**).
- Tie each free end up to the top coil, making two knots across the coil and finishing with a double hitch (**e**). The top of the spring will slope downwards towards the seat rail and help to produce a nice domed shape later.
- Now repeat the whole process, going from side to side, rather than front to back. Each spring will now have two fixings with additional knots where the cords cross (**f**).

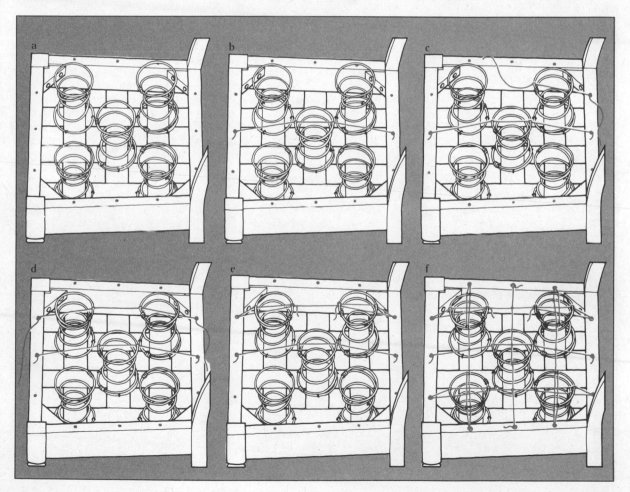

Covering with hessian

The springs are covered with a heavyweight hessian. Tack it lightly to the top edge of the frame until it is evenly distributed, then turn over the edge and tack all round. The hessian should be tight enough to take out any slack but not so tight that it compresses the springs, or the spring ties will be ineffective.

● The tops of the springs are sewn to the hessian in a similar way to that described earlier for fixing their bottoms to the webs.

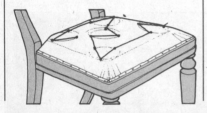

The first stuffing

The first stuffing is a thick layer of hair or fibre.

● Begin by making a series of stuffing ties in the hessian (see *Drop-in seat pad* page 94) about 18mm (¾in) from all four sides of the seat frame.

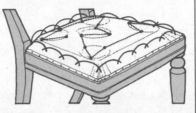

● Stuff a roll of hair or fibre under the ties to produce a firm edge about twice the height of the finished seat. The roll should overhang the edge by about 18mm (¾in).

● Fill the centre evenly with hair so that when compressed by hand it does not fall below the level of the stuffed edge.

● Cut, fit and tack a piece of medium-weight hessian over the stuffing. Use a similar method to that described for fitting a calico lining to a drop-in seat pad on page 94 but in this case tack to the bevelled top corner of the rail.

● Starting at a back corner with a slip knot, make a series of large stitches through the stuffing and hessian, using a mattress needle threaded with No 1 twine as shown in the panel below.

Stitching the hessian

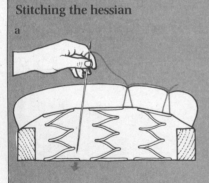

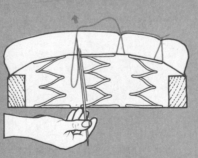

a

b

c

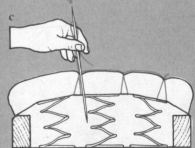

d

Stick the needle through both layers of the hessian, past the springs and out of the webbing below the seat (see **diagram a**).

● When you can feel that the needle is free of the lower layer of the hessian, move it to one side and stick it back in again (**b**).

● Pull the needle out from above to make a stitch (**c**).

● Re-insert the needle about 100mm (4in) to one side and repeat the process, building up a square spinal pattern (**d**) inset about 100mm (4in) from the edge of the seat. Finish with a double hitch (see page 85).

Stitching the edge

The edges of the seat are stitched through with twine to compress the stuffing and give a firm edge. One or two rows of 'blind' stitches are used, depending on the height of the stuffing, and then one row of through stitches to form an edge roll.

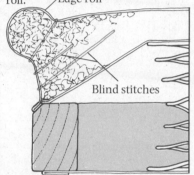

Edge roll

Blind stitches

Blind stitching

Thread a mattress needle with about 2 metres (2 yards) of No 2 twine. Starting on the side of the chair, make the first stitch about 40mm ($1\frac{1}{2}$in) from the back leg, just above the tack line. Push the needle up into the stuffing at an angle of about 45° (see panel below, **diagram a**).

● Before proceeding with the stitching mark both positions where the needle penetrates the hessian, using a felt tipped pen to draw two lines, one on the side and one on top of the seat. These lines will help you to keep the stitching even.

● Pull the needle through until its eye just begins to emerge and, without pulling it out, push the needle back down to the edge and left of the first stitch. Pull the needle and twine right through (**b**).

● Slip knot the end of the twine (see page 85) and pull it tight (**c**).

● Insert the needle 50mm (2in) to the right of the first point of entry. Angle the needle at about 45° and also towards the first stitch, so that the point emerges 25mm (1in) further back on the seat (**d**).

● Do not pull it right through but push it back through the edge so that the eye emerges next to the first knot, to make a triangular stitch (**e**).

● Before pulling the needle back out of the stuffing, wind two or three turns of twine around the needle to bind the stitch (**f**).

● Pull the needle through and make another stitch 50mm (2in) to the right.

● Follow this procedure round three sides of the seat and tie off at the back leg with a double hitch.

● Make a row of stitches across the back of the seat in the same way.

● If the seat pad is 75mm (3in) or more deep, make a second row of stitches 18mm ($\frac{3}{4}$in) above the first.

Blind stitching

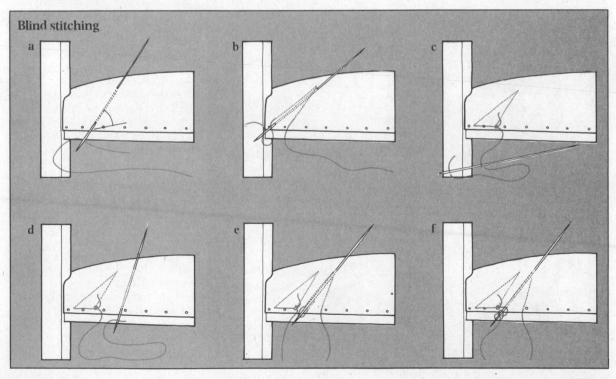

a

b

c

d

e

f

Making an edge roll

To make the edge roll, draw a guideline along the top and sides of the seat about 25mm (1in) from the edges. Insert the needle into the side of the seat about 25mm (1in) from the back leg on the marked line. Push it through until it emerges on the top line.

● Pull the needle through and insert it from the top as close to the leg as possible, pulling it right through the seat pad (see panel below, **diagram a**). Tie the end of the twine with a slip knot and pull it tight.

● Insert the needle 25mm (1in) to the right of the first stitch and pull it through on the top line (**b**).

● Pass it back next to the first stitch on the top line. As the point of the needle emerges, wind two or three turns of twine around it before pulling it right through (**c**).

● Repeat this process all round the chair to form an edge roll (**d**). Use the regulator as you proceed to pull stuffing into the roll and achieve an even density.

The second stuffing

The second stuffing is a layer of fibre and cotton felt distributed over the seat to fill depressions left in the top by the stitching.

● Tease out the stuffing, building up a layer of even density in the form of a shallow dome running out to the edge roll. If the centre of the seat is fairly hollow, requiring a thick layer of stuffing to build it up to the correct height, use stuffing ties (see page 94) to hold it in place.

The calico lining

A calico lining is fitted over the second stuffing as described for a foam-filled seat pad (see page 97) but in this case it is tacked to the seat rail above the show wood edging. The corners are made in a similar way except that it is not necessary to allow for turning under the seat rail. Simply form neat pleats as described on page 97, and when the cover is finally tacked in place, trim the surplus below the tack line with a sharp knife. Do not come too low with the line of tacks, to leave room for the top cover.

Fitting the top cover

Before fitting the top cover, cut a layer or two of cotton wadding to fit the seat. This prevents the stuffing working through.

● Fit the top cover as you would a calico lining, ensuring that it fits neatly up to the show wood edging of the rail. The tacks will be covered by a decorative edging known as braid or gimp.

Making an edge roll

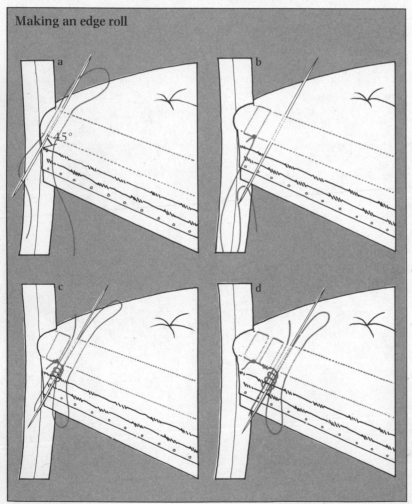

Finishing the edges

Gimp or braid is available in different colours to match woven covering fabrics. A special edging is available for leather or plastic which is designed to conceal the pins which fix it to the chair frame. Gimp can be attached by sewing, with latex adhesive or by gimp pins, which are fine nails with coloured heads to match the fabric.

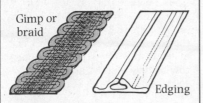

Gimp or braid

Edging

Pinning

To fix the gimp with pins only, fold one end under your thumb and pin it close to the back leg. Keeping the tension on the gimp, work around the chair, fixing every 100mm (4in) with another pin. When you arrive at the other back leg, leave an extra 9mm (⅜in) for turning under.

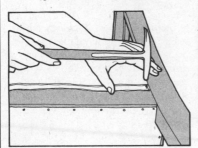

Gluing

To apply adhesive, pin the gimp face down to a bench, keeping it under slight tension. Apply adhesive sparingly with a narrow spreader or bristle brush.

● Apply a narrow band of adhesive to the seat frame, just above the show wood edging. Allow the adhesive to dry.

● Pin one end as before and carefully position the gimp to follow the edge. It will stick on contact.

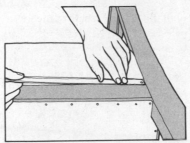

● Pin the other end of the gimp.
● Tap the gimp all round, using a hammer and softwood block to make a firm bond.

Sewing

Sewing produces a better finish than other methods but it takes longer. Pin one end of the gimp and sew along the top and bottom edges with a simple hem stitch, using a small half circle needle.

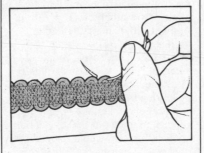

Upholstery nails

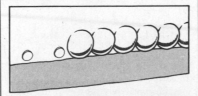

Close nailing with upholstery nails is used on PVC or leather and sometimes on heavy woven fabrics. These nails have large dome heads which are either coloured or metal

finished. They can be used to cover the fine tacks holding fabric or to take their place. The nails are driven in with an upholsterer's hammer so that the heads are touching. Draw a centre line parallel to the edge to help you line up the nails. Try to use solid brass nails rather than the plated variety, which may mark when you drive them in.

Upholstering a chair back

Some dining or bedroom chairs have a back pad, which is upholstered using methods similar to those we have described for upholstering a seat.

Webbing

A chair back which is flat is webbed in exactly the same way as a seat frame (see page 92) and is then covered with a hessian panel. Chairs which have a small back pad may not need to be webbed at all. The hessian panel is all that is required.

Those chairs which have a curved back should be fitted with the vertical webs first. Interlace the horizontal webs, keeping them under slight tension only to maintain the curve of the back.

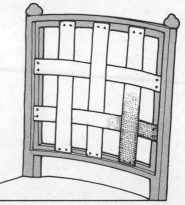

Some chair backs have a central vertical tacking rail to which the webs, which run only from side to side, are fixed. Little tension is needed as the webs simply follow the curve of the back.

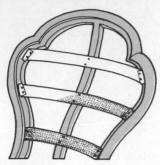

Adding a foam pad

Cut a piece of 25mm (1in) medium density foam 6mm ($\frac{1}{4}$in) larger than the pad area. Cut a bevel on all the edges (see page 84).

● Lay the foam over the back, bevel side down, and cover with a calico panel. Cut 50mm (2in) larger all round.

● Temporarily tack the covering to the frame on all four sides, starting with a few improved tacks in the middle of each rail. Apply more tension from top to bottom than across the width.

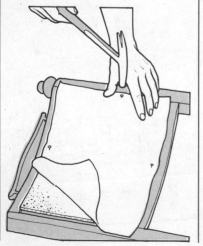

● Complete the tacking by driving fine tacks between the improved tacks, which are then removed. Trim away the spare fabric level with the tacking rebate in the frame.

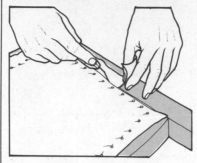

● Cut the top covering at least 25mm (1in) larger all round and tack to the frame as described above. Finish the edge with braid as described on page 103.

Using traditional stuffing

Distribute an even layer of hair over the back panel so that it tapers towards the edge to form a shallow dome. If the stuffing is deeper than 25mm (1in), stuffing ties can be used (see page 94).

● For a thin pad, use a couple of layers of cotton felt instead of hair. The edges of the pad can be tapered by tearing the felt.

● Cover either stuffing with a calico lining and, in the case of hair, apply a thin skin wadding over it to prevent the hair working through.

● Cut and fit the top cover and apply the braid.

Covering the reverse of the chair back

Neaten the reverse of the chair back by stretching a medium-weight hessian panel across the frame to reinforce the top covering.

● Apply a top covering panel as described for fitting a dust panel (see page 95). Braid can be applied when required.

Upholstering a simple armpad

To upholster simple armpads, tack a series of stuffing ties along the framing.

● Add a pad of fibre which compresses to about 30mm (1$\frac{1}{4}$in) thick. Allow plenty of overhang along the edges.

● Tack hessian over the pad in a similar way to that described for covering a seat (see page 100).

● Drive some 2 inch nails along the centre to prevent distortion as it is sewn along the edges. Make one row of blind stitches and an edge roll (see page 101).

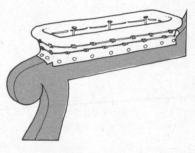

● Remove nails and add a second layer of fibre and wadding, covered by calico tensioned first along the arm. Cut away excess fabric at both ends to produce neat pleats.

● Add the final cover in a similar way covering the line of tacks with gimp (see page 103).

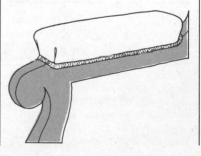

Repairing cane chairs

Cane has been used for chair seats, backs and arms, stools, bed heads and cabinet doors since the seventeenth century. Chairs upholstered with cane have a graceful, lightweight look but unfortunately the cane is often damaged. Many a beginner has been put off a beautiful set of cane chairs because one of them has a broken seat but it is in fact a relatively simple task to repair it. In the instructions below we describe the repair of a seat but the method is basically the same for any cane panel.

Cane

Cane comes from the long stems of the rattan, a palm which grows in South East Asia. Thin strips are taken from the hard, glossy surface below the bark and cut into standard widths. The remainder of the rattan stem is converted into canes for basket making. The intermittent notches found along the surface of the cane mark the places where thorns on the stem have been removed. Slide a strip of cane between your finger and thumb and you will notice it is smoother in one direction than the other. The cane should be woven in the 'smooth' direction to prevent it catching.

There are six sizes of split cane in common use, numbered from 1 to 6. The choice of cane will be determined by the size of the woven panel, the distance between hole centres and to some extent the pattern of the weave. Bedroom chairs, which usually have the holes spaced about 12mm ($\frac{1}{2}$in) apart, require the thinner No 2, No 3 or No 4 sizes. Wider canes are used when a long span is required and to finish the edges of the weave on smaller chairs. The pegs which fix a cane permanently have to be a good fit in the holes. They can be cut from small diameter birch or ramin dowelling or from basketry cane.

Tools

You will need only a few tools for cane work, most of which will be found in an average tool kit or can be improvised from basic tools. The most important ones are:
- A light hammer, to drive in the pegs holding the canes.
- A sharp, stout knife for cutting the cane and shaping the pegs.
- A pair of strong scissors or side cutters to crop the canes.
- A hole clearing tool for driving the old pegs out of the holes. Use an improvised tool such as a small screwdriver with the tip cut off, or a wire nail of a suitable diameter with the point cut off.

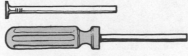

- A stiletto or else a small electrical screwdriver with the tip rounded, for lifting tight canes over the frames to assist further weaving. A bayonet pointed sack needle with a handle can be used. The bend keeps the handle clear of the work.

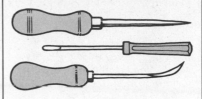

- Long-nosed pliers, to pull the cane through.
- Temporary pegs. Long golf tees, about 38mm ($1\frac{1}{2}$in) long, make ideal pegs for holding the cane as work progresses.

Preparing the chair

The caning of a chair is the last process required to complete its restoration, so the frame must be made sound and properly finished before weaving the cane.
- Before stripping old cane work it is well worth recording the original method of weaving by taking a clear photograph from above. This can be a considerable help when deciding which holes to use for an even pattern, particularly when the seat shape is not rectangular.
- Cut away the old cane with a sharp knife, following the inside of the seat frame. Carefully cut through the ends of the beading and the ties holding it in place. Pull out the loose ends of cane from the hole and punch out the pegs from below with a clearing tool. Should glue have been used, the holes will have to be drilled out.
- The frame should now be finished as required (see *Finishes and polishes* pages 7 to 17).

Preparing the cane

Cane should be dampened to make it pliable before it is woven. Working with a few lengths at a time, dip them in warm water for a minute or two then leave them in a plastic bag or wrapped in a damp cloth. Replenish your prepared supply as work progresses. Wipe the canes with a damp cloth if they dry out as you are working.

Weaving the cane

The cane can be woven to give a variety of patterns but the most popular, both for appearance and strength, is known as the six way pattern (see diagram below). This process has six stages, plus an optional seventh stage:

1 Lacing from back to front with No 2 cane (*vertical*).
2 Lacing from side to side with No 2 cane, overlaying stage 1 (*horizontal*).
3 Lacing from back to front, again with No 2 cane, overlaying stage 2 (*vertical*).
4 Lacing from side, again weaving through the cane strung in stages 1 and 3 (*horizontal*).
5 Lacing diagonally from right to left with No 3 or No 4 cane.
6 Lacing diagonally from left to right with No 3 or No 4 cane.
7 Covering the holes with beading cane.

Instructions for weaving each stage are shown in the panels from this page onwards. The frame is worked with the chair facing you. We have described a seat which is narrower at the back than at the front, since this illustrates some of the problems of shaped frames.

Stage 1

Find the middle of the back and front rails. If there is an odd number of holes, a hole will be at the centre. An even number of holes will place a hole on either side of centre. Mark the centre hole, or one of the two off-centre holes, at the front and back. This is where you should start threading the first cane.

- Thread a long strip of No 2 cane through the back hole for about half its length. The shiny surface of the cane should be uppermost.
- Trap the cane in the hole with a golf tee. Pass the cane down through the hole immediately opposite in the front rail. Slide it through your fingers as you work, to ensure that the cane is not twisted and that you are working in the 'smooth' direction.

- Apply slight tension to the cane and make a half twist so that it faces the adjacent hole. In this way the cane lies flat on the underside to give a better finish. Fix the cane in the hole with another tee peg. Do not over-tension the first canes or the weaving will be difficult later on.

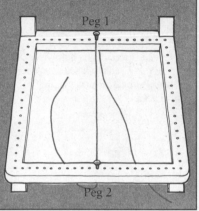

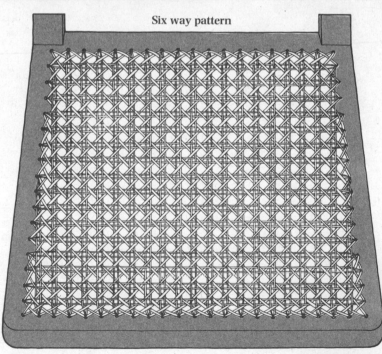

Six way pattern

Stage 1 (continued)

• Pass the end of the cane back up through the next hole in the front rail, making a half twist so that the cane lies flat on the top of the rail, pointing to the back of the chair. Keeping the tension on, transfer the second peg into this hole.

• Take the cane across to the back rail and pass it down through the hole opposite, make the half twist and transfer the second peg once again. This peg is transferred from hole to hole until the end of the cane is reached.

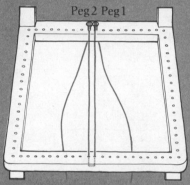

Peg 2 Peg 1

• Pass the cane up through the next hole in the back rail, twist and peg. Continue in this way across one half of the seat but do not use the last hole in the corner. Work across the other half of the seat in the same way, using the remaining half of the cane left hanging from the central hole.

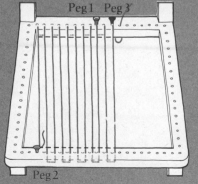

Peg 1   Peg 3

Peg 2

• It is unlikely that you will be able to complete the run of caning with a single strip. When you come to the end of a strip, fix its end with a peg, leaving a minimum of 75mm (3in) hanging under the seat.

• Now go back to the next available hole on the opposite rail, and peg in the new strip of cane, again leaving 75mm (3in) hanging under the seat. Working this way, you do not have two ends hanging side-by-side on the same rail, which is a help when you have to tuck them up at the edge finishing stage.

• All the holes in the back rail should now be caned except the corner holes but because the seat is wider at the front, we must now fill in each side. The aim is to thread the cane so that it runs parallel with the rest of the seat caning to fill all the holes in the front rail except the corner holes. Select holes in the side rail which will produce this effect, pegging the ends each time.

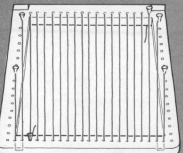

Stage 2

In the second stage the cane is passed from side to side, overlaying stage 1 and making no attempt to weave it up and down. The cane is threaded through the frame in the same way as stage 1, starting one hole from the front corner. The corner holes are not used until stage 5.

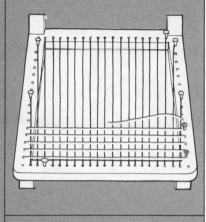

Stage 3

Proceed as for stage 1. Run the cane from front to back on top of stage 2, again making no attempt to weave up and down. As the cane passes through the holes, work it so that it lies to the right of the first cane. This may mean pulling the first cane over to the left slightly. This process will make the weaving in stage 4 easier and ensures that the canes overlay one another in the correct way for weaving the diagonals in stages 5 and 6.

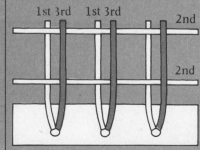

1st 3rd   1st 3rd   2nd

2nd

Stage 4

This stage repeats stage 2 but the cane is woven through the vertical canes of stages 1 and 3.

- Starting at the front, peg the end of the cane into the first hole in the right hand side rail. Leave the corner hole free as before.
- Take the free end and, working towards the left, weave it over and then under the canes in the first vertical pair. Take care to prevent the cane twisting by passing it from hand to hand above and below the seat without allowing loops to form. Repeat this operation through each pair of canes across the seat. Work no more than two or three pairs before pulling the cane through.
- Pass the cane up through the next hole in the usual way and work back to the right through each pair, under the first, over the second and so on.

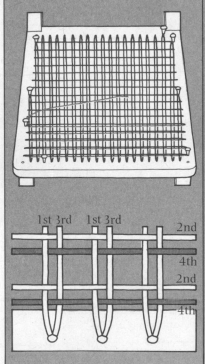

Stage 5

The diagonal canes are now fitted. Use a larger size, preferably No 3 or No 4.

- Begin at the back, using the right-hand corner hole for the first time. Insert the first 75mm (3in) of the cane in the hole, and peg it. Run the cane through your fingers to ensure that it is not twisted.
- Pass the free end over the first pair of vertical canes to the left, then forward under the first pair of horizontal canes. Continue over the next pair of vertical canes and under the next horizontal ones and so on.

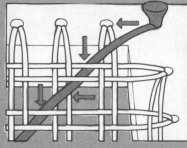

- Work three or four pairs at a time before carefully pulling the cane through, proceeding in this way across the seat. On a tapered seat, the cane should finish on the front rail two or three holes in from the corner.
- Pass the cane up through the next hole on the right and weave it in the same way, parallel to the first diagonal cane, *finishing in the same corner hole that it started from.*

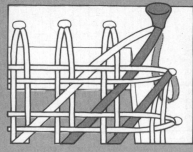

- Take the cane up through the next hole in the side rail and work toward the front, repeating the sequence until you have a triangle of cane on the right.

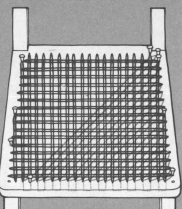

- The left hand 'triangle' is worked in the same way, starting from the next hole in the back or front rail. When there is an even number of holes remaining in the front rail, start at the back. When there is an odd number start at the front. When you get to the front left hand corner, pass the cane through it on two successive runs to keep the pattern symmetrical.
- As stated above, two diagonal canes are fitted in the corner holes and one in each subsequent hole. As this seat tapers from front to back, some adjustment must be made when weaving the diagonal canes in order to keep them parallel. This is achieved by fitting two canes into one hole on the side rails as circumstances dictate. The decision must be made by the individual caner. When you have used one hole twice, miss the hole directly opposite on the other side rail so that two canes can be fitted into it during stage 6, thus keeping the pattern symmetrical.

Stage 6

Repeat the previous stage, but reverse the sequence. The cane starts from the left hand back corner and is worked to the right. The weave now goes under the first vertical pair of canes to the right and over the horizontal pair, and so on. Remember to fit two canes in the side holes that were missed and to miss the holes that were previously fitted with two diagonal canes.

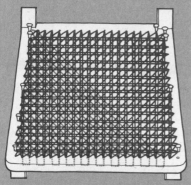

● It is important when working diagonal canes in stages 5 and 6 that they pass under and over the vertical and horizontal pairs in the correct way so that the canes can slide under each other to prevent wear on the edges.

Correct

Incorrect

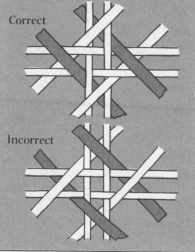

Finishing the edge

The edge of a cane panel may be finished in one of two ways. In early examples the canes were fixed with small permanent pegs in each hole. In later cane chairs, a cane beading was added for a neater finish to the edge, in which case only alternate holes were pegged.

Pegging

Peg each hole with a prepared length of basket cane or dowel rod. The pegs are cut to the required length, which should be a little less than the thickness of the rail. They should be a tight fit in the hole; a slight taper trimmed with a knife will make fitting easier.
● Tap the pegs in part way with a hammer and finish by carefully driving them just below the surface with a clearing tool. Remove the temporary tee pegs as you go, holding the loose end of the cane under tension while fitting the permanent peg.
● Cut all loose ends of cane flush with the underside of the seat rails.

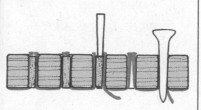

Beading

Beading is the neatest and most popular way of finishing the edge. As previously described, only alternate holes are pegged and the rest are left open for the beading cane, including the corner holes. You will find that a row with an even number of holes will have either two open or two pegged holes together at the centre.

● Peg alternate holes as described under *Pegging*. Should you find that a hole you wish to miss has a loose end of cane in it, turn the end of the cane up through the nearest hole to receive a peg. Pull on the loose end of the cane above the seat as the peg is driven in, to prevent the cane slackening.

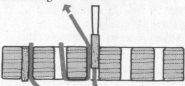

● Use the widest No 6 cane for the beading and No 2 cane for binding it in place. Cut four pieces of No 6 cane about 50mm (2in) longer than each side rail. Taper the first 25mm (1in) on one end of each strip to fit into the corner hole.
● Begin the beading by passing the end of a long piece of No 2 cane up through the rear corner hole. Bend it to follow the line of the holes in the side rail about 38mm (1½in) from its end. Insert the prepared end of No 6 beading cane into the same hole from the top and hold both canes with a tee peg. Fold the No 6 cane to cover the line of holes.
● Pass the free end of the No 2 cane up through the first open hole, over the beading and back down the same hole. Pull the cane through to tighten the loop. Continue in this way through each open hole.

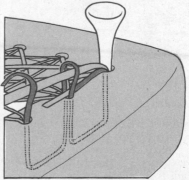

- Before tightening the last loop, trim the end of the beading cane and tuck it into the corner hole. Pull the No 2 cane tight and pass it diagonally underneath the corner and up through the first clear hole in the front rail.
- Insert the prepared end of the front beading cane in the corner hole. Drive a permanent peg into it to secure both canes. Bend the beading cane so that it covers the peg and the holes in the front rail.

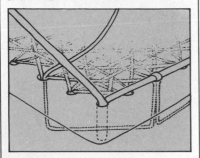

- Continue binding the beading and securing the corners all round the seat frame. When you reach the corner where the beading started, remove the tee peg and insert the prepared end of the back rail beading. Pass the binding cane up from underneath and fit a permanent peg into the hole to fix them. Trim the ends of the cane flush.

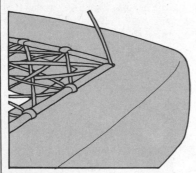

- When a seat frame has round corners the beading is worked in one piece and carefully bent to follow the curve. The No 2 binding cane is worked in the same way.

Rush seating

Woven rushes make attractive seats for traditional country style chairs. Real rushes are only available from a few specialist suppliers and are relatively expensive. Consequently, twisted cord substitutes such as seagrass are often used. The methods are identical except that a pair of rushes must be twisted together to form a cord on the upper surface of the seat only as it is woven. Always twist away from a leg towards the centre of the rail. Rushes or seagrass must be soaked in water for about 10–20 minutes to make them pliable. Wrap them in wet towels to keep them moist.

A square frame

Starting at the front left hand corner, tie the end of the cord to the side rail with string. Wrap the cord over the front rail next to the leg, up through the frame and over the side rail. Pass it through the frame again to the right hand corner, continuing around the frame back to the left hand corner.

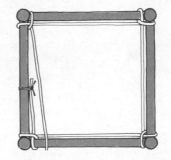

- After five or six rows have been woven press them together with a piece of wood ensuring that they lie evenly and that the diagonals are straight.
- Join lengths of cord as necessary with a reef knot so that it is on the inside of the seat.

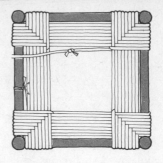

- The pockets formed at the corners between the cords should be filled with offcuts of rush or folded card to pack out the inside of the seat and prevent the cords rubbing on the rails.
- Tie off the last length of cord to another underneath the seat with a couple of half hitches. Trim and tuck the knot into the weave.

Rectangular frames

The extra space in the centre of a rectangular frame is filled by weaving the cord in a figure of eight pattern.

Tapered frame

Start weaving a frame that tapers in the normal way working round the front corners only, tying the end to the right hand rail.
- Tie another cord to the left hand rail and repeat the procedure adding more cords until the space between the cords on the front rail equals the length of the back rail. At that point, weave the seat as a square frame.

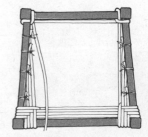

CHAPTER SIX

Hardware

A lot of old furniture is fitted with metal hardware. Some of it is purely functional, such as wood screws, but in most cases the fitments combine function with decoration, for example in solid brass handles or castors.

It is probably a mistake to polish old brass work until it gleams like new. The metal acquires a colour or patina with age which perfectly complements the quality of the old woodwork. However, if the metal has oxidised beyond the normal acceptable level, wash the fitting in warm soapy water with a nail brush. Dry it carefully with a soft cloth. If absolutely necessary, polish it gently by hand with a liquid metal polish.

Screws

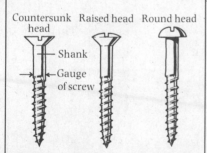

Countersunk head — Shank — Gauge of screw
Raised head
Round head

Screws used for furniture are made from steel or brass, which may be self coloured or plated. A wide range of sizes is available, specified by the length of the screw and the gauge of the shank. The length refers to that part of the screw which is actually sunk into the wood and is therefore measured from different parts of the screw according to the shape of the head (see above).

Curiously enough, screws are not yet measured in metric units and are supplied up to a length of 4 inches. The gauge of screws ranges from 0–20, but it is unnecessary for the amateur restorer to know all of these. In most cases, if you want to replace the screws in an old piece of furniture, all you need to do is take one of the old screws to your supplier who will match it for you. In older pieces of furniture, the screws may not conform to any modern pattern, but a new equivalent can nearly always be found.

There are three types of head for screws; countersunk, raised head and round head. Screws found in old furniture will have a single slot across the head so that they can be driven by a standard bladed screwdriver. Some modern screws are cross slotted and require a special screwdriver.

Fitting screws

Apart from very small screws which can be fitted by making a hole with a bradawl, most sizes will require a pilot hole to guide the thread and a larger clearance hole to accommodate the thicker shank.

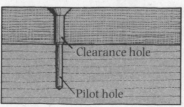

Clearance hole
Pilot hole

- The diameter of the drill for the pilot hole should be slightly less than the full screw thread. The easiest way to choose the drill bit is to compare it directly with the screw. The hole should be as deep as the entire length of the screw.

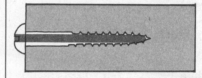

- Follow up with the clearance hole which should match the diameter of the shank.
- Drill the countersink if required with a countersink bit.

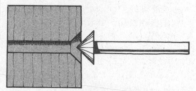

- Alternatively, a special bit will drill all three together for a given size of screw.

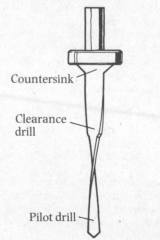

Countersink

Clearance drill

Pilot drill

111

● A screw which is recessed deeply into the wood requires a deep hole known as a counterbore.

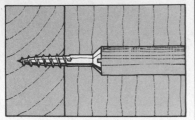

● Always use the correct size of screwdriver to suit the screw. If the tip is too wide it will damage the wood surrounding the screw head. If it is too small, it may ruin the slot, particularly of brass screws. The tip of a driver should always fit snugly into the slot. A worn tip can slip out causing serious damage to surrounding timber.

● When fitting screws in hardwood, put a touch of vaseline on the thread to lubricate it. Run a matching steel screw into the wood to cut the thread before fitting brass screws.

Removing screws

Screws which have been undisturbed in old timber can be quite difficult to remove. The most important requirement is a screwdriver which fits snugly in the screw slot, with as large a handle as possible. This will provide maximum torque and the best chance of freeing the screw.

● Rusty screws are particularly difficult to remove. Try placing the screwdriver in the slot and giving it a sharp tap with a mallet. This will often 'shock' it free.

● Another method is to heat the screw thoroughly with a soldering iron, then let it cool. The resulting expansion and contraction should release the screw.

● If the screw head is so damaged that the screwdriver will not grip it, indent the centre of the head with a centre punch.

● Drill down to the shank so that the head breaks off.

● The component that the screw was holding in place can now be lifted clear to reveal the shank, which can be gripped with pliers or a mole grip to remove it. File flats on two sides of the shank so that you can grip it firmly with the jaws of the tool.

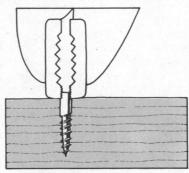

● A screw that has broken off at the thread is very difficult to remove. If you cannot fill the hole and reposition the screw, it may be possible to drill it out using a fine twist bit, followed by successively larger bits to remove the metal.

● Alternatively, try making a hollow drill from steel tube which is a close fit over the screw thread (see page 64 for making the drill).

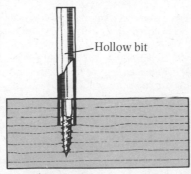

Hollow bit

● Glue and plug the hole with dowelling to receive the new screw.

Making and fitting wooden plugs

Screws which are fitted through show wood, usually to facilitate a repair, are often counterbored below the surface so that a matching wooden plug can be fitted to hide them. The grain of the plug should run in the same direction as that in the component, and the plug should fit the hole accurately.

● Making plugs with hand tools is a difficult and time consuming business for the amateur. The best way of assuring a good fit is to make the plug with a special plug cutting bit which is matched to certain drill sizes.

● Fit the cutter into a power drill, preferably set up in a drill press.

● The revolving cutter is simply pushed into a piece of scrap timber to cut the plug.

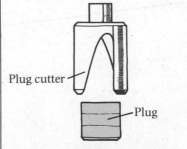

Plug cutter

Plug

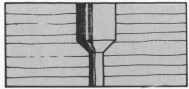

● Glue the plug into the hole, aligning the grain as closely as possible.

● Wipe away excess glue with a damp cloth. When it has set, plane the plug flush.

● Finish the plug to match the colour of the surrounding wood (see page 11).

Hinges

Should you wish to replace a set of hinges the panel opposite shows the main types which you are likely to encounter. They are available from ironmongers or by mail order.

Butt hinge

Butt hinges are used extensively for hanging doors. They are made in a wide range of sizes from both steel and brass, although the latter is preferable for furniture. For better quality work, choose a hinge made from solid brass rather than the cheaper variety made from rolled brass sheet. The hinge bears screw holes which are countersunk on the inside face for screws which are in proportion to the size of the hinge.

Piano hinge

A piano hinge is in effect a long butt hinge, originally used to fit piano lids but used on many other boxes as well. Although it is made from relatively lightweight metal, it is a strong fixing by virtue of its continuous central pin and its many evenly spaced screw holes.

Back flap hinge

The back flap hinge is another type of butt hinge with a relatively short knuckle joint and wide flaps. It is used for bureau fall flaps and some drop-leaf tables.

Card table hinge

Card table hinges are double jointed so that they lie flat when open. Two types of hinge are found on card table flaps. One which is widely available is let in flush with the surface as shown, while the other, more often found on older tables, is recessed into the edges.

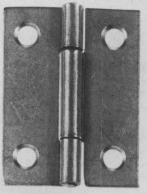

Butt hinge

Table leaf hinge

Back flap hinge

Card table hinge

Table leaf hinge

The table leaf hinge has one long flap and one short, and these flaps are countersunk on the outside face. It is used for drop-leaf tables which incorporate a rule joint (see page 54), the longer flap being fixed to the leaf. The knuckle and flaps are recessed into the underside of the table top and leaf.

Face mounted hinge

These hinges are screwed on to the face of the cabinet. A feature is often made of this type of hinge, which has large and decorative flaps.

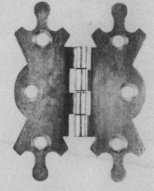

Face mounted hinge

Fixing a hinge

During the renovation of a cabinet you may have had cause to replace part of a door frame or a door jamb. In this case you will have to cut a housing in the new wood to take the hinge flap.

• Place the hinge flap in its intended position and draw round the edge with a sharp pencil.

• Using a try square, cut along the top and bottom lines with a craft knife as shown in **diagram a** in the panel below.

• With a marking gauge set to the distance between the centre of the hinge knuckle and the edge of the flap, mark the back line (**b**). Mark the depth of the housing with the gauge set to half the thickness of the knuckle (**c**).

• Use a chisel and mallet to chop across the waste several times before paring away the wood with a sharp chisel to make the housing (**d**). When the housing is of the correct depth, the centre pin of the hinge will lie flush with the surface of the wood.

• Repeat the process for the other side of the hinge. Fix the hinge with countersunk wood screws.

Problems with hinges

Doors that sag and table flaps that bind are very often the result of worn hinges. They bear the full load of the moving part, which is quite considerable in the case of, say, a mirrored wardrobe door. The wear affects not only the hinges but also the screws holding them in place.

Any hinged component should move freely and hang square to the frame or carcase to which it is attached. An uneven gap along the hinge line, slackness in the hinges themselves, or scuffing on the woodwork are all signs that the hinges are in need of attention.

Worn hinges

If the hinges are excessively worn, the door will begin to drop. Check by lifting the door while it is half open to see if there is any vertical movement. Look for wear on the edge of the door, particularly towards the top corner, as well as that part of the cabinet with which it is in contact. Similar marks will often be found on the bottom rail if the door is fitted inside the frame. When a hinged component is prevented from moving freely, it is said to be 'binding'. Although a warped carcase or component may be the reason, binding is very often caused by badly fitting hinges. For a binding rule joint see page 56.

Slightly worn hinges, or those which cannot be replaced easily, can be swapped top for bottom, which puts the load on another part of the knuckle and remedies the fault for some time.

When hinges are very badly worn or damaged it is advisable to replace them. Normally you will have to trim the old housing to fit the new hinges and if new wooden parts have been fitted, you will need to cut a new housing altogether (see panel).

Protruding screw heads

If you can only close the door of a cabinet with excessive force, or if it tends to spring open unaided, check that the heads of the screws holding the hinges are completely flush. Tighten any loose screws. If screws of the wrong gauge have been used to replace stripped screws, the heads will be too large for the countersinks in the hinge flap. Replace them with screws of the correct gauge. To do this, you will need to plug the holes.

• Having removed the screws, trim tapered wooden plugs from dowelling to fit the hole.

• Apply a little glue and tap them in until they fit tightly. Remove any excess glue and when set, trim the plugs flush with a chisel.

• Drill pilot and clearance holes for the screws (see page 111), using the hinge as a guide to their position.

A split frame

If the frame has split at the hinge point, the movement on the door can encourage the loosened screws

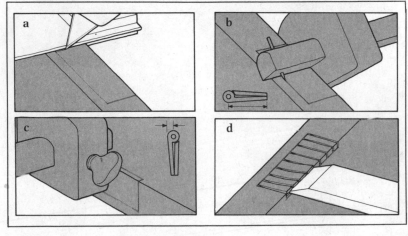

to ride out of their holes. The door will be reluctant to close or it will bind against the opposite framework.
- Remove the door and hinges and work glue into the split with a brush or knife blade.
- Cramp up the repair with a G-cramp and softening blocks.

- Wipe away excess glue and refit the hinges when it has set.

Re-seating a hinge

A hinge will bind if its housing is too deep. Pack the badly fitted flap until it is flush with the framework.
- Cut thin card or veneer to the size of the flap and punch holes through it to correspond with those in the hinge.

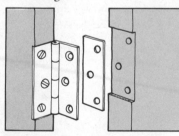

- Fit the hinge with one screw in the central hole to try the door, adjusting the thickness of packing if required.
- When the door operates properly, complete the fitting of the hinge.
- If you find that a lot of packing is required, glue a piece of matching timber into the hinge recess and re-fit the hinge completely.

Castors

It used to be the custom to fit castors to heavy pieces of furniture, so that they could be moved more easily. Castors were not confined to mobile furniture such as chairs or settees, but were also fitted to cabinets and tables. Although the function was primarily practical, they were often a decorative feature adding a touch of 'style'.

Castors are often missing from an old item, usually because one or two have become damaged or worn, and, rather than replace them, the previous owner has removed them altogether. This often gives the furniture an awkward, heavy appearance, since the proportions of the piece were designed with the castors in mind. Tell-tale screw holes, or rebates for cup castors at the end of the legs, will soon tell you if castors were once fitted. A little research at the library or around old furniture shops will help you decide what type of castor was used originally, and a new set can then be purchased from a specialist supplier or by mail order.

Types of castor
Old castors had brass or sometimes brown or white glazed china wheels running on a steel axle pin. There were two basic methods of fitting them, cup or screw fixing.

Cup castors

Cup castors have a brass socket into which the bottom of the leg is fitted. It will be round for turned legs or square for straight tapered legs. The toe castor is a variety of cup castor which has the opening to one side for fitting over the end of outward curving legs such as are found on pedestal tables (see page 61). The cup is sometimes decorated, or cast in the shape of a claw foot.

Screw castors

Screw castors have a large central screw which is inserted into a hole or socket in the end of a leg. Wood screws are used to hold a flat brass plate against the underside of the leg. These castors are usually found on heavy furniture.

A separate, brass capping with a moulded edge was sometimes used with a screw castor on a square leg.

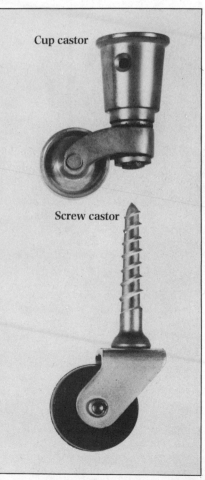

Cup castor

Screw castor

Worn castors

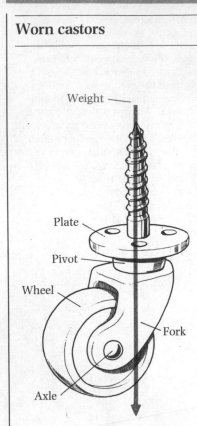

Weight

Plate

Pivot

Wheel

Fork

Axle

The small wheel of a castor is offset from the central pivot by a fork which carries the axle. As the furniture is moved, the fork swivels around the pivot, so that the wheel trails behind. It is this action that allows the furniture to be guided or steered easily. However, because the wheels are not directly under the pivot point, the weight of the furniture puts a greater strain on the swivelling mechanism. The weight also produces considerable wear in the small bearings of the wheel. Many castors are so badly worn that the fork can no longer revolve freely and the hole in the wheel is so over size that the wheel binds in the fork. A castor which is worn as badly as this is not worth repairing and should be replaced.

Replacing a cup castor

To replace a cup castor first remove the brass screws fitted through the side of the cup.

● Pull the cup from the end of the leg, tapping it all round with a wooden block and hammer to release it.

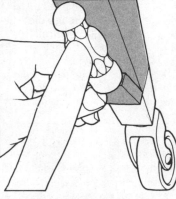

● Alternatively, tap a screwdriver wedged between cup and fork.

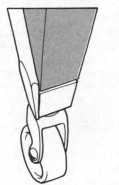

● Try the new castor to check its fit on the end of the leg. The leg may have to be trimmed carefully with a chisel or file, or alternatively packed out a little with thin veneer.

● The screw fixing holes are unlikely to line up exactly. If necessary, plug the old holes and drill new ones (see page 121).

● Fit the new castor and seat it firmly by tapping the end of the central pivot. Insert new brass screws.

Replacing a toe castor

Remove a toe castor by taking out the screws from the side of the cup and from the lug on the underside of the leg.

● Tap a new castor in place, protecting the toe with softwood.

Replacing a screw castor

Having removed the wood screws from the plate, place a nail punch against the edge of one hole and tap the plate in an anti-clockwise direction. Once free, it should be possible to unscrew the castor by hand.

● To fit the new castor, insert the tip of a small screwdriver in one screw hole, using the shaft as a lever against the fork to provide the turning force and lock the swivel mechanism at the same time.

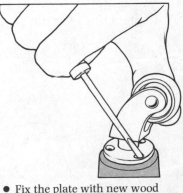

● Fix the plate with new wood screws.

Knobs and handles

Handles for cabinet doors and drawers vary enormously in their use of material, shape, size and style. However, they can be categorised roughly into groups for the purposes of identification.

Knobs

A knob is a one piece handle usually in the form of a bulbous mushroom, although many varieties of cylindrical knob exist.

Cabinet handles

Cabinet handles, used as drawer pulls, are roughly D-shaped and hang vertically from a pivot at each end. Variations will include plate handles, where the pivots are linked by a decorative metal backing plate, pressed into relief or fretted from solid metal. Another version is the 'swan neck' handle, a name which is derived from the distinctive S-shaped curve at each end of the handle.

Drop handle

Drop handles are for small drawers or lightweight doors, having a tear drop shaped grip suspended from a single pivot. A variation known as a 'Dutch drop' has a decorative D-shaped grip.

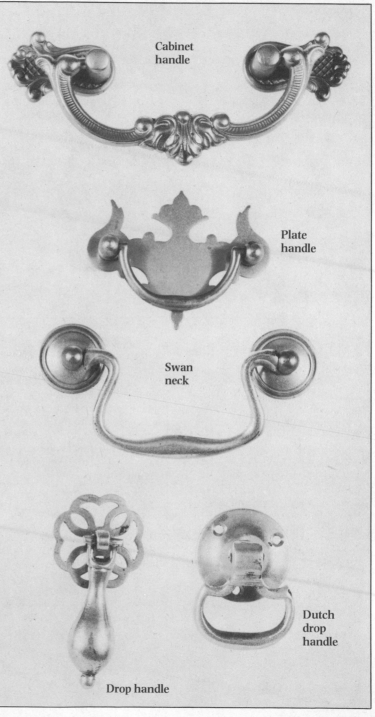

Cabinet handle

Plate handle

Swan neck

Drop handle

Dutch drop handle

Ring pull

A ring pull, as its name implies, has a circular grip suspended from a single pivot like a drop handle. It may have a decorative backing plate in the form of an animal or human head.

Flush handles

Flush handles can be found with ring or D-shaped grips which are recessed into their backing plate. The plate itself is let into the woodwork, so that the entire handle is flush with the face of the cabinet.

Ring pull

Flush handle

Replacing handles

Metal handles rarely break with normal use. Any pivots are subject to a certain amount of wear, but a slack fit does not detract from the function or appearance of the handle.

Wooden knobs on the other hand, suffer from short grain near the edge of the base. If a section is broken off and is now missing, it can be repaired in a similar way to that described for the foot of a pedestal table (see page 65). A small item like a handle can be shaped on a lathe.

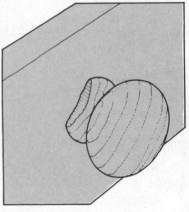

If the wooden thread has been stripped, it can be glued permanently in the hole.

Missing handles present more of a problem. With luck an identical handle can be purchased, as all the handles described are available as reproductions from specialist suppliers. If you cannot match the original, it may be better to buy a complete set of replacements which resemble them closely. You will probably have to plug old fixing holes, and some colour matching or refinishing may be necessary if a new backing plate does not fill the area of wood covered by the original (see pages 114 and 11).

Methods of fixing handles

Most handles on old furniture are made from solid brass, except for a few in cast iron or plated steel. Knobs however, are also made from wood and china.

Knobs are usually fixed by means of a single screw projecting from the back face. Even wooden knobs are provided with their own coarse thread which screws into a matching hole in the door or drawer front.

A small drop handle may be fitted in the same way, but most handles have threaded rods which pass through the woodwork and are secured on the inside by nuts. Better quality versions have fine bolts which screw into the back of the handle, showing as a neat countersunk or raised head on the inside. Flush handles are usually face fixed with brass wood screws.

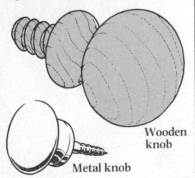

Wooden knob

Metal knob

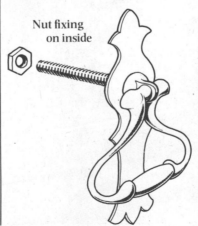

Nut fixing on inside

CHAPTER SEVEN

Tools of the trade

As explained in the introductory chapter, we have assumed that you are familiar with most of the basic woodworking skills, in which case you probably own many of the relevant tools. However, for less ex-perienced readers, we give below an account of the tools which are necessary for basic repairs, followed by those tools which, although not essential, are particularly useful in renovation work. Specialised tools, such as those used for upholstery or veneering, are described in the sections dealing with those subjects. You may consider hiring some of the more unusual tools for one or two jobs only.

Basic tool kit

Rule

A folding boxwood rule is the traditional cabinet maker's tool, but an extendable steel tape will prove to be more versatile.

Try square

A try square is used to check that a section of timber is accurately planed to a right angle or that framing or joints are square. It is also used as a guide to marking lines at right angles to an edge.

Marking gauge

A marking gauge which scratches a line parallel to an edge is used for marking out a variety of joints, rebates and so on. You will find it easy to use if you push the tool away from you while holding the guide fence or stock against the edge of the wood.

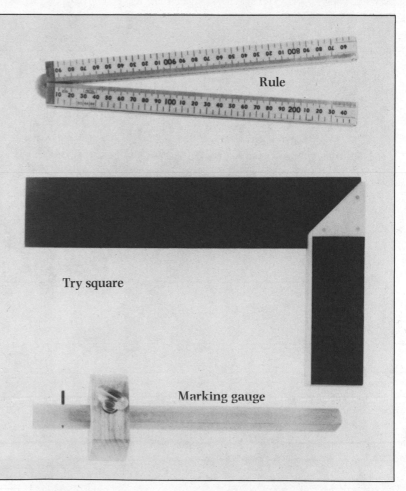

Rule

Try square

Marking gauge

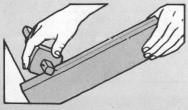

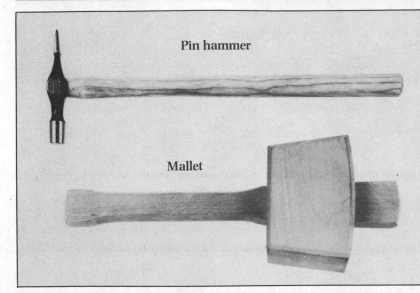

Pin hammer

Mallet

Pin hammer

A lightweight hammer used for driving pins and brads. Choose one with a crosspein to help you start small pins held between fingertips.

Mallet

A beech mallet is useful for driving chisels as well as dismantling frames and carcases in old furniture. A heavyweight hammer can be used to knock a structure apart, so long as a block of softwood is used to prevent any marking of furniture (see page 29).

Tenon saw

A tenon saw is designed to cut joints accurately. The blade is held rigid by a heavy strip of metal along the top edge. It is the most versatile saw for a cabinet maker but it is too crude for really delicate work (see *Dovetail saw* page 126).

Panel saw

A panel saw is primarily for cutting composite boards such as plywood, chipboard and so on, but it will also cut large sections of timber, which are difficult to tackle with a tenon saw because its backing strip gets in the way.

Coping saw

A coping saw has a very thin blade for cutting curves in boards and solid timber.

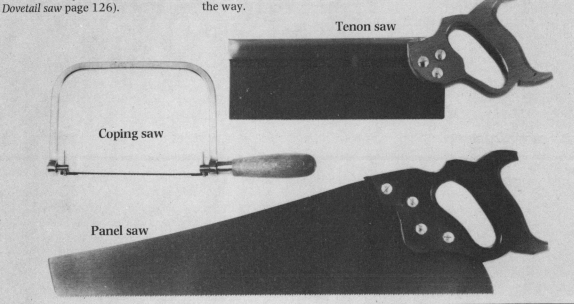

Tenon saw

Coping saw

Panel saw

Bench plane

The family of bench planes includes a short smoothing plane, a try plane which has a very long sole to square up long edges, and the medium size Jack plane. This is the best bench plane to start with as it can cope with most planing operations reasonably well.

Block plane

The block plane is a small lightweight plane which is invaluable to any renovator. Originally designed to plane end grain, it is also used for fine smoothing and shaping of timber.

Chisels

Any renovator will need a selection of chisels of various sizes. Firmer chisels, with their strong, rectangular section blades are the best general purpose chisels. Bevel edged chisels are for lightweight work only, due to their greatly reduced section. The bevels along both edges allow the chisel to work undercuts, for example letting in a patch of new wood. You may find at least one or two paring chisels useful. Their extended blades are for cleaning out the waste from long housings. Mortice chisels have narrow but stiff blades for levering out the waste from a mortice.

Gouges

Gouges are chisels which are curved to cut hollow or rounded sections. An in-cannel gouge is ground on the inside; an out-cannel gouge is ground on the outside.

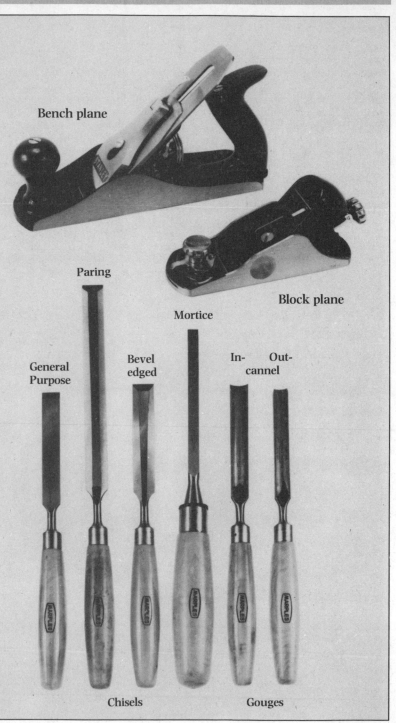

Bench plane

Block plane

Paring

Mortice

General Purpose

Bevel edged

In-cannel

Out-cannel

Chisels

Gouges

121

Scrapers

The cabinet scraper is a thin, rectangular piece of steel with sharpened edges for smoothing flat wooden surfaces. A scraper which is cut into a series of curves is used for scraping mouldings and shaped work. To use a cabinet scraper, press both thumbs into the back of it to produce a slight curve and angle the tool away from you. Scrape diagonally in two directions, finishing with the grain to avoid hollowing the wood locally (see diagram page 9).

Scratch moulding tool

A scratch moulding tool, or scratch stock, is one of the most useful tools for furniture renovation, being both cheap and extremely versatile. It is a home made tool cut from wood and fitted with a piece of steel scraper which has been filed to match the required moulding. The burr formed by filing the shape in the metal is enough to form an efficient cutting edge. Two wood screws close the slot sawn in the handle to hold the blade in place.

With the fence held against the edge of the work, the moulding is produced by scraping a little at a time starting at the far end of the workpiece and working back towards yourself.

Files and rasps

Round, flat and half round files and rasps are available for shaping metal and wood. Rasps have coarse teeth for cutting wood which would clog the finer teeth of a file.

Tyzack
SONS & TURNER
SHEFFIELD ENGLAND

Scrapers

Scratch moulding tool

File    Rasp

Screwdrivers

A large cabinet screwdriver is an essential tool for freeing old screws (see page 112) as well as replacing them with new ones. In addition, you will need at least one small screwdriver for fixing small hinges or similar fittings.

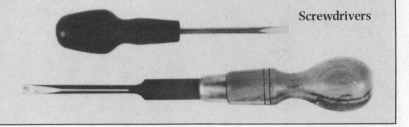

Screwdrivers

Pincers

Carpenter's pincers are ideal for removing nails, so long as at least the head is protruding from the surface. Grip the head and rock the tool away from you to draw the nail out of the wood. A small claw at the end of one handle is for removing tacks.

Pliers

A pair of strong pliers with wire cutters is always useful, and a pair of long-nosed pliers will prove to be invaluable for reaching into confined spaces.

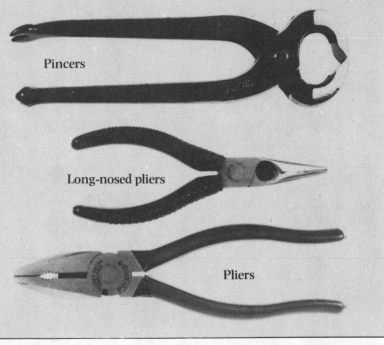

Pincers

Long-nosed pliers

Pliers

Centre punch

A drill bit is prevented from wandering off centre by first marking the job with a centre punch. Position the tool upright on the spot and strike it with a hammer.

Nail punch

The nail punch is used in a similar way to the centre punch but the tip is ground square to drive the heads of nails below the surface of timber.

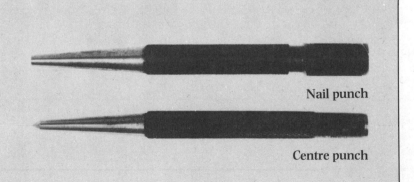

Nail punch

Centre punch

Sash cramps

You will need at least two medium sized sash cramps for re-gluing frames and boards (see pages 30 and 49).

The *jet cramp*, a variety of sash cramp, is a useful addition to a tool kit, especially as its heads can be reversed to produce outward pressure to dismantle a frame (see page 29).

G-cramps

G-cramps in a range of sizes will be required to clamp workpieces while glue sets.

Trimming knife

A strong trimming knife is required again and again in many aspects of furniture renovation. Choose one that has replaceable blades so that the knife is always razor sharp. For delicate work, you may prefer to use a surgeon's scalpel, available from any artists' suppliers.

Sash cramp

G-cramp

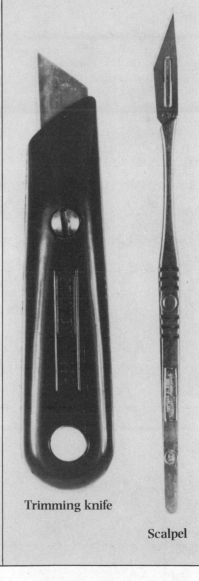

Trimming knife

Scalpel

Power drill

A variable speed power drill will repay its purchase price in no time. Using standard twist drills, power bore bits or spade bits, the drill can be used to make a range of holes from 1mm to 38mm in diameter. In addition, by acquiring a range of accessories you can build up a miniature power workshop (see page 128).

Safety note
Always turn off the mains supply to your power drill between operations to guard against accidents, particularly if children come into your workshop.

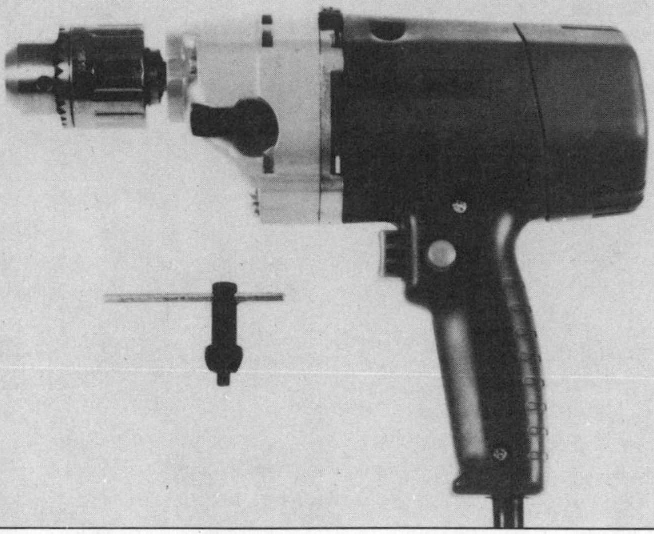

Bench

Although a sturdy carpenter's bench with a built-in woodworking vice is perhaps the ideal work surface for furniture renovators, many amateurs do not have the space for a fully equipped workshop. A folding bench will solve the problem of restricted space as it can be set up quickly and conveniently and folded away after use. The long adjusting jaws which form the entire worktop can be used to hold all manner of workpieces.

Vice

A small clamp-on vice for working on small items can be used in conjunction with any bench or work table.

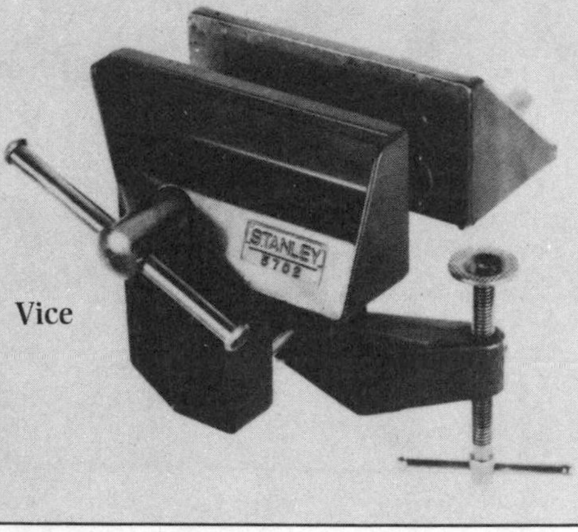

Vice

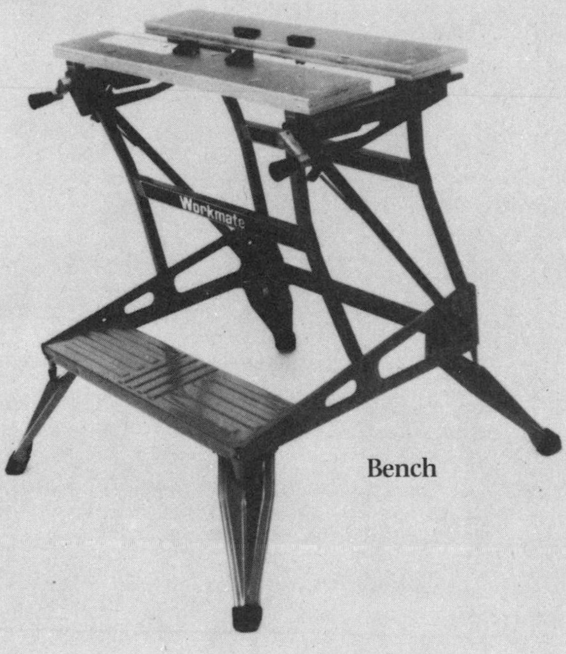

Bench

Additional tools

Mortice gauge

A mortice gauge is a marking gauge with two scribing pins. One is fixed while the other is adjustable. Both sides of the mortice and tenon can be marked out simultaneously with the gauge.

Needle template

Sometimes referred to as a profile gauge, the needle template has a row of steel pins which when pressed against the workpiece reproduce its shape.

Dovetail saw

A smaller version of the tenon saw for fine jointing work and for cutting small sections of timber to length.

Pad saw

The pad saw has a narrow blade held in the handle by two locking screws. It is used to cut holes in a panel. The tip of the blade is inserted in a small hole drilled in the work to start the cut.

Mortice gauge

Needle template

Dovetail saw

Pad saw

Spokeshave

A spokeshave is a form of plane for curved surfaces. A handle is held in each hand while the thumbs control the angle of the tool in relation to the surface. A spokeshave with a flat face will cut convex shapes but you will need one with a curved face to accommodate concave curves.

Spokeshave

Shoulder plane

Also known as a rebate plane, this tool is ideal for planing the square shoulders of joints or rebates as the blade runs the full width of the sole. Choose one with a detachable nose or body, so that it can be converted into a chisel plane which will allow you to plane into a corner.

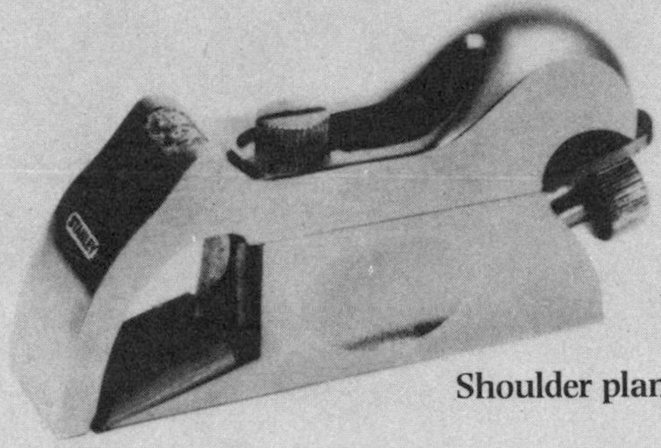

Shoulder plane

Hand router

The cutter of a router is adjusted vertically so that the tool will accurately level the bottom of a groove or housing.

Hand router

Combination plane

All the mouldings on old timber were cut by a special purpose plane that had a cutter and sole shaped for that one profile. A modern combination will take a variety of cutters for planing common mouldings as well as grooves and rebates. Having adjustable guides and fences, it is an extremely useful tool.

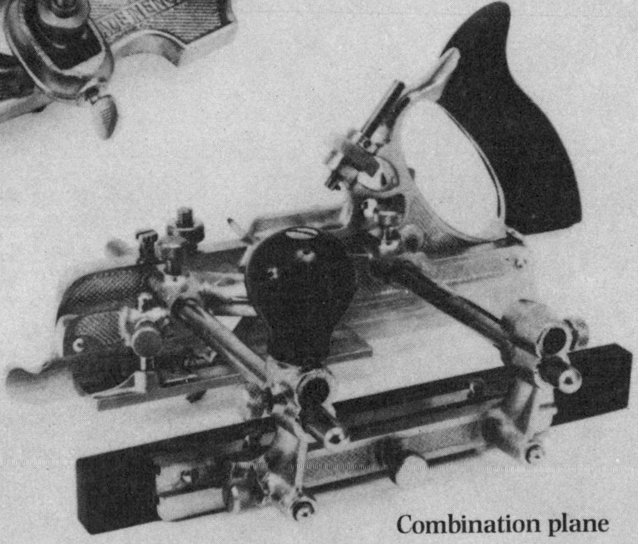

Combination plane

Attachments for a power drill

A *circular saw* attachment will enable you to cut timber to size easily. Not an essential tool for a renovator, the circular saw is fitted with guide fences and a depth gauge, so it will make accurate parallel and angled cuts, rebates and grooves. The addition of a saw bench attachment increases the use of the circular saw, since it has an adjustable sliding fence for making cross cuts.

An *orbital sander* will cut down preliminary sanding (see page 10).

A *drill stand* will convert a portable electric drill into a drill press. This combination will improve your ability to drill holes accurately and vertically.

Curved cuts are performed easily with a *jig saw* attachment on the drill.

A *lathe* attachment will enable you to produce small turnings to replace missing knobs or sections of damaged legs or rails (see page 41).

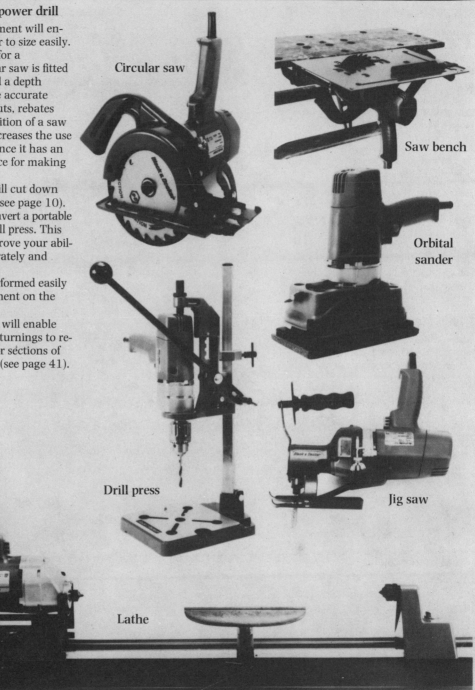

Circular saw

Saw bench

Orbital sander

Drill press

Jig saw

Lathe

Rubber headed mallet

A mallet with a relatively soft head which will not damage the surface. Useful for dismantling and re-assembling carcases and frames.

Bradawl

An awl with a wedge shaped tip to make starting holes for small screws. The blade is positioned across the grain to prevent splitting, and pressure is applied while twisting the tool from side to side.

Wheel brace

A hand operated drill which takes twist drills up to 8mm ($\frac{5}{16}$ in) in diameter.

Brace and bit

Another hand operated tool which takes a variety of bits for drilling large holes. Countersink and even screwdriver bits are available to fit the brace.

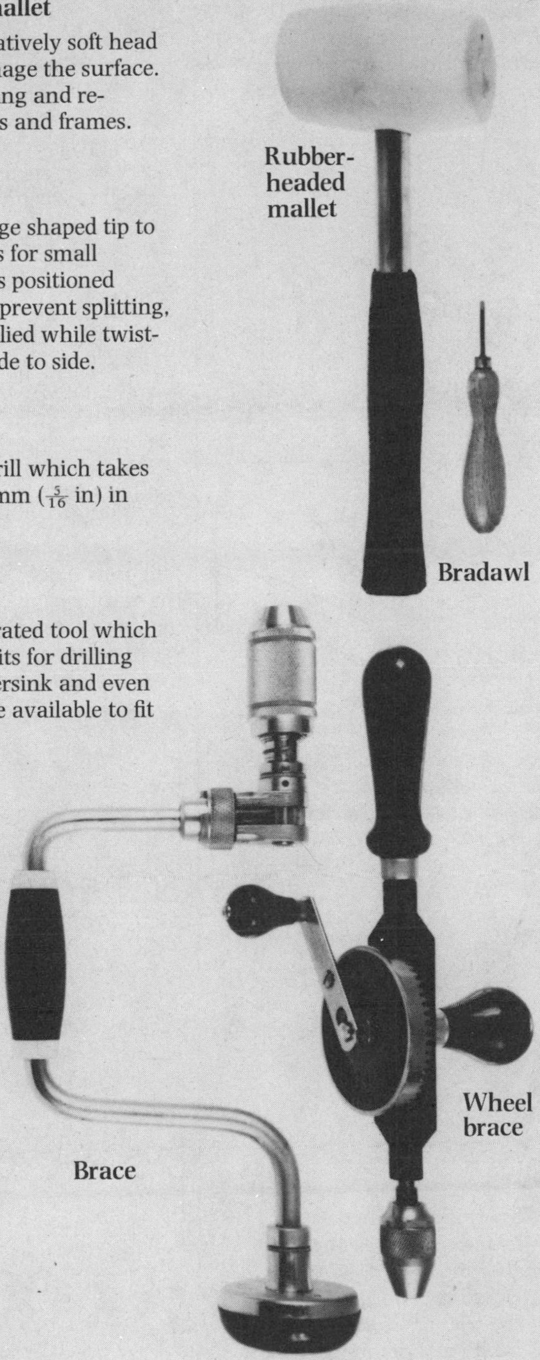

Rubber-headed mallet

Bradawl

Wheel brace

Brace

Sharpening tools

Chisels, planes and spokeshaves

Chisels, planes and spokeshaves should be kept as sharp as possible. Not only will they produce better quality work, but they will be safer to use. Blunt tools resist pressure behind the blade until they slip suddenly and damage the work or the user.

You will need a combination oil stone, which has a medium grit on the one side to remove metal quickly, before a final edge is produced by the fine grit on the other.

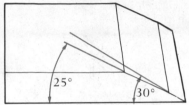

A new plane or chisel blade has a 25° bevel ground on the blade. A second angle of 30° is honed on the oil stone to produce a stronger cutting edge. The small blades which fit into a combination plane for cutting rebates or grooves should be honed to an angle of 35°.

A honing guide, a device which clamps the blade at the required angle to the surface of the stone, will simplify the sharpening process.

Using a honing guide

Put a few drops of oil on the fine side of the stone and remove the machining marks from the flat back of the blade by rubbing it up and down the length of the stone, maintaining even pressure with the finger tips.

● When the area immediately behind the cutting edge is shiny and smooth, fit the blade in the honing guide to sharpen it.

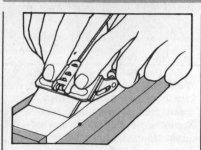

- Use the entire width of the stone as well as the length to reduce uneven wear. If the blade is wider than the stone, angle it until it fits.
- When the burr is raised on the back of the blade, remove it by rubbing it flat on the stone. Alternately raising and returning the burr eventually breaks it off to produce a sharp edge.

- A final stropping on a leather strap will produce a razor sharp tool.

Gouges

A gouge is sharpened by moving it from side to side along the stone while rocking the blade to treat the whole cutting edge.

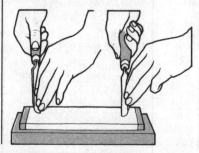

- Remove the burr with a shaped 'slip' stone, rubbing it flat on the inside of the gouge. Oil the stone slightly.

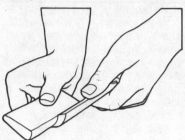

- An in-cannel gouge is sharpened in reverse, raising the burr with the slip stone.

- Remove it by rubbing the outside of the gouge up and down the oil stone while rocking the blade.

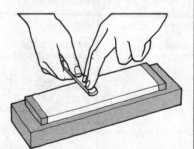

Saws

Saws are sharpened with special files and must be set to angle the teeth alternately. Unless you are sufficiently experienced at this, it would be wise to take your saws to a specialist for sharpening. Seek the advice of your local tool stockist.

Drill bits

Twist drills are sharpened on a grind stone. Unless you own your own bench grinder, once again take them to a professional.

Drill bits used in a hand brace can be sharpened by stroking the cutting edges and inner edge of the spur with needle files.

Scraper

A cabinet scraper has a burr raised on its edge which cuts minute shavings from the wood. If dust only is produced by the scraper it should be sharpened.

- Produce a square edge on a scraper with a file and finish it on an oil stone.
- Hold the scraper on the bench and draw a hard steel strop along the cutting edge, keeping it almost flat on the scraper. This action raises a burr which is turned over to form a sharp scraping edge.

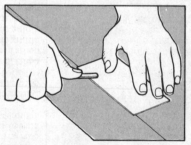

- Stand the scraper on end and stroke the strop firmly along the edge keeping it at an angle of slightly less than 90° to the face.

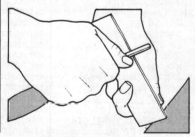

CHAPTER EIGHT

Some basic techniques

Ideally, a book on furniture renovation should include all the techniques which would enable a beginner to tackle any form of repair. Unfortunately, that involves a complete account of all the skills of woodworking and it would take a book of twice this size to cover the field adequately. In the following pages, we describe some basic procedures which may prove useful as a back-up to the instructions in the main part of the book, but the only safe way for a beginner is to go to a course of evening classes in woodwork before tackling some of the more intricate repairs. In woodworking, as in many other skills, practice makes perfect.

Woodworking joints

Dowel joint

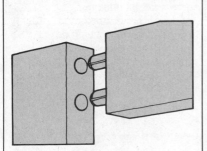

A dowel joint is often used to join the rails to the legs on old dining chairs, particularly when they are upholstered. Hardwood pegs or dowels are glued into holes in each half of the joint. Use dowels which are from one third to half the width of the component.

Making a dowel joint

Make a centre line through the thickness of the upright using a marking gauge.
● Using a try square, mark two positions for the dowel centres. It does not matter exactly where these are but they should match sensibly with the side member.

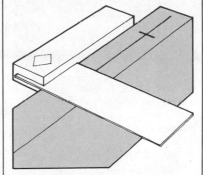

● Drive a panel pin into each dowel centre, cutting the head off with a pair of pliers to leave short spikes projecting from the surface.
● Align both halves of the joint on a flat surface and push them together. The pins in the upright will mark corresponding centres in the end grain of the side rail.

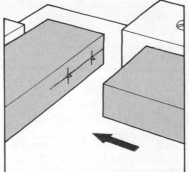

● Remove the pins and drill holes in both halves. If possible, use a drill stand for greater accuracy and to limit the depth of the holes.

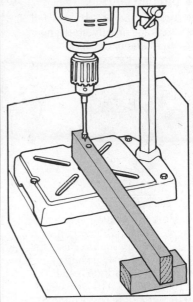

● Cut matching dowels 1mm or 2mm shorter than the combined depth of opposing holes.
● Use a saw to cut a glue clearance slot along each dowel to prevent excess glue from splitting the wood, and use a pencil sharpener or a file to cut a chamfer on each end so that they enter the holes easily.

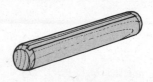

● Glue each half of the joint and the dowels and assemble the joint in cramps. Leave to set.

Housing joint

A housing joint is used to fit shelves, dividers or draw runners in cabinets and chests of drawers. The main component (say a shelf) fits into a shallow groove cut into the upright.

A through housing

A through housing runs the full width of the upright emerging at the front and back edges.

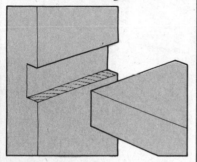

- Mark the position of one edge of the shelf across the upright with a knife and a try square. Place the shelf against this line and mark the other edge. Continue both lines across the back and front edges of the upright to the depth of the housing.
- Mark the depth of the housing on each edge with a marking gauge. It should not be more than one third of the thickness of the wood.
- Use a tenon saw to cut on the waste side of each line across the upright down to the depth of the housing.

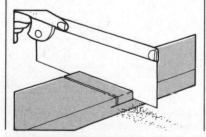

- Chisel out the waste from each edge to the middle of the housing.
- Fit the component to ensure that the bottom of the housing is flat and level.

A stopped housing

A stopped housing does not emerge at the front edge of the upright, thus concealing the joint.

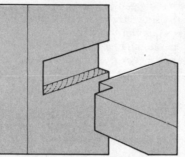

- Mark out the housing as before leaving out its depth on the front edge. Instead, mark a line across the housing about 12mm ($\frac{1}{2}$in) from the edge.
- Use a chisel and mallet to chop out the first 50mm (2ins) of the waste at the stopped end of the housing to allow clearance for a tenon saw to cut along each edge.

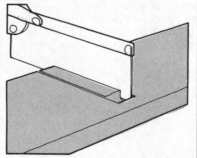

- When you have sawn down the edges, chisel out the rest of the waste. A paring chisel may be helpful (or even a hand router) to level the housing accurately.
- Cut a notch in the front corner of the shelf to match the stopped end of the housing.

Mortice and tenon

A mortice and tenon joint is used in the construction of tables and chairs where a strong joint is needed. It has a tongue known as a tenon, which fits into a slotted hole which is the mortice.

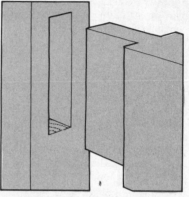

The tenon should be approximately one third of the thickness of the side rail but its length will differ depending on the type of joint. A through tenon passes right through the upright, whereas the stopped tenon is obviously shorter. As a rough guide, make the length of a stopped tenon three times its thickness.

Pegged tenons are locked in the mortice by dowels which pass through the leg and tenon at right angles to the rail. Stub tenons are short tenons which are usually grouped in pairs.

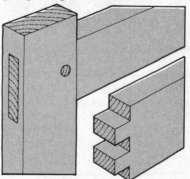

Marking out the joints

Mark out the shoulder line of the tenon around the rail, using a try square and knife.
● Using the rail as a guide, mark its position and width on the upright with a try square and pencil.

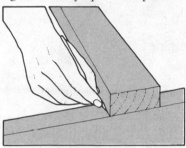

● Set a mortice gauge to the width of the required tenon and mark out both mortice and tenon.

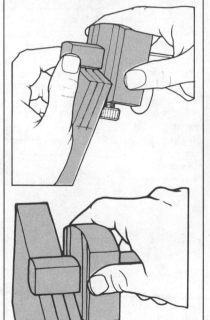

● Use a knife to cut across the grain at top and bottom of the marked mortice.

Cutting the tenon

Hold the rail in a vice at an angle. Using a tenon saw, start at one corner, cutting on the waste side of the line down to the shoulder.
● Turn the rail to cut from the other corner down to the shoulder.

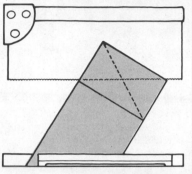

● Hold the rail upright to cut square across the tenon down to the shoulder line.
● Cut the other side of the tenon in the same way.
● Finally cut both shoulders with a tenon saw and remove the waste.

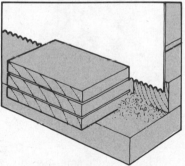

Cutting the mortice

The easiest way to remove the waste from a mortice is to use a drill on a bench stand (see diagram page 131). Bore out successive holes side by side.
● Chop out the remaining waste with chisels.
● Check that the joint fits together before gluing it. Leave in cramps till dry.

Repairing tenons

Shown on page 32 are three methods for repairing a broken tenon depending on how much of the tenon remains.

Method 1
Less than half the tenon damaged

Cut away the broken part of the tenon with a saw.

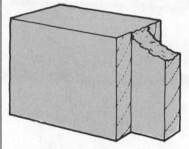

● Lay a steel rule on each shoulder against the tenon and use a knife to mark lines on the end grain to define the area of the tenon which is missing.

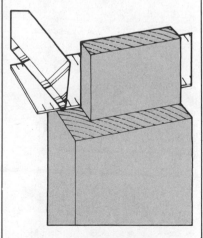

● With the rail held upright in a vice, use a chisel which fits the width of the tenon to pare away the waste between the lines to form the undercut. Cut at an angle towards the tenon removing a little at a time.

● Cut a piece of timber to fit the width of the tenon and the undercut. Glue it in place and hold it with a small G-cramp until it sets.

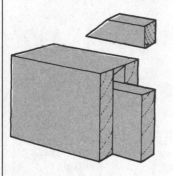

Method 2
More than half the tenon damaged

Cut the broken tenon square and mark lines on the end grain as before.

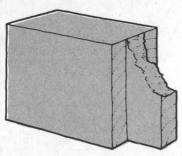

● Mark out a stopped housing by continuing these lines along the rail, using a mortice gauge. They should be as long as the tenon.

● Cut each side of the housing with a saw held at an angle up to the end of the housing.

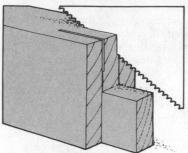

● Chop out the waste between the sawcuts with a mortice chisel.
● Alternatively, drill out the waste with a drill, as described for cutting a standard mortice.
● Cut and fit the new section of tenon.

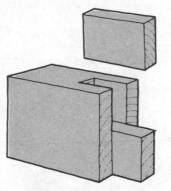

Method 3
All or most of the tenon damaged

Cut off the broken tenons squaring the end of the rail.

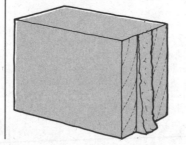

● Use a mortice gauge to mark out an angled bridle joint across the end of the rail and along its underside. It should match the thickness of the mortice and it should be three times the length of the original tenon.

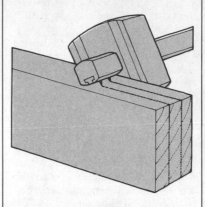

● Hold the rail in a vice and make a saw cut along each line on the waste side. Pare out the waste with a chisel working in the direction of the grain.
● Cut a new tenon which fits in the bridle joint. The grain direction must match that of the rail. Leave it slightly oversized top and bottom for planing flush.
● Glue the tenon in place, pinching across the rail with a G-cramp until it is set.
● Drill and fit a glued reinforcing dowel from the inside of the rail which stops short of the outer face.

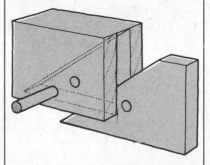

● Plane the top and bottom of the tenon flush with the rail.

Halving joint

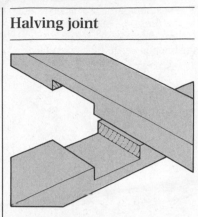

A halving joint allows two components to interlock, so that one lies within the thickness or width of the other. It is found in some draw-leaf table underframes and on the hinged leg frames of a gate-leg table.

● Mark one edge of the joint across a component. Lay the other component against this line to gauge the width of the joint and score both lines with a knife and try square.

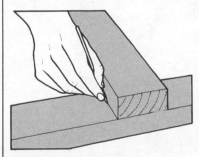

● Lay the components side by side and mark one component from the other.

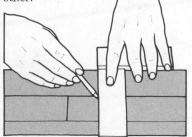

● Mark the depth of each half of the joint using a marking gauge. This should be exactly half the thickness of the components. Link the lines marked across each component with the depth line, using a try square and knife.

● Cut the lines across each half of the joint down to the halfway mark. Remember to keep on the waste side of the line. Make several more cuts across the waste to make it easy to remove.

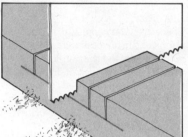

● Chop out the waste with a chisel working from both sides of the component towards the middle.

Bridle joint

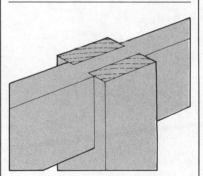

A bridle joint is used to join a thick leg in the centre of a thinner rail. This type of construction will be found on some side tables.

● Use the methods described for marking out and cutting a halving joint to cut a 5mm ($\frac{3}{16}$in) deep housing on each side of the rail.

● Use a mortice gauge set from the cut rail to mark out the joint on the top of the upright.

● Bore out the base of the waste just above the base line.

● Saw down both sides of the waste with a tenon saw and remove the waste. Clean out the bottom of the groove with a chisel.

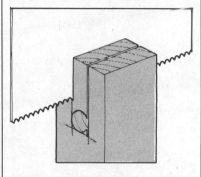

Scarf joint

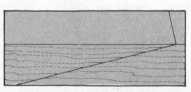

A scarf joint is used to join two pieces of wood end to end, providing a large gluing area by cutting a long taper on each piece of wood. The length of the joint should be four times the width of the wood. There is more than one method of cutting the scarf joint but the simplest is as follows:

Cutting the scarf

Hold both pieces of wood together to cut and plane a matching angle.

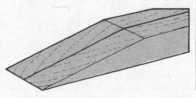

• Reverse one piece of wood and glue them together with G-cramps and long softening battens.

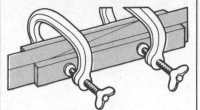

• Scarf joints used in the repair of chair legs must be reinforced (see page 33).

A shouldered scarf joint

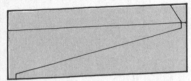

A skilled craftsman could cut both halves of a shouldered scarf joint together, but another method is to mark one half from the other as described in the panel below.

Dovetail joint

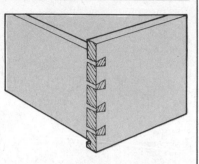

There are many sophisticated variations of the dovetail joint, but the most basic is the through dovetail used to joint the back of drawers to the sides. This joint needs practice, and you should try it on some spare softwood before setting to work on old furniture.

Cutting a dovetail joint

Having squared up the ends of the components, mark the shoulder lines using a knife and try square.

The position of the shoulder should be the thickness of the other component plus 2–3mm for planing flush when the joint is assembled.

• The number of tails is dependent on the size of the component. Three 25mm (1in) tails for every 100mm (4in) is a rough guide. Space them evenly.

• The easiest method for marking out the tails on one of the components is to draw round a dovetail template, squaring across the end grain with a try square.

• Using a dovetail saw, cut the tails on the waste side of the line down to the shoulder.

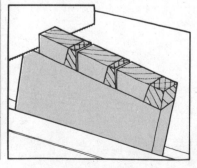

Cutting a shouldered scarf joint

Cramp the two halves of the joint together side by side, marking the shoulders across top and bottom. Mark the depth of the shoulders which should be between 3mm ($\frac{1}{8}$in) and 6mm ($\frac{1}{4}$in).

• Separate the components and draw the angled face of the joint on one half with a straight edge.

• Cut the shoulders and the angled face with a tenon saw, finishing with a chisel plane or paring it with a chisel.

• Clamp the two halves together again, lining up the shoulders and draw round the cut component.

• Cut out the second component as before, trying the joint for fit as it is trimmed with the plane or chisel.

- Cut out the waste with a coping saw, finishing off at the shoulder line with a small bevelled edge chisel. Cut from both sides toward the middle to prevent splitting out.

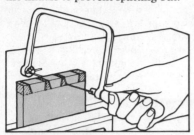

- To mark the pins, use the tails as a guide, holding them in position on the end of the other component held in a vice. The end of this component should be chalked first. Use a pointed scriber or the dovetail saw to scratch the shape of the pins in the chalk.

- Square down to the shoulder line with a try square.
- Cut the pins down to the shoulder line removing the waste as before.

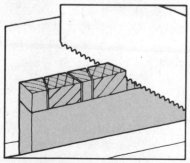

- Test the joint for fit, trimming as necessary before gluing up and cramping.

Mitred butt joint

When two pieces of wood meet at a right angled corner, the ends are often cut at an angle of 45° so that the end grain does not show. This is the only way to join moulded sections of timber.

- Use a mitre box, a specially made jig which has slots to guide a saw blade at the required angle. Hold the wood against the far side of the jig and place scrap timber under it to protect the bottom of the mitre box from saw cuts.

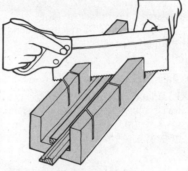

- The joint can be trimmed with a finely set block plane. Make up a mitre shooting board if you are making a lot of joints.

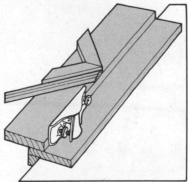

- The joint can be glued in a special mitre clamp or a mitred frame can be held together with a cord tourniquet, protecting the corners with card.

Adhesives

In old furniture, animal glue was used universally for bonding joints and fixing veneers. For this reason, many restorers use animal glue only in the repair of old furniture. Modern glues are far stronger, however, and more resistant to damp and fungal attack. Providing all the original animal glue has been removed from the joint, they can be used very successfully on old furniture.

The only real disadvantage is that a joint which is bonded by modern glues cannot be dismantled easily, should that ever be necessary in the future. This may be an important factor when considering the conservation of valuable antique furniture, but most people want a glue that will stand up to the strain of constant use, in which case the modern glue is superior. Veneering has its own particular requirements and a number of glues can be used (see page 21).

Animal glue

Traditional animal glue is made from animal bones and skins. Some glues are supplied as beads or cakes which must be melted and applied while hot and runny. It is not a gap filling glue so joints must be close fitting and must be cramped.

PVA glue

PVA glue is a white, creamy adhesive which is used cold directly from the container. Paint the glue on to both joining surfaces and cramp the joint for up to an hour under normal conditions. The bond will not be strong for about twenty-four hours. As with most glues, leave the work in cramps overnight wherever possible.

Urea formaldehyde glue

UF glues cure by chemical action. The process begins when a resin and a catalyst (or hardener) are mixed together. With some types of UF glue, each constituent is painted on to a different half of the joint, so that the reaction begins when the joint is assembled. More commonly, the resin and hardener are mixed together in a dry power form and do not react with each other until they are mixed with water. This type of glue has good gap filling properties and is therefore preferable for a poorly fitting joint. It is also water resistant. UF glues must be cramped while they are setting.

Contact adhesives

These are rubber-based adhesives which produce a strong bond immediately on contact. Glue is spread on to both of the surfaces to be joined and left to dry. When the two surfaces are brought together, they bond firmly without recourse to cramps and the piece may be handled immediately. Some glues are designed for plastic foams, while others are for laminates and veneers.

Latex adhesive

Latex adhesive is a white, milky glue used by upholsterers for attaching gimp or for patch repairs.

Epoxy adhesive

Epoxy adhesives are general purpose adhesives used only rarely in furniture renovation. They may prove useful in repairing a broken metal component. The two constituents react when mixed together to produce an extremely strong bond. The work must be cramped while the glue sets. Setting time can be accelerated by the application of heat from a hairdryer.

Abrasives

Abrasives used to produce a smooth surface are categorised as coarse, medium or fine, referring to the size of the grains glued to the backing paper. Each category may also be specified as closed or open coat. A closed coat abrasive has the particles packed together for fast cutting, whereas an open coat abrasive has more space between the particles to reduce clogging, which makes it more suitable for resinous softwoods. Although the term sandpaper is widely used to describe abrasives, it is in fact no longer available, having been superseded by superior materials.

Glasspaper

Glasspaper is a relatively cheap yellowish abrasive paper which wears quickly and is really only suitable for rough work.

Garnet paper

Garnet paper is much harder than glasspaper and is preferable for fine finishing of timber. It can be recognised by its red/brown colour.

Emery

Emery is a dark abrasive material which may be backed by paper or cloth and used to finish metal. It is used dry but can be lubricated with paraffin.

Silicon carbide

Silicon carbide abrasives are used extensively for furniture renovation. They are often referred to as wet and dry paper as they can be lubricated with water when rubbing down between coats of clear finish or paint.

Turning techniques

The shapes that make up common turned legs and rails can be formed from a combination of parallel or tapering, lines, punctuated with grooves, coves or beads.

Professionals carry out this work on a full scale motorised lathe, but such a machine is beyond the purse of most amateur restorers. Simple turned work can be carried out, however, using a lathe attachment to an electric power drill provided that the tools are sharp and in good condition.

Using a lathe attachment

The illustration in the panel opposite shows a lathe attachment set up ready for use. The work is held firmly between the tailstock at one end and the headstock on the drill at the other. The drill is fixed, but the tailstock slides on the lathe bed to accommodate work of different lengths. The tool rest supports the blade of a turning tool at a convenient height to cut the wood.

Turning tools

Special chisels and gouges are used which have long handles. These provide sufficient leverage to resist the turning force of the wood. They have square, skew or curved ends and can be used with a cutting or scraping action. The cutting method will give a good finish straight from the cut but needs experience: the scraping method is easier for beginners, but it will take longer and will require sanding.

Holding a turning tool

Hold the tool firmly, one hand over the blade to guide it and the other steadying the end of the handle. Advance the blade slowly into the work and remove a little at a time ensuring that you do not damage the work with the corners of the cutting edge. Close the gap between the work and the tool rest as the work progresses, to prevent the tool snatching.

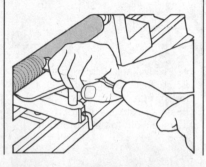

● For lighter finishing and shaping, the hand can be positioned under the blade with the thumb lying on top. The forefinger is held against the rest to control the depth of cut.

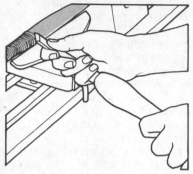

Lathe speed

Start rough cutting at a slow speed. Increase the speed for shaping and use the high speed for sanding and finishing.

Turning a cylinder

Having planed the corners off the work and set it between centres (see page 42) it can be turned roughly with a large gouge. The gouge is primarily a cutting tool and will remove the wood quickly.

● Hold the blade at right angles to the work with the handle below horizontal to present the middle portion of the cutting edge to the wood. Advance the blade slowly to make a cut about 2mm deep and then move the tool parallel to the work from one end to the other. If the wood is longer than the tool rest, the rest must be moved along the lathe bed and re-clamped.

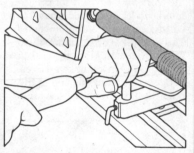

● Continue in this way, reducing the work to approximate size and checking periodically with calipers. Move the tool rest towards the work as it diminishes in size, to maintain the 3mm ($\frac{1}{8}$in) clearance.

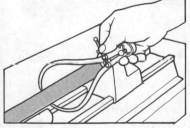

● A faster cut can be made with the gouge almost on its edge with the middle to bottom part of the cutting edge making the cut. The tool

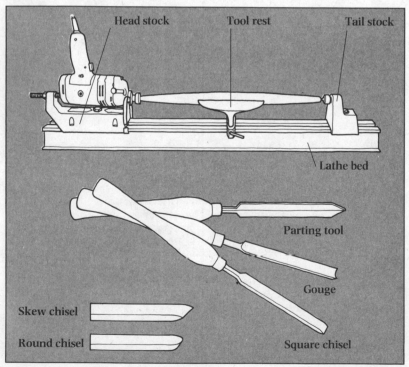

Head stock   Tool rest   Tail stock

Lathe bed

Parting tool

Gouge

Skew chisel

Round chisel

Square chisel

is angled to face the direction of the cut as it is moved parallel to the work.

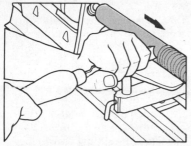

● The skew chisel is used to bring the work to size and to give it a smooth finish. Raise the tool rest above the work centre line so that the chisel cuts near the top of the cylinder. Start the cut with the bevel of the cutting edge held flat on the work and carefully lift the handle to feed the middle part of the cutting edge only into the wood. The amount of movement controls the depth of cut. Move the tool across the work to make an even cut, working from one end to the other until the required size and finish is achieved.

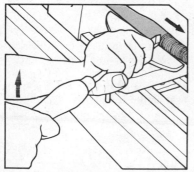

● A square chisel can be used to scrape the surface smooth instead of using the skew chisel. Set the tool rest below centre and hold the chisel horizontally with the blade square to the work. Move the blade steadily across the work making a shallow cut and keeping the blade square to prevent the corners catching.

Cutting decorative features

Grooves

Grooves are made with narrow-edged tools like the skew chisel and parting tool. The narrow groove formed by the parting tool is also used to form a clean shoulder where the waste is cut from the end of a cylindrical turning. A deep groove is made, leaving a narrow piece at the centre which is cut through with a dovetail saw when the work is removed from the lathe.

● To use the parting tool, hold it square to the work with the bevelled edge on the surface and the handle held horizontally. Lift handle to feed the cutting edge into the work.

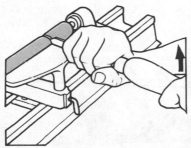

Coves

Set the tool rest just below the centre line of the work. Make V-grooves on the waste side of the lines with a skew chisel to establish the extremities of the coving.

● Cut away the waste with a narrow gouge, handle held below horizontal and working from each side of the centre. Start with the gouge on edge and roll it on to its back as the handle is swung away from the direction of the cut. Advance the cutting edge slowly into the work as the sweeping movement is made. Work down to the depth required checking the curve with the template.

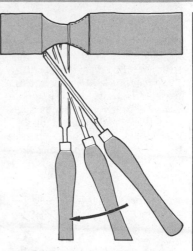

● A round nosed chisel can also be used to form coves. The tool is held horizontally and at right angles to the work. Advance it into the work to make a cut to the required depth.

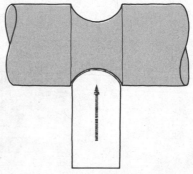

● Wider coves are made by pivoting the tool while it is held flat on the rest working from each groove down to the centre of the cove. Finish with abrasive paper wrapped around a block to match the curve.

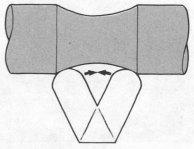

Beads

Mark the width and centre of the bead on the work. Set the tool rest level with the centre. Cut narrow grooves straight into the work on each side of the centre. If the bead is a single raised feature, first cut away the wood on either side with a gouge and straight chisel.

● Cut the bead with the skew chisel starting with the handle below horizontal. Position the heel of the cutting edge to one side of the centre line of the bead with the bevel flat on the work.

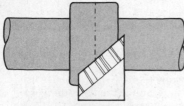

● Lift the handle while slowly rolling and advancing the cutting edge towards the groove. The blade should finish on its edge. Turn the chisel over and work from the centre around the other groove to form a complete bead.

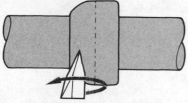

● A bead can also be shaped by scraping with a skew chisel. Place it flat on the rest and slowly feed the toe of the cutting edge round into the groove. Make successive cuts to form the shape.

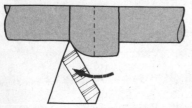

Sanding turned work

Remove the tool rest and set the lathe to maximum speed. Use only fine grade paper as light sanding should be all that is necessary.

● Hold the abrasive paper on the back of the turning between both hands. Cylinders and straight tapers can be sanded with relatively wide pieces of paper. For convex shapes use narrow strips.

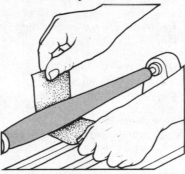

● Fine details and concave shapes should be sanded with folded paper or paper wrapped around shaped blocks.

Shaping wood

The components of old furniture are frequently curved or rounded and if you find it necessary to replace one of the components, you will have to shape it to match the rest. This can be a difficult job for the beginner and as usual it is wise to practice on some spare wood until you are familiar with the use of the tools. These will mainly be planes, rasps, files and spokeshaves.

Where you are replacing an entire component, use the damaged one as a pattern for its replacement. More often though, you will be making a patch to an existing component and this must be shaped so that the surface flows uninterrupted from old to new work. For this reason most additions are left slightly oversized, so that they can be shaped after they have been glued in position. To avoid unnecessary work, retain as little extra material as possible. A small patch let into a flat surface or square edge should be very slightly proud so that a finely set plane can be used to skim the patch flush with the surface. Some of the surrounding finish and material will be planed at the same time, but this is unavoidable and it will be necessary to touch in the repair with stain and polish at the finishing stage.

For more extensive shaping, such as a moulding or the replacement of one end of a curved leg, several tools may be required to gradually reduce the profile of the new work to match that of the original. Saws are used to cut away any obvious waste until only that wood which contains the required shape remains. Circumstances will dictate which tools are used to sculpt the roughly shaped addition.

Single curves can be worked with a spokeshave, a moulding plane or a scratch stock, whilst fully three dimensional curves can be worked with rasps or gouges. Having blended the new work into the existing component, it will often be necessary to smooth the surface with abrasive paper. Use a pad of paper under the finger tips (see page 10), or cut a softwood block to match the profile of the work. Carved components, particularly those incorporating decorative motifs, require a standard of work which is only acquired with considerable experience. It would be advisable to seek expert tuition before tackling anything of this kind, but wood carving is an absorbing hobby which can greatly add to your skills as a renovator.

British-American terms

The clarity and thoroughness of this book, which was first published in Great Britain, are so fine that we thought that American craftspeople would be entirely comfortable using the British edition and we have reprinted it without change. However, a few terms may be unfamiliar to U.S. and Canadian readers, and we have defined them here:

brace and bit—hand drill
buttons—small hardwood blocks into which rebates have been cut to prevent shrinkage
carcase—the body or main bulk of a piece of furniture
caustic soda—sodium hydroxide (lye)
coach bolt—stud bolt
cock bead—rounded corner for drawer front
cold cure lacquer—clear, high-gloss cold enamel, such as "Boss Gloss"
cotton wool—absorbent cotton
DIY shops—"Do-it-yourself" shops

drawing room—living room
fillet—a narrow flat molding
fitment—fitting
fox-wedged—applies to hidden wedges in a mortise-and-tenon joint
G-cramp—C-clamp
glass paper—sandpaper
glazing bars—muntins
"go off"—to harden or begin to harden
hessian—burlap
high street—a part of town where the principal shops are located
hire—rent
ironmonger—dealer in metal utensils, hardware dealer
litre—approximately 2.11 pints
meths—methylated spirits
moving house—simply moving or relocating
ply—plywood
pot life—shelf life
pound (monetary unit)—approximately $1.50 at time of printing
prise—pry, pull away
proprietary grain fillers—name brand wood grain fillers, such as "Plastic Wood"

proud—slightly raised; not flush with a certain surface
PVA—polyvinyl acetate, normal white woodworking glue (like "Elmer's")
rubber—a cloth used for polishing or buffing
scarf joint—joint made by notching and gluing two pieces of wood together
screw fixings—metal plates used to reinforce the positioning of wood screws
"skips"—"dumpsters"
softening blocks—padding to protect wood from clamp marks
spanner—wrench
stockist—a retailer, shop owner
timber—used here in the sense of cut timber, or lumber
try square—T-square
upholsterer's skin wadding—cotton padding often used to make a "rubber"
vice—vise
white spirit—colorless liquid obtained from petroleum, substitute for turpentine

Index